Praises
for
The Shadows in My Heart

"In this brave memoir, Mary Havens reveals the secrets of her upbringing as the oldest daughter of a large family where stoicism was valued more than truth and where unspoken rules trumped any cries for help. Havens' story reveals how family secrets are kept and how they are perpetuated through tangled loyalties, misplaced religion, and corrosive self-doubt. For any woman wondering how to find her way clear of a thicket of lies, this book offers encouragement. And for any woman who celebrates having found her way free, this book is a captivating reminder of how far she has come. Honest and engaging, readers are the beneficiaries of Havens having found her voice in the storm."

—Kaylene Johnson-Sullivan,
Author of *Our Perfect Wild* and other books

"Author Mary Havens never flinches in her powerful memoir about the hardest-to-speak-about problems in families. With great courage, she leaves the elephant in the room question up for grabs: 'Why did she stay?' In order to protect those she most loves, she struggles to protect herself. Try as we might, we can never build perfect families. With tenacity and tenderness, Havens offers a road map, resources, and hope for healing the fissures."

—Lois Rafferty,
Author of *Carnie's Child*

"'I never told a soul.' Mary Havens is telling us now, not only of sexual abuse, but also the warmth of four generations of extended family, transporting the reader to southwestern Wisconsin rural life in the past seven decades. Eventually she reassures us and herself, 'We're a family now.'"

—E. Reid Gilbert, PhD
Author of *Shall We Gather at the River*

"Mary Havens' deeply moving story is a reminder that the good ol' days—when appearances were valued above safety, secrecy above truth, and stoicism above healing—were the perfect breeding ground for incest and domestic violence to flourish."

— Lizbeth Meredith,
Author of *Pieces of Me: Rescuing My Kidnapped Daughters*

"An emotional roller coaster. *The Shadows in My Heart* captures one woman's struggle to conquer past demons of sexual assault, loss, and denial. Mary Havens winds her way into your heart and leaves you with emotions that range from unbelievable sorrow to heartwarming hope while recounting a life of tragedy, lies, abuse, and victory. A quick read that will leave you with deep sorrow, and yet, a heartwarming feeling for the woman who conquered her past and proved that the past can be overcome."

—Pam Garner, Sexual Assault Response Coordinator

the Shadows
   in My Heart

1974 Elbert & Illene Mullikin Farm

the Shadows
in My Heart

Mary A. Havens
with
Lynn Wiese Sneyd

The Shadows in My Heart

Tumbleweed Mask Press

ISBN: 978-0-692-94754-8 (paperback)
ISBN: 978-0-692-94760-9 (ebook)
LCCN: 2017936098

Thank you to:
The Wisconsin Historical Society for use of Kitty Korner Kafe picture

Vintage Aerial - Historic Aerial Photography
vintageaerial.com/photos/wisconsin/crawford/1974/KCR/6/31

Cover & Interior Layout Design by Lori Conser

Web Design by Atilla Vekony & Mindy Burnett

Author Photograph, Photography by Gayle Warren

Permissions:
Mary Oliver, Thirst "The Uses of Sorrow"

Alan Pastman for (Ruth Wallis) "The Dinghy Song"

OWN TV Material License for three transcribed interviews on
The Oprah Winfrey Show

To all families who have experienced
unexplained death, unexpressed grief,
unresolved injustice, and unrealized expectations.

To my family

Shawntel, Tim—Vincent, Vanessa, Valerie, and Verrick

Shannon, Sean—Jacob, Jonah, and Elijah

Shayne —Josephine

In Loving Memory of Josephine "Lilly" Wolf

Sunrise September 3, 1999 to Sunset August 10, 2015

The Uses of Sorrow

(In my sleep I dreamed this poem)

Someone I loved once gave me
a box full of darkness.

It took me years to understand
that this, too, was a gift.

—Mary Oliver, *Thirst*

Author's Note

This memoir does not include my entire life's story, but the content in this book is true to the best of my knowledge. The story begins at my mother's death, which captures the essence of my loss. Then begins my journey with the writing of this story.

I am reminded of the biblical story of Joseph's coat, sometimes referred to as "Coat of Many Colors," as my life was filled with many characters; a life that held as many trials and tribulations as are characters in the story. Lynn Wiese Sneyd, my ghostwriter, brilliantly captured, intertwined, and wove the intricate colorful details of my life in *The Shadows in My Heart*.

Certain dialogue is quoted from love letters, diaries, audio and video tapes, especially my conversations with my mother near the end of her life and with Oprah Winfrey as guests on three *Oprah* shows.

Contents

PART ONE

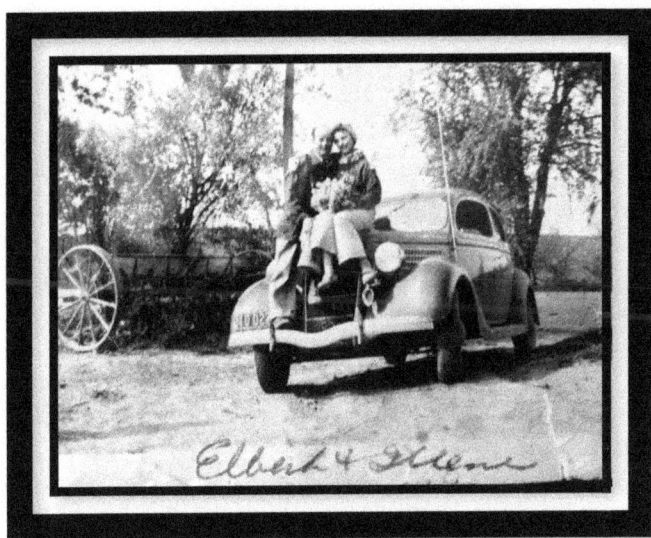

Elbert & Ilene

"Mary! Where's Mary?" My brother's raspy voice turned the corner of the farmhouse before he did. "Mom's asking for Mary. Where is she?"

I considered crawling behind one of the bridal wreath bushes growing on either side of the cement stoop where I had sought refuge. Long ago I learned snakes like to slither in their shadows, and I wasn't keen on meeting one. Footsteps swished closer.

"Mom wants you."

I squinted into the late-afternoon sun. Walt's backlit shoulders slumped with weariness, resignation, or something else; I couldn't be sure. He extended a hand. I pushed myself up and began walking, afraid if I uttered one word, a flare of them would erupt and ignite a fire. We had enough chaos in the family as it was.

I started up the stairs to the deck, ignoring Walt and the rest of the family milling around the yard. Everything felt heavy—the humid air, my legs, my heart. I paused at the top to gather myself before heading into Mom's apartment. I dreaded the request I presumed she was going to make.

Inside, my eyes took a moment to adjust to the dim light. The door between her apartment and the rest of the farmhouse, where Walt and his wife, Isabel, lived, was closed. A small fan sat on the kitchen counter, trying to expel the stale air. Every time I had visited during the past months, I found my mother resting or sleeping in Dad's recliner. The metal-railed hospital bed that recently took over the room looked sterile and cold. Thirty minutes ago, Mom had insisted on being moved to her own bed. I walked over to her bedroom.

My mother looked small under the light blanket. Her eyes were closed, her pale face quiet. Her hands rested on her chest, atop my father's pajamas, her source of comfort during lonely nights. Someone had woven a strand of rosary beads through her fingers—probably my sister Barbara. I wondered if the move had been uncomfortable for Mom. Had the photos in the room given her strength to deal with the cancer's pain? The photo of her and Dad sitting on their new car, newlyweds full of hopes and dreams, her dark brown hair, her thin waist. Photos of her twelve children and her many grandchildren. Or maybe she focused on the two crucifixes on the wall, the framed image of an angel hung between them. I settled on the rickety chair next to the bed. A floorboard creaked beneath the shag carpeting. My mother's eyes fluttered.

"Hi, Mom. It's Mary," I said, leaning over, smoothing wisps of white hair from her forehead. Her eyes had a glazed look. "Mom, it's Mary. I'm here now." Her hand felt soft and dry. Weren't the dying supposed to be cold? I had been around so much death, yet at the moment I didn't seem to know.

Mom turned her head. A light sparked in her eyes, and she squeezed my hand. Right then I knew she wasn't going to ask me to return to the Catholic Church. For whatever reason, it didn't matter. But I sensed something else did. She inhaled, furrowed her brow, and looked at the ceiling as if she saw something. She started twitching and moaning, her legs growing restless. Suddenly, she gripped my hand hard and cried out. "My babies!

My babies are on the road. The cows are coming. Look! The babies, they'll get hurt. Please, please help them!"

Her shrieks startled me. "Shhh, it's okay, Mom. The babies are safe," I said, enfolding her hand in both of mine. "They're safe." I half expected someone, alarmed by the commotion, to come running into the apartment.

Her mouth moved. I leaned closer. "What did you say, Mom?"

"They want me to come with them."

"Who wants you to come with them?"

"My babies." Her voice sounded tired and sad. I assumed she meant my siblings who had died. "What about my babies here? How can I leave all of you?"

I fumbled for an answer. "We're all grown now, Mom. We can take care of ourselves. It's okay to join them." Dear God, I silently prayed, this is my mother's journey. Help me keep my emotions in check.

Mom relaxed into the mattress. The fan whirred, and somewhere beyond the window a meadowlark sang. I watched the shallow rise and fall of her chest. Just when I thought she had fallen asleep, my mother turned and looked at me in a way I had never experienced. So direct, so aware of my needs and who I was. In a hoarse whisper, she said, "Follow your heart, Mary. Trust it. You'll find what you've been searching for all these years."

I was stunned. My mother never had encouraged me to follow my heart. For decades, my brothers, sisters, and I had followed the beat of *her* heart. I placed my hand on her forehead and leaned close. She smelled fresh and clean, like sheets drying on a sun-drenched clothesline. "I promise, Mom. I promise to follow my heart."

I sat next to her for a while longer. If only I had followed my heart years ago. How different life would be. I was too emotionally exhausted to dwell on those matters.

Though she never regained consciousness, my mother held on through the night and into the next day waiting for my brother-in-law, the last of the family, to arrive. Soon after he spoke to her, Illene Krachey Mullikin slipped away from the Wisconsin dairy farm where she had lived most of her life and joined her deceased children and her husband of sixty-one years in heaven. It was Saturday, August 2, 2003. The previous day, my mother had spoken her last words to me.

After my mother's funeral and the will reading, my siblings and I cleaned out her apartment. That's when I found the box hunkered in a corner. I sifted through its contents. Farm records, invoices, bank statements dating back decades. Then, stuffed under a stack of account payables, I noticed two small books, one with a leather cover, the other coverless and bound by a string. Sneezing, I lifted them out.

My mother's handwriting filled the pages of what appeared to be diaries. I had no idea she had kept diaries. I rummaged through the rest of the box and discovered a bundle of brittle papers. I carefully removed the rubber band. Based on the dates and handwriting, the signatures and salutations of endearment, these were missives my parents exchanged before marrying. Resisting the urge to read, I tucked the diaries and letters back in the box, carried the box to my car, and stowed it in the corner of my trunk. The only other thing I took was my mother's ceramic cookie jar in the shape of a donkey. One of my daughters had asked for it. Over the years, pieces of it had broken off, and

Mom had glued them into place as best she could. I imagined her, hurriedly spreading glue on a piece of ear, pressing it into place, not quite lining it up, but not willing to toss out something that still served its purpose, even if it wasn't pretty.

All I wanted to do now was get home to Minnesota. I had a four-hour drive ahead, so I quickly said my good-byes and turned the car west on the county trunk road toward Prairie du Chien and the Mississippi River. Within a few miles, Mom's absence slammed into me. I grabbed a tissue from the box on the passenger seat. I didn't shed tears for the farm or its current owners. As far as I was concerned, I had no reason to visit either again. I forced myself to focus on the surroundings, the Ocooch Mountains, the terrain untouched by glaciers, now blanketed in soothing summer greens. The crests of the rounded hills offered a panorama of patchwork farmland. Small-town water towers poked up their heads to peer at the view. In the valleys, the Wisconsin River wound in and out of sight, its placid surface concealing unstable sandbars. Its tributary, the Kickapoo River, never showed itself. I imagined Mom driving along this road, a corner of the world she had occupied for so long. How different my life was from hers. I was a fifty-seven-year-old woman about to take early retirement, divorce her husband, and let her adult children fend for themselves. I had protected my family long enough, or at least tried to protect them.

In Prairie, I turned north onto Highway 35, the Great River Road bordering the Mississippi. The highway swooped down into the floodplains, the mighty river on one side, forested bluffs towering on the other side. Grain-loaded barges floated south, empty ones chugged north. The river waters ran high from the summer rains that filled the sloughs and created lush forage. My mother had forbidden us to swim in those waters. Every year, the river's crafty currents consumed some poor soul. Yet seeing the river, watching the waters as I drove, calmed my inner turmoil.

My mother had instructed me to follow my heart. I felt the familiar edge of irritation. Why had she waited until now to say that, after everything I'd endured? Was she suggesting I change course to break the patterns that ran so deeply within our family, those heavy, chain-linked patterns that inexplicably seemed to hold me hostage? Or was she merely telling me the time had come to find my happiness, my voice? Even the Mississippi's course could be altered through dams and levees, spillways and weirs. Maybe during her last few days, Mom had looked back on her life with more regrets than she had revealed to me. Maybe she didn't want me to do the same someday. But that was my mother, never fully explaining herself. Leaving it up to me to finish her story while dealing with my own.

My mother had always wanted to be a teacher. I suspect her lifelong love of learning began in first grade, back in 1931, when her family's dairy farm was feeling the one-two punches of the Great Depression. Being the eldest child, she was the first Krachey to cross the threshold of the one-room schoolhouse. Before I graduated from grade school, her story ran like a film in my mind, one that I watched reruns of repeatedly.

Act One began on a bright September day with my Grandma Krachey accompanying my mother the one-and-a-half miles to school. They walked along the county trunk highway, veering to the road's edge when a car or horse and buggy team passed. Dogs on farms barked greetings or warnings. Illene was excited to have new pencils and a notebook. "I always had good penmanship in school. You should too," she said more than once to us kids. For the remainder of that school year, through sun, mist, fog, wind, rain, or snow, she journeyed alone. The following year, her younger sister, Virginia, joined her, and each year thereafter, another sibling of first-grade age tagged along.

The teacher, who rode a horse to school, taught twenty students in grades one through eight. Each day, students cleaned the blackboard and erasers, stoked the wood stove that warmed the room, swept the floors, and hauled drinking water in buckets from the closest farm a quarter-mile away. They sat in rows by grades. Each subject was taught for fifteen minutes to each class. Mom liked when it was her turn for lessons because she and the other first-grader could sit on the bench next to the teacher. Her favorite subject was history. She made sure we knew that she excelled in her studies and that we should do the same.

Most students, including my mother, carried lunch in a gallon syrup pail. A few fortunate pails held a thermos, but no pail toted store-bought food, only homemade breads with jelly, soups in jars heated in pots of hot water on the stove, cakes, cookies, and occasionally homegrown fruit. At recess, the kids played games like tag, Red Rover, and hide-and-seek and climbed the big rock in front of the schoolhouse. When bad weather kept them indoors, I'm sure my mother pouted. She loved the fresh air and spent recesses picking flowers, carving her initials in the sandstone outcroppings, petting the teacher's horse, playing house on warm days, sledding on cold. I suspect that by second grade she directed activities in the schoolyard.

When I was seven or eight, my brother Bobby and my Uncle Lyle, my mother's much younger brother, used to sneak along the county trunk road to the schoolhouse. Though no longer in use, the white clapboard building was never locked. We'd sit at the dusty wooden desks with the iron legs bolted to the floor. The boys weren't interested in playing school as I was. They wanted to climb the big rock out front, and since it was my self-appointed job to keep up with them, I'd scramble around the granite in my dress, scraping my bare knees. We never did find my mother's initials on any of the rocks. Mom had hoped her children would attend school there, but by the time we started we had to attend school in Wauzeka, the town closest to our farm. Later in her life, she fervently petitioned to keep the schoolhouse from being torn down. Her editorials in the local newspapers, her mailed fliers, and her verbalized opinions made a difference. The school-house remained intact, though it was relocated to a historical preservation site about twenty miles north.

Act Two began in 1938, when my mother entered high school. Then she had to walk two and a half miles each way, downhill from the dairy farm into Wauzeka, then uphill on the way home. High school was not mandatory. Some children had to forgo the education because they needed to work the farm. Others looked for paying jobs to help support their mostly large families. Still others were forced to stay at home because of a family illness. Mom wanted to attend school despite having to help her dad milk cows, spread manure, clean the barn, throw hay from the loft and silage from the silo, feed pigs and chickens, and gather eggs. At school, she joined the band and glee club, extracurricular activities that meant she didn't start the long trek back home, lugging her clarinet case and books, until 4:00 p.m. After helping with supper and supervising her younger siblings, she was free to do her homework. If she could keep her eyes open.

In the spring of my mother's sophomore year, her father decided to purchase a pony that she could ride to school, a black-and-white paint named Dick. A slower horse couldn't be found in the county, my mother always claimed. By the time the two made it to school and she tied him up and fed him, she was late and in trouble again, so she returned to walking. I wonder if she ever thanked Grandpa Krachey for buying Dick.

In 1942, my mother graduated from Wauzeka High School, along with fifteen or so other kids. Her boyfriend, Bert Mullikin, gave her a Brownie camera. Her graduation photo remained on her dresser until the day she died. She was so proud of that certificate. She had finished in the top quarter of her class. "A good education, that's what this country needs more of," she would say when conversations turned to school and learning.

When I was a senior in high school, I shared with her my dream of going to college. "That's ridiculous," she said. "You don't need an extra piece of paper. You'll have your high-school diploma. That's what counts. By the time you pay back what it costs to get that extra piece of paper, you'll have ten years behind you, and you'll be back at first base. Besides, you'll get married and have babies."

I had no intention of getting married a year after graduating, as she did, then have a baby the following year. As graduation neared and I realized college did cost a lot of money, I changed my tune. When I suggested that I enlist in the air force, Mom had a conniption. "The only women joining the military are nurses, and you don't have a nursing degree," she argued. So I applied to be an airline stewardess. When the airline responded that I had to be twenty-one to qualify, Mom pursed her lips and raised her eyebrows, her patented I-told-you-so look. I still wonder if the plans for what we once wanted ever collided in the wastebasket of unfulfilled dreams.

Yes, I knew my mother's story by heart, or thought I did. Some months after she died, I read her diaries and the love letters between her and my dad, Elbert "Bert" Mullikin. It took a bit of squinting and concentration to decipher the words she had scratched across the pages.

Tuesday, February 24, 1942:

School was usual. Glee club. Ness got awful mad. Letter from Mary & Joyce. Uncle Bill shot himself. They are taking him to the hospital. Nice day.

Wednesday, February 25, 1942:

I didn't go to school. Uncle Bill is still alive. I was sick. Bert went to Prairie du Chien to see about the army. He came down to the farm tonight. Virginia came with him.

Thursday, February 26, 1942:

School. Glee club. Ness wants me to speak. Joe, Dad, Uncle Leo & Bert pulled pump at farm. Bert, Ma and I went to see Uncle Bill. About the same. Swell day & night.

Friday, February 27, 1942:

School as usual. Reports. Boy, Hughes really brought me down. Uncle Bill was swell until this p.m. Much worse tonight. Swell day. Nothing unusual. 2 B- and C+ and C on reports.

Saturday, February 28, 1942:

Uncle Bill died 3:30 a.m. I didn't do much. Just chores and fix fence. Bert and I, Ma, went down to town. Ma stayed down and Bert and I went back to farm. Swell day.

Monday, March 2, 1942:

> *I didn't go to school. Uncle Bill's funeral. Swell day. Of*
> *course I went to the funeral. I didn't do much more after*
> *at home.*

Granted, Mom only had three lines per day on which to
write. Still, how could days be swell when someone shot himself
and died? My mother never had much to say about Uncle Bill.
Dad, on the other hand, claimed Uncle Bill had a mean streak
longer than the Kickapoo River and was quite jealous. After
Uncle Bill died, his only child, a daughter, suffered a tough life,
which bothered my dad for decades.

Based on earlier diary entries, I knew Mom was pining for
her first love, Ruben Infield, a vagrant farmhand who was two
years older and had enlisted in the navy the previous September. "No letter again from the sweetest boy on earth," she wrote
on February 17, 1942. Rube was fighting somewhere overseas.
Dad must have seen the opening. He made himself helpful to
Grandpa Krachey on the farm, easy enough to do as he only
lived a mile away. I can just see him teasing my mother as she set
off for school in the morning. Perhaps those days surrounding
Uncle Bill's death were swell for Mom because my father was
starting to wheedle his way into her heart.

After Uncle Bill died, Dad asked Mom out on a date. Soon
they were going to dances, movies, parties, Miller Hill Cemetery
in the dark. By April, the tone of my mother's diary entries had
changed. Bert's name replaced Rube's. Sparks didn't exactly fly
off the page, but a relationship was developing, one Grandpa
Krachey didn't appear to appreciate. Dad's father had up and left
the family when my dad was about twelve years old, and Dad

had to quit school after the eighth grade to help on the farm. He was thirteen years older than my mother.

In June, after my mother graduated from high school, Grandpa sent Mom out to California to live with his sister, Hattie. It was a decision that took my mother by surprise. One day Grandpa mentioned the trip, and a week later Mom was singing "California Here I Come," whether she wanted to go or not. Correspondence between my parents began immediately. Based on those letters, I think Grandpa Krachey's plans backfired.

I brought my parents' mildewed letters on a sisters' trip. My four sisters and I began reading and soon were giggling and laughing, our cheeks blushing as red as the wine in our glasses.

Day 5, June 25, 1942 from Bert to Illene

HI, honey, Well hear it is Thursday nearly a week sins I saw you how are you any way feeling fine I hope it seems like a month to me sure is lonsum around hear I was shire glad to get your letter yesterday. I have bin looking for one every day sins you have bin gone. With lots of Love Your future husband Next year at this time XXXXXXXXXXX O yes I kiss your picture every nite silly isent it or is it I don't thing so you have bin getting kissed every nite and you dident no it did you.

Day 11, July 1, 1942 from Illene to Bert

As I am writing this letter, sweetheart, I am listening to the song I wanted you to sing that last night we were together—remember "The Waltz you saved for me?" It is very beautiful. I loved that song ever since I heard that little bit you knew from Boscobel one night a long time ago. Probably you don't even remember but I do…Well, good-bye, for now Daddy & take good care of yourself & don't worry about me & don't work to hard. With all my love XXXXX "Just Mommie"

They wrote about the weather, about Dad getting drafted, then deferred, because farmers could do that during World War II. Mom wrote about working in a factory that produced parts for bombs and about her and Aunt Hattie seeing movies in downtown Los Angeles, like *Somewhere I'll Find You* with Clark Gable and Lana Turner. Dad informed Mom that she had a lot of hens among her chickens and to remind her folks not to sell them because those hens would bring in good egg money next year after they married. When he told her the farmhand who was helping her father had quit, she wrote, *The only person that can work for my dad is me and then sometimes he gets pretty sore at me, too, doesn't he? Oh well, he gets over it so that's the important thing.* When Dad worried that maybe Mom couldn't read his handwriting, she assured him that she could and hoped he could read hers too, as she noted "I sure can scribble." They wrote about their wedding, planned for the following June, unbeknown to anyone else, and their future life together forever and always. They already had chosen the name of their first child: David, if a boy, and Barbara, if a girl. My mother sealed her letters with a lipstick kiss and signed them "Your Loving Wife."

After five months, Illene Krachey returned to Wauzeka and to Bert Mullikin, the man who would be the love of her life. As planned, they married on June 8, 1943. Their first child, David, was born less than a year later, in May, and a second boy, Robert, was born fourteen months later. I was born on July 28, 1946. Mary Alice Mullikin. My parents' first daughter. I like to think

Mom was excited to have a girl, but I'm not so sure. She wasn't keeping a diary then, as she did when David was born, though never once did she mention being pregnant with him. After his birth, she wrote entries like *I did my work and took care of baby.* Odd in its feeling of disconnectedness, especially for a woman who gave birth to a total of twelve children over seventeen years. Then again, why was I surprised? That was my mother.

My earliest memory was of my brother Johnny. He entered the world on a blustery March day trying its mightiest to transition southwestern Wisconsin from winter to spring. While my mother suffered through contractions, my father loaded his brood of five into the car and delivered us next door to my grandparents' house. He then raced to the hospital in Boscobel, the next town, the pale sun guiding the way. As the shadows lengthened in the waiting room, my father knew he had to get back to the farm to do the evening chores. I'm sure it tore him apart to leave my mother laboring. It would be the only birth out of twelve that he missed. By the time he returned to the hospital sporting a clean pair of bib overalls, a six-pound, nine-ounce, twenty-inch bundle of baby awaited him.

Johnny appeared to be a healthy, apple-dumpling-cheeked child with the trademark Mullikin blue eyes and cue-ball, bald head. Within a few weeks of arriving at the farmhouse, he began coughing. It wasn't a new sound to any of us. David and my sister Bonnie made the same sound, only louder. Sometimes while I held him, Johnny's mouth would form a small circle, and he would cough and gasp so much that I became unnerved and passed him back to my mother or grandmother. My mother would pat him on the back and pace with him, then hand him to my grandmother when she needed a break. She wasn't nursing him because she had mastitis with Barbara, my sister born before Johnny, and Mom's doctor had advised her not to breast-feed the next baby. My parents worried, but my mother was not one to rush a child to the hospital. "Another child with bronchitis," she told her friends. She did her best to keep him on a regular feeding schedule, but eventually those wet coughs left her no other option. In early May, she and my dad brought Johnny back to the hospital where he had been born.

"The doctors wanted to take care of him for a while," my mother said to us when my parents returned empty-armed. "He's in the best place he can be. Right now, I need to get supper ready."

Even at three years old, I could feel the world go topsy-turvy. Dad still got up to milk the cows. Mom still whipped up a breakfast of eggs, bacon, pancakes, toasted homemade bread, and orange juice. But after Dad finished the outdoor chores and Mom cleaned up the dishes and made sure everyone was dressed and ready to go to school or stay at home with our babysitter, Grandma Krachey. Then my parents drove to the hospital to be with Johnny. The sun was on the other side of the fields by the time they returned. Whoever spotted their car first would yell, "Mommy and Daddy are home," the code to drop what we were doing and race outside to greet them. Each time, I half-expected a swaddled Johnny to appear. "The doctors are taking care of him," my mom would say, then catch up with Grandma at the kitchen table in a whispered, unsmiling sort of way. I didn't understand what the doctors were doing or why Johnny had to be with them for so long or why my mother seemed just a little bit sadder and quieter each day.

I still recall the morning the phone call came. I was playing with a doll on the kitchen floor. My mother stood at the old porcelain sink that drained into a bucket below, washing dishes. The phone's ring made her flinch. She quickly wiped her hands on her apron, then picked up the receiver and spoke into the mouthpiece.

"Yes, this is she." There was a long pause. Her face paled, and she gulped for air as if she couldn't breathe. I thought she was going to start coughing like David and Bonnie, but then she whispered into the phone. "We'll be there as soon as we can." She hung up and sat down at the table.

I went over and pulled on her dress. "Mommy?"

She looked at me, or maybe through me. She took my hand, and out the door we went. I had to run to keep up. We headed to where my dad was sawing wood into fence posts, the roar of the Allis-Chalmers tractor fueling the saw blade and overpowering the sound of our footsteps. When he looked up, my mother practically fell into his arms. It was one of the few times during my childhood that I saw my parents embrace or my mother cry.

Not quite three months old, Johnny had died in the hospital without a parent at his bedside. The cause of death was listed as pneumonia. Near the end of her life, Mom told me that when she got to the hospital and saw Johnny lying in the crib, she wasn't allowed to pick him up and hold him. Hospital rules. For the rest of her life she regretted not being with him when he died, and even worse, that she did not break the rules, take him in her arms, and kiss him good-bye.

Johnny was buried behind Sacred Heart Catholic Church in Wauzeka. A small white cross marked his grave near the ditch where waters ran. The last time I saw him was in the church vestibule. The memory that lingers is strange, mainly because the only two people in it are Johnny and me, which certainly couldn't have been the case. No one held my hand or picked me up or explained why my baby brother lay with his eyes closed in what looked like a white basket. Instead, I approached him alone, tentative yet curious. I only could see the upper part of his body. His little face rested on a white satin pillow. How did he get there, I wondered as I looked down at him. What was he doing? Would he be there long? I felt as if I were looking at a real-life angel, the littlest angel of all, the one I held in my arms, and the one I would hold in my heart forever. From that point on, every time I walked into the vestibule of that church, I thought of Johnny. Sundays, Fridays, Christmas, Easter, baptisms, funerals. Hundreds of times I entered that narrow space, and every time I'd shiver and see an image of the little white basket with a baby in it.

Johnny had appeared in the family and, just as abruptly, disappeared from it. The thing was, no one talked about his absence. Mom would visit his grave, gently clear the weeds from the site and leave bouquets of fresh bridal wreath and lilacs or peonies without speaking his name. If one of us kids did ask about Johnny, she would clamp her mouth shut and hang her head or simply turn and walk away, ignoring whoever had spoken. Soon enough we stopped saying Johnny's name. I didn't understand why.

A few months later, spring rounded the bend and flowed into summer like the Kickapoo River flowing into the Wisconsin. The earth breathed fresh scents after rainstorms, and vases of sweet-smelling lilacs filled the house. The hay grew, the calves grew, I grew, and my brother's hair grew.

One day, Grandpa Krachey called my mother on the phone. She was staring out the window, at what I wasn't sure. The bird feeder was empty of finches, and the boys were on the other side of the house. She startled when the phone rang, but her mouth softened during the conversation. "Okay, Daddy, we'll be right over." The next thing I knew, she herded us into the car. It was only a half-mile to Grandma and Grandpa's house, but driving meant she didn't have to carry Bonnie, who was a year younger than me, or keep David from running after Bobby and me.

"Grandpa's giving you boys haircuts," Mom said. The boys whined, unhappy at their play being interrupted. I suggested he cut my hair too. "You don't need your hair cut," she said. I knew better than to argue.

When we arrived, my uncles Larry and Lyle were playing on the tire swing in the yard, sporting fresh crew cuts. We entered the big kitchen through the side porch. Grandpa stood next to a wooden chair, an overturned pot on its seat, a plastic cape draped over its back. Clippers and a comb were on the table.

"Welcome to Grandpa's barber shop. I understand your ma made some haircut appointments," said Grandpa, winking. David edged closer to Mom. "Who's gonna climb up first?" He patted the pot. "David, how about you? You're the oldest." David ducked his head.

"Daddy," said my mother. "Let him be. Bobby can go first." She grabbed Bobby by his arm. "Now, don't you go cutting off all those curls."

Grandpa snapped the cape to attention, and Bobby carefully climbed onto the pot. "Don't you worry. I've done this hundreds of times. And don't you go babying David so much." Grandpa turned the shears on and tugged one of Bobby's ears. David and I watched hair fall to the floor. The soft buzz of the shears sounded comforting. When Bobby was done, he hopped down and ran outside to play with Larry and Lyle.

"Okay, big boy," said Grandpa. He put his hands on his knees and looked David in the eyes. "Ready to get your ears lowered?"

Grandpa picked him up and gently set him on the pot. "Can you sit up tall for me, David?" he said, his hands on David's back.

David took his job seriously and sat stiff and straight. He stared ahead while Grandpa maneuvered the clippers around his ears, then giggled and scrunched his shoulders when they moved across the back of his neck. This was not like the haircuts my mother gave me. She flattened her hand against my forehead and clipped my bangs with scissors, then trimmed the bottom of my hair. Fascinated, I watched Grandpa. Inadvertently, I inched closer and closer, until my head accidentally bumped his elbow. His arm jerked and he looked down. I braced myself for a tongue-lashing.

Instead, he said, "A little mouse come to visit." He brushed my cheek. "It's okay, Mary. No harm done." I was so unaccustomed to such a loving gesture that my cheeks grew warm. I felt special, a rare feeling. I tucked the feeling in my heart. This is my only memory of Grandpa Krachey. Although I don't have a clear image of Grandpa, I can still feel his weathered hand against my face. Amazing how one touch can last a lifetime.

Grandpa must have inspired the boys, because shortly after their haircuts, they decided I should have a new do. I thought it sounded like a good idea. We were playing in the fruit-tree garden, overgrown with grass and weeds. The blooms of the burdock plants surrounding the rusty water tank had turned into cockleburs that stuck to everything. The boys wanted to use the burrs to make hair rollers like the rags my mother rolled in her hair at night and took out in the morning. Lyle clumped together some burrs, then rolled the wad in a swath of my hair. Bobby and Larry did the same. Mom always griped about how fine my hair was and how it wouldn't comply with her plans for pigtails or braids. Maybe this would make things easier for her. Pretty soon I had a head full of burr rollers. I skipped and twirled around in my bare feet holding the hem of my dress. "I have curly hair, curly hair," I sang.

It didn't take long for the rollers to start prickling my scalp. I decided my hair would be curly enough. I pulled at a burr clump, just like my mother pulled at her rag curlers, but nothing budged. I tried another one. The burr roller held my hair in its spiny grip. "I can't get these out," I said, anxiously hopping around. The boys came over and started tugging.

"Owww! Stop!" I began to cry. The pain of their rough tugs wasn't nearly as painful as the thought of what trouble I was in. The boys had no sympathy.

"You'll have to sleep on 'em forever," said Lyle, doubling over with laughter.

I needed help, and the only person who could help was my mother. I ran through the tall grass toward the farmhouse, the boys tagging behind. The last I had seen Mom, she was tending to her vegetable garden. I spied her blouse between tomato plants.

I ran up to her, panting. "Mommy, the boys stuck burrs in my hair, and I can't get them out. They were supposed to make my hair curly, but I think they're stuck for good." I couldn't stop the tears running from my eyes.

Mom took one look at me, and her peaceful countenance disappeared. "Oh for Pete's sake," she said, dropping her trowel and yanking at her garden gloves. "Mary, what on earth have you done?" She pulled at a burr roller. I winced. The boys arrived, still full of giggles. "Did you boys do this?" Her irritation was enough to wilt cornstalks.

"Mary wanted curly hair," said Lyle. He lunged for a burr curler, but my mother swatted his hand.

"You shouldn't have let them do this," she said, trying to peel hair from a burr. "I'm going to have to cut your hair, and you have hardly any hair to cut." She stood up and grabbed me by my arm. "Larry and Lyle, you get on home right now. Bobby, you come with me."

Giggles subsided. I sniffed, instantly feeling guilty and ashamed. I shouldn't have let the boys do this to me. Now I had caused a mess. My mother made Bobby stand in the corner of the living room while she clipped all the burrs from my hair. She pulled and cut. The burrs poked and pricked. All I could do was sit and endure, awash in guilt. Instead of helping, I had become a burden.

That fall, Grandpa Krachey had a heart attack and was admitted to the hospital in Boscobel where Johnny had died less than six months earlier. The doctors had him transported to a larger, better-equipped hospital in Madison where he was diagnosed with heart disease. I can just see Mom racing the ninety miles to Madison, her hands tense on the steering wheel, a nervous Grandma in the passenger seat. Once there, Mom must have recognized the gravity of the situation. She knew Grandpa didn't have a will, so she called the family lawyer and told him to come to the hospital so the document could be drawn up and signed. My mother was not present at the signing. She only knew that Elbert Mullikin was named executor. She assumed her father had divided his estate fairly.

On October 17, 1950, at the age of fifty-four, Grandpa died. My poor mother. She had lost her son and now lost the father she worshipped. Mom attended the reading of the Last Will and Testament of Walter Krachey. The estate was divided equally among the eleven Krachey children.

Many years later, Aunt Virginia told me this infuriated my mother. "Larry is two years old!" Mom had said. "He's never even helped on the farm. The one who worked the hardest deserves the most." She was twenty-five. Without a doubt, she had worked on the farm the longest, and, as Virginia vouched, had worked the hardest. Seeds of bitterness were planted deep in my mother's heart.

Thank goodness for the holidays. That year, while the cold outside grew heavier, a warm lightness filled the farmhouse. My brothers and I hauled wood from the porch into the kitchen to fuel the stove. My mother rolled out piecrusts and cookie dough and wiped her hands on her apron with a hint of cheerfulness and sometimes even a smile. Soon after Thanksgiving, the Sears Roebuck catalogue arrived. Bonnie and I would snuggle on the couch, where she spent most of her days, and ooh and aah over dolls and dresses and candy. After perusing the catalogue only once, Bonnie could flip to her favorite pages.

When we kids became too rambunctious, Mom bundled us up in snowsuits, boots, hats, and mittens and sent us outdoors with reminders to Bobby and me not to get David and Bonnie running too fast. I loved feeling the cold air on my face. It usually sent Bonnie into coughing fits.

"Sit here," I said to Bonnie, pointing to the snow that had drifted into a pile during the night. It looked clean and as white as the sheets on our bed. Bonnie plopped down, her little legs stuck out in front of her. I scooped up some fine, dry snow and rubbed my mittens together over her head. "It's a snow shower," I said. She giggled and stuck out her tongue.

A few weeks before Christmas, Bobby suggested we go up to the attic. Bonnie and I had been playing on the floor, but she had tired and crawled onto the couch.

"But we aren't supposed to go up there," I said, tucking a blanket around Bonnie's slight frame. Whenever I asked to play in the attic, Mom said absolutely not. The floorboards didn't cover all the insulation, and we might fall through to the kitchen. I had been up there with her once. Boxes and an old trunk filled half the space. I imagined a sparkling treasure lying in the corner of the trunk. I had suggested opening it, but she said no.

"I think Ma's hiding something," said Bobby. "Don't be such a scaredy-cat. Let's go look."

Through the window, I watched Mom walking outside toward the barn, tying her wool scarf around her neck. I knew she would be furious if she caught us. As soon as we saw her enter the barn, Bobby ran outside to the porch, but the door to the attic was locked. He then ran into the kitchen and tried the door that opened to the cellar and attic. It was the more precarious option, because it required crossing a board that connected to the staircase. One misstep and I would land in the dank, damp dirt of the root cellar. Bobby trotted across the board and turned up the stairs to the attic. I cautiously followed. The dry air smelled dusty. He was halfway up when he turned with a box in his hand. Behind clear plastic was a beautiful doll with bright blue eyes, dark hair, and a creamy face. She wore a pink dress with a white Peter Pan collar.

"What is that?" I said, confused as to why a doll would be on our attic staircase.

"It's a present, dummy."

"Why is a present here? Santa brings presents."

Bobby rolled his eyes. "There is no such thing as Santa Claus. He's just a made-up guy."

My chest hurt. I didn't like what Bobby was saying.

"Oh wow! There's more stuff. A truck." He scrambled up a few steps. "A cowboy hat!" Just then we heard the porch screen door open and slam shut. I froze. We had left the kitchen cellar door wide open. Bobby tried to make his way down past me, but before he could get to the door, Mom's head popped into view.

There was one second of horrible silence and then, "What are you doing up there? I told you not to go up there! Get down here now." I had never heard her yell so loudly.

I headed down the stairs, my hand pressed against the log cabin wall for balance.

"Can't you two listen to anything I tell you?" She hauled Bobby out and swatted his behind. I cautiously stepped onto the board between staircases. She reached over, grabbed my arm, and yanked me into the bright kitchen. It hurt, but at least I wasn't going to tumble into the basement.

"Santa knows when you're naughty, and you two are very naughty," said Mom. "I hope you know he won't be coming to this house now." She was far madder than a wet hen, as my Grandma always said, far madder than I had ever seen her. Her fury frightened me.

Bobby and I sat in separate corners. She threatened to get the paddleboard, threatened to leave us in the corner until Dad came in, practically threatened to cancel Christmas. Her voice was angry, but it didn't match the disappointment in her eyes.

Many years later, it occurred to me that what she sought was something in her life to remain untarnished and perfect. Bobby and I had marred her expectations not only of Christmas, but of what her family should be like.

In spring, the Ocooch Mountains exploded in shades of green, bringing life back to us. By May, the redbuds and crab apples boasted pink blossoms, and the purple strife had invaded the moist soil along the valley roads. Dad spent most of his working hours on the seat of the Allis-Chalmers tractor planting crops—rye, wheat, corn, oats, and whatever new grain he decided to try. At breakfast, Mom would ask him where he would be plowing that day. If it fit in her schedule, she would bring him lunch, which meant it would be a picnic day for me, Bonnie, and Barbara. David and Bobby were in school and only joined Sunday family picnics.

One day at breakfast, between reading the paper and talking crops with Mom, Dad mentioned the upcoming coon hunt. Once a year the local farmers gathered with their hound dogs down on our pasture land in Stuckey Hollow, near the Kickapoo River, to see who had the best tracking and treeing dog. Someone would drag a dead raccoon through the woods, then place it in a tree. The dogs were timed on how fast they could locate that tree. The previous year, Bobby and David accompanied Dad, but I was too young. Now, at age four, soon to be five, I wasn't about to miss my chance to join in the special day. I quickly piped up. Dad made me stand up to see how tall I was, winked, and gave me the okay. Bonnie was sitting at the table and looked interested. She didn't complain or argue when Mom told her she needed to stay home because it would be a long outing.

The following Saturday after the morning chores, Dad, the boys, and I, barefoot as always, climbed into the pickup. Dad already had loaded the wooden planks and tools that he said would be used to build a concession stand. The morning air was still damp, and my breath fogged the passenger window. I still thought it unfair that I had to wear a dress.

We drove down County N, turned on Plum Creek Road, then bumped onto a gravel road. We followed it down into Stuckey Hollow and pulled into an open pasture. The sun sparkled on the Kickapoo where the river curved near one end of the grassy expanse. A smattering of pickups were parked, most with leashed hound dogs pacing and howling in the back beds. Some of the men came over to our truck to unload the boards. David, Bobby, and I took off to explore the area and look at the dogs. I didn't much like the coonhound dogs because they were noisy and jumped and pulled on their leashes, unlike the collie we had for fetching the cows or the hunting dog Dad had that sniffed out fox in the brush piles near the fence lines.

Pickups continued to arrive. When the men began taking their dogs off the trucks, we hightailed it back to Dad. We found him at the registration table. A generator hummed near a stand that had heaters warming coffee and hotdogs. Boards had been set across tree stumps to serve as benches.

The owners and their dogs lined up, the dogs tugging on their leashes, feeding off each other's hysteria. Their bays reverberated off the bluffs and through the valley. I'm sure our coonhound hunts had a very different flavor than the ones in Britain where the tradition originated. Certainly, bib overalls, flannel shirts, and straw hats were not the attire there, as they were in Stuckey Hollow.

A gunshot cracked, and the owners unleashed their dogs. The

coonhounds put their noses to the ground, sniffing and zigzag-ging, tails wagging, occasionally howling to each other as they searched for the coon's scent. The group reached the edge of the pasture, and dogs and owners disappeared into the woods. The owners wanted to make sure the person at the tree recorded the dogs' times correctly. For me, the show wouldn't start up again until the hounds returned. The boys went over to play with some other boys they knew. I saw Dad standing a short distance away, rocking on the heels of his boots, his arms crossed over his bibs, talking to a fellow farmer. I walked over to him. He smiled and swooped me up in his arms.

"Hey there, Frinkles." I was never sure why he called me that. "How about something to drink?"

We walked over to a milk tank filled with glass bottles. He reached into the tank and pulled out a bottle filled with orange liquid and another with brown liquid.

"I'll take an Orange Crush and a Hires Root Beer," he said to the man behind the makeshift counter. He dug out a dime from his pocket.

The boys noticed and came running over. "Can we have some too, Daddy?" Bobby asked.

"How about you all share, then you can see which you like best." Dad handed me the Orange Crush.

I took a swallow. Up to that point in my life, I only had drunk milk and water, and occasionally fresh juice. But this, oh, this was sweet and bubbled on my tongue. "It's my favorite," I said, handing the bottle to Bobby, who started to guzzle.

"Whoa, there," said Dad, taking it back and passing it to David.

I tried the root beer. Its spicy caramel flavor agreed with me just as much. I was stumped. "I think this is my favorite." Dad laughed. I tugged at his overalls. "Can I have something to eat too?"

He bought us all hotdogs to go with our pop. It didn't matter that we each got half. It was so much fun being there in the pasture with my father, feeling that rare moment of being spoiled.

When a chorus of yelps erupted, we knew the hounds had reached the tree. Soon after, the dogs and men reappeared. The times were tabulated and awards dispersed. Then came story-telling and beer drinking. The boys and I played tag and hide-and-seek around the trucks. The spring grasses had dried in the sun, but they still felt soft, and the thistles hadn't yet sprouted prickers.

We returned home weary, with dirty feet and the feeling that as long as there were coonhound dogs, bottles of cold pop, and dads with a dime or two in their pockets, the world wasn't such a scary place. If only the feeling could have lasted.

Mom and Dad repeatedly told us not to play in the barn. So of course, that's what we did. The barn was a weathered wooden structure in need of fresh paint. Occasionally, you could see red, but mostly, the barn looked gray. The ground floor had poured cement. Each morning, the cows plodded into their stalls and were milked by hand to the sound of twangy country music playing on Dad's radio. The radio sat on a board perched atop a post, the extension cord across the ceiling to an outlet near a light switch. He believed the music calmed the animals and increased milk production. On the second floor, above the milking stan-chions, was the haymow that held loose and baled hay. To get up there, we had to climb a wooden ladder that was permanently attached to the inside of the barn wall close to the big doors. At age five, my hands couldn't fully grasp the two-by-four pieces of lumber that served as rungs.

Every evening, the cows returned to the barn for their second milking. My mother assigned Bobby and David the job of driving the small herd from the pasture to the cow yard. After the last cow entered, my job was to pull the wire gate over to the post, so Bobby could hook it. Usually there was a farmhand around, and I often wondered why that person couldn't do my job, but Mom worked hard to keep us all busy, and we worked hard to try to please her.

One day, I sat in the shade on a grassy embankment near the silo, waiting for the cows and boys to return. The only other person around was Raymond Bushey, the farmhand my dad had hired in early spring. He was stork-like, with slender arms and legs and a long face that always had stubble on it. His eyes reminded me of a hound dog's, droopy and watery. He usually had brown stains around his mouth and on his teeth from chewing tobacco. Bushey popped in and out of view while cleaning out the milking stanchions and the gutters where the cows pooped.

"Whatcha doin' there?"

I looked up. Bushey was standing in the barn's doorway, holding a pail and looking at me. I held up the clover chain I was making.

"Well, ain't that pretty?" He flashed his brown teeth at me. "You goin' to school this fall?"

I shook my head. "I have to wait one more year."

He set the pail down and ambled over. "Well, you're a big girl. I seen you do lotsa things 'round here to help."

I liked that he knew that.

He continued. "I got somethin' you can help me with in the barn. Come with me, and I'll show ya." I dropped the clover chain and followed him into the cool barn. "It's up there in the haymow," he said, extending a long arm and flashing brown teeth.

I hesitated. I was still nervous about climbing the ladder, even though the boys and I had snuck up there a bunch of times. Bushey set me on the ladder. "I'll help ya," he said. I climbed up to the top, and he helped me through the opening into the mow. The stuffy air smelled of pungent drying hay. The next thing I knew, I was on my back, my legs spread apart, my panties at my feet. Hay prickled through my dress. Bushey knelt between my legs and leaned over me. He smiled and breathed his stinky tobacco breath on me. I had never seen teeth so brown. He smelled so bad I almost gagged. He grabbed my hand and put something warm and hard in it, then spit on his finger and rubbed my bottom. Somewhere far below, a calf bawled. I let go of the object, but he grabbed my hand and placed it back on the hard thing. I had no idea what it was or why he insisted I hold it. I was paying more attention to it than what Bushey was doing between my legs. A cowbell tinkled in the distance. Bushey abruptly sat up on his knees and listened. Again, the tinny sound filtered through the haymow. Bushey went into action. He lifted me up, pulled up my panties, then stood up and tucked the hard thing back into his bib overalls.

"This is our little secret," he said, buttoning his fly. "We're not gonna tell anyone about it, okay? It's just you and me that knows."

My underwear felt wet and gross from where his brown spit had touched my butt. But his narrowed eyes and creased brow encouraged me to nod in agreement.

Bushey hurried me to the ladder, and we climbed down, he practically carrying me. He set me on the ground. "Remember, this is our special secret," he whispered in my ear, then slunk off into the shadows of the barn. I could see the cows almost at the gate. I ran to let them in.

That night, when I thought of telling Mom what happened, an image of Bushey flashed through my mind, and a strange shame rose from my center. I wasn't exactly sure what had happened in the barn, but I knew I didn't want to be a burden to my mother and I didn't want to be punished. If I told, I thought one or the other would happen. All I wanted was for my mother to love me. So I kept quiet.

A few days later, the boys insisted on playing King of the Mountain in the haymow. I suggested other games we could play outside the barn, but they began climbing the ladder. For the first time in my life, the smell of hay made me queasy. We bounded shoeless around the bales and loose straw, pushing and shoving each other. All of a sudden, a patch of slippery straw catapulted me toward the window, and before I knew it, I was hanging half out of it, looking thirty feet below at boards with protruding nails. I screamed in pure terror. No one came running. I unfroze my muscles and inched backward. When I sat up, my heart felt huge and angry in my chest. I knew what had happened. The haymow had threatened me. Watch out, it warned. If you do not keep my secrets, I will spit you to death. From that point on, the haymow, the barn, and I were not friends.

It was September, and I was in first grade. No longer would I have to sit on the porch steps picking at peeling paint while waiting for Bobby and David to get home from school. Although Bobby was a year older, he was in my first-grade class. The previous year, he had missed too much school due to polio and had to repeat the grade. David should have been in third grade, but he'd had an appendectomy the year before and often was sick, so he was in second grade. School offered a steadiness, a predictability that felt grounding and comforting.

While I liked my teacher and learning, I wasn't fond of the bus ride. First graders through high-school seniors rode the bus. The big kids picked on the little ones, and I was definitely one of the little ones. I'd be sitting in the front seat, and out of the blue, my head would jerk back because some boy had yanked my pigtail. Had I known then that I would have to ride the bus for only two years, I would have been relieved, but at the time, I thought it was a grade-school sentence.

In addition to starting first grade, I started catechism classes at our church. Although Mom's family was not religious, my mother began attending church while in high school. Sometimes she was the only one in her family at the service, having walked there or gotten picked up by a fellow parishioner. The church must have filled an empty space in her heart, because by the time she had kids, she was a devout Catholic. Every night, she made all of us kids kneel on the floor next to our beds and say our prayers.

In catechism class, our lay teacher told us the story of Adam and Eve. The serpent came alive for me. I could see it wrapped around the tree limb, hanging its head and fangs in front of Eve, taunting her. It was a thick and scaly beast. Like the rattlesnake in the kitchen that Grandma Krachey killed before it attacked my two-year-old mother. Like the snakes I imagined slithering between the blackberry bushes when Bobby and I picked fruit from their branches. Like the snakes my uncles held as they chased me through the fields, my legs and adrenaline pumping as

fast as they would go. Or the snakes they said lived in the drain
in the basement, the drain they threatened to shove me down. It
didn't matter that my mind said I wouldn't fit down the drain.
Part of me feared it and thought I would. And then there was the
snake that Raymond Bushey had made me hold in the barn.

By second grade, I had been tormented on the bus one too
many times. It was late fall, and two large boys had me sandwiched
between them and were pushing me back and forth and pulling
my braids. I ran down the steps of the bus, up the driveway, and
right into the kitchen. No one had a right to push me around. I
was going to let my mother know about this. Mom was at the
stove. I could hear her before I even entered the kitchen. She
was expounding on the trials of raising children, her arm jerkily
stirring the stew. Bobby was leaning against the counter. He had
stayed home from school, complaining of a headache.

"Children bring about their own grief," Mom said as I walked
into the kitchen. "If they would behave like they're supposed to,
these things wouldn't happen."

My indignation deflated. I wasn't sure what things she was
talking about, but her message rang out loud and clear. I must
have done something that warranted being bullied on the bus.
Maybe there were other things that I had done, too. Maybe something that made Bushey take me up to the haymow. I reminded
myself that no one was to blame when I was in trouble but me.
I took my mother's words, packaged them up, and tucked them
deep inside me.

Mom had finished mopping and waxing the linoleum floor in
our bedroom and had moved to the dining room. Bonnie woke

up from her nap on the couch and followed me upstairs. The sweet smell of the wax mingling with the summer breeze streaming through the window made me feel lighthearted. Bonnie must have felt so too, because she said, "Mary, let's play house."

"Okay," I said, happy that Bonnie felt well enough to play. It was two weeks before I would start third grade and she would start first grade. I hopped on the bed and bounced a few times. I took off my dress to better feel the fresh air and bounced some more. House would have to wait. I had a better game in mind.

"You sit on the bed here," I said patting the quilted bedspread, "and take off your dress." I helped Bonnie with the buttons and positioned her cross-legged in the center of the bed. I stood in front of her. I bounced, little bounces that pushed Bonnie up and down. Her eyes widened, and she smiled. I bounced higher, my arms extended for balance, my feet landing square and steady on the mattress. Bonnie bounced higher, her little body easily defying gravity. She giggled. I pushed my weight into the mattress. Bonnie went higher, her flyaway hair framing her round face. Her eyes sparkled. She came down, I went up. Our laughter pinged around the room, and I felt suspended in the moment. Bonnie bounced and squealed uncontrollably. Then, in a flash of a bounce, her laughter halted. She fell on her back and began coughing that deep, dry cough I knew so well. Panic seized me. Hot and sweaty, I bent over her. Her face was already turning red and her lips blue. Her tiny rib cage protruded above her barrel tummy as she gasped for air. I had caused this. I felt dizzy and weak. Bonnie gasped and convulsed. I jumped off the bed, sucking in foul-tasting air, hit the slick linoleum, and fell hard on my butt. I scrambled up. "Ma, Ma," I screamed, racing down the stairs. "Bonnie's coughing. She can't breathe!"

My mother dropped the mop on the kitchen floor and ran

past me up the short flight of stairs. I watched from the foot of the bed as she picked up Bonnie, bent her over her knees, and firmly patted her on the back. Gradually, Bonnie's cough weakened, and her breath returned. Mom checked Bonnie's rectum, and sure enough, it had popped out. She worked to push it back in. Bonnie's painful cries cut through my gut. Mom turned Bonnie over and held her close. Bonnie whimpered.

Mom glared at me. "I've told you over and over—you're not allowed to jump on the bed. Now see what you've done? What if I hadn't been here?"

Tears jammed in my throat, and shame and guilt stung me sharper than any willow switch could ever do.

My mother never talked about it, but looking back, I think she had a premonition. Maybe she had it in the middle of the night in a dream. Maybe an angel came and told her what to do, maybe Johnny's spirit spoke to her, or maybe she woke up one morning and the thought popped into her mind as strong and bitter as a cup of black coffee. At any rate, she made an appointment to have Bonnie's portrait taken. She ordered her a new dress out of the Sears catalogue. It had a navy top with a white collar and three white buttons, then flared into a patterned skirt. Bonnie's thin arms stuck out of the short sleeves. Mom tamed her curly hair with clips. In the photo, Bonnie is tilting her head and has a shy, sweet smile. It was taken two weeks before Thanksgiving.

Bonnie wanted her doctor, Dr. Randall, to have one of the photos. She liked Dr. Randall. He had his clinic over the drugstore in Boscobel, and after each appointment, Mom bought her a jellied orange slice at the store. My mother told me many years later that Bonnie, while in the hospital that fall, had told her she wished she could go to heaven to be with Sharon Kilburg, a teenage girl who had died in August. Then Bonnie asked, "If I go to heaven, do I get to be with God?" It must have been one of those moments where my mother had to swallow hard and take a deep breath before answering. Before the proofs were even ready, Bonnie was back in the hospital.

She was still there the day I came down to breakfast and Mom had her apron on over a dress instead of her usual blouse and slacks. I knew she was going to visit Bonnie. My sister had missed more of first grade than she attended. Bobby, David, and I ate our breakfast. David sprinkled extra salt on his eggs and bacon. I fed Walt in his high chair and wiped his face, instructed Barbara and Kathy to put their dirty dishes in the sink, then ran upstairs to get dressed for school. When Bobby, David, and I were ready to leave, Mom made sure our shoes were tied, hair combed, and coats buttoned, then sent us down the driveway to wait for the bus. I was hoping for snow, but the blue sky didn't look like it was going to share any. It wasn't until I plopped down in the seat next to David that I realized we didn't have our lunch boxes and thermoses.

"What are we going to eat?" I asked David, pretty certain my stomach had just growled. He shrugged.

By the time the lunch bell rang, my stomach really was growling. The other third- and fourth-graders began to spread out their sandwiches and fruit and cookies on their desk, and the milk monitor passed out cartons of milk. At least I had milk. I looked over at Bobby two rows over. His chin was resting on his arms, and his little milk carton looked empty. David was a few seats behind me. He sat in his seat looking out the window. We weren't allowed to get out of our seats during lunch.

"Mary, where's your lunch?" said the teacher, appearing by my side.

"My ma forgot to give it to us," I said.

She put her hand on my shoulder and glanced at Bobby, then David. Mom would be annoyed if the teacher bought us lunch. School lunches weren't fresh, and the district overcharged, according to Mom. The teacher looked at me and smiled one of those sad, concerned smiles that people gave me when they asked how Bonnie or my mother was doing. A few kids were starting to pack up their food. I didn't want her to ask other kids to donate part of their lunches. It would be embarrassing, and the other kids would tease me again about being poor. Maybe she would have if it were just me.

During math, someone knocked on the door. The teacher opened it, and in walked my mother carrying three lunch boxes. I sat up straight. Heads swiveled toward her and then me, David, and Bobby. Though I was too far away to hear the whispered conversation, I imagined it. Mom was saying that Bonnie was in the hospital again and having trouble breathing, so the doctors were keeping her there for more treatments. They were good doctors, and everyone was hoping she would be home by week's end. Sometimes life gives you these challenges, and the Lord willing, you can work through them. Though sometimes you forget things like lunches. A slight smile.

The teacher called the three of us over, and we stepped into the hallway. I felt big and small at the same time. Ma handed us our lunch buckets. The school secretary was there and escorted us to the small lunchroom in another building. Mom came too. "You eat, then go back to class. I'll see you after school," Mom said to us. She and the secretary spoke in whispers. I knew better than to ask about Bonnie.

Bobby, David, and I returned to our desks after eating. The incident remained unspoken among all the students; they knew something was going on with our family, and they took care that day to be nice to us. I was happy to have food because I was hungry. Although the attention felt special, below it lay a sadness that felt weighty, like I had eaten a sandwich made of pebbles instead of the peanut butter and jelly my mother brought us.

By Thanksgiving Day, the Ocooch Mountains had retreated into wintery browns and dark greens. A few inches of snow had fallen, and the air felt crisper, lighter. Or maybe it was my mother's steps. She moved around the kitchen with a light-footedness I hadn't witnessed in some time, stuffing the turkey and the goose, her favorite, boiling and mashing potatoes, and baking fresh bread. Pies and tins of popcorn balls lined the counters. My dad had killed one of her geese the day before, and by early morning, its rich scent filled the house and made mouths water. Cranberries with orange slices, green beans, apple pie, carrots, and gravy vied for attention. We attended church in the morning, and Grandma Krachey and all my uncles arrived mid-afternoon. We sat at tables set up around the house. Mom laughed when Dad teased her about making enough food to feed our first, second, and third cousins. I overheard Mom tell Grandma that the nurse at the hospital had called. "We can bring Bonnie home tomorrow," she said. Happiness pumped my heart.

Early the next morning, my parents left for the hospital. I heard the car rumble down the driveway, but I was tired and the air was cold, so I pulled the blankets under my chin and fell back asleep. No one woke me up, and by the time I finally found my way downstairs, Grandma was in the kitchen washing dishes.

"Happy birthday," I said.

"Thank you, honey. Another year older, not sure about wiser."

"When will Ma and Daddy be back?" I said, wrapping my arms around my middle.

"I suspect they'll be back by lunchtime," Grandma said. She must have seen my shivering. "You skedaddle upstairs and get some warm clothes. I'll make you breakfast."

I scurried upstairs. Barbara and Kathy were awake and sitting up.

"Bonnie's coming home," I said. I would have her little body next to mine. I wouldn't jump on the bed anymore. She wouldn't be in pain. We all went downstairs and ate breakfast. Grandma didn't assign us chores like Mom did, so we had time to play with our dolls.

I was in the kitchen with Grandma lining up bread slices for sandwiches when the phone rang. "Hello," said Grandma. Her voice was never very loud, but this time it quickly petered to a whisper, and she hung up the phone without saying good-bye. She sat down at the table, her hand over her eyes. I held my breath as my heart flip-flopped, searching for oxygen.

"Bonnie went to heaven," Grandma said. She sat very still.

I stood at the counter, a piece of bread in my hand. My eyes and mind said that Grandma was at the table, my sisters, brothers, and uncles were in the other room, my parents were within driving distance. Yet I felt abandoned, as if I was standing alone in a room, the door locked, and the key in someone else's hand. But who that someone else was and where they were, I had no idea. I felt like crying, but instead I swallowed and hoped I wouldn't choke.

Bonnie was to be buried in the same cemetery as Johnny. The thought of her being lowered into the hard, cold ground hurt my stomach. A viewing of her in a casket took place at our farm-house. The casket was set out in my parents' bedroom. She was dressed in a white dress with a flowered wreath over her curly hair. She looked frail but peaceful, like she could finally breathe. Years later, Barbara, who was two years younger than Bonnie, told me that she had touched Bonnie's arm. It felt cold. A rosary had been placed in Bonnie's hand, and Barbara's touch caused the rosary to slide to the bottom of the casket. Barbara thought she had done something terribly wrong and never told anyone what happened.

My mother told me years later that Bonnie had an incredible memory, almost a photographic memory, and could assemble a jigsaw puzzle at an early age. One time Mom lost the mop handle, and Bonnie knew it was behind the couch. She must have watched us all as she lay on the couch forcing air into her lungs, too weak to move. What she saw and understood, I'll never know. I was too young. At the time, I only knew Barbara was her sister, Ma was her mother, I was her guardian, and I had failed her.

PART TWO

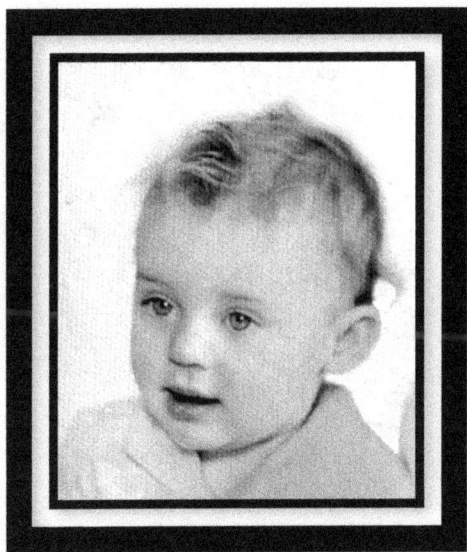

My parents intended to move into town at the start of the New Year. They had rented the farm to a young couple and bought a house in Wauzeka. Without chickens, pigs, geese, horses, and cows to care for, Mom figured she'd have more time to care for Bonnie. After Bonnie died, Mom wavered on leaving the farm but in the end stuck with the plan. The eight of us moved into a small five-bedroom, two-story home. Like most of our neighbors, we didn't have a phone, but for the first time we had indoor plumbing and the luxury of a toilet and bathtub. I've always had a sense of adventure, and even back then the move felt like an exciting new beginning. None of us would have to do farm chores, so it almost seemed like vacation, though without Bonnie beside me in bed, an emptiness persisted.

The park across the street had a bandstand, baseball field, and big hill crested with woods. During the winter, the town flooded the field and turned it into an ice-skating rink. I didn't get my first pair of skates until high school, but I spent a lot of time sledding down the hill and across the ice. Sometimes we built small jumps. The first winter, an airborne toboggan clipped David and sent him into a coughing fit. My mother was really upset, and rightfully so. It frightened all of us.

After Bonnie's death, my parents took David to the hospital in Madison for testing. I overheard them use the term cystic fibrosis. I didn't know exactly what it was, but I figured that's what Bonnie had too. Occasionally, classmates would say something about how David was sick and was going to die. They stopped when they saw my quizzical looks. Their statements frightened me. Instinctively, I knew not to bring up the subject at home. Mom's whole demeanor would melt into sadness at the mention of it, just as when someone mentioned Johnny or Bonnie's name. Though I wanted to ask what cystic fibrosis was, I didn't know whom to ask and frankly was afraid to ask. I was tired of seeing sadness.

School was two blocks away, so I could walk and avoid the bus. Church was three blocks away. My friend Mouse lived across the street. My mother didn't like Mouse's father because he went to the tavern after work to drink beer and smoke Camel cigarettes. He worked at the Wauzeka Box Factory, which manufactured wooden cheese boxes. Soon after we moved to town, Dad began working there during the week. He continued to work at the farm on weekends. The factory was located near the artesian spring down by the Kickapoo River. The wooden building had a tin roof and windows constantly covered in sawdust. A few times, I went in to get candy money from Dad. Whirring drive belts and band saws released the scent of fresh pine. Stacks of finished round boxes destined to hold seventy pounds of cheese filled tables along the back wall. I usually found Dad maneuvering wood through a table saw or working a lathe.

"What are you doing here, Frinkles?" he'd say, then tease about Ma not wanting to part with her money. I'd leave with a few dimes in my pocket and sawdust clinging to my shoes, ankle socks, and bare knees. Later in life, I wondered what it was like for my dad to transition from a dairy farmer to a factory worker. Instead of a blue sky or moody clouds, a wood-beamed ceiling with fluorescent lights hung over his head. Maybe the change eased his grief.

Before moving, Dad purchased a TV without Mom's input. It was a good distraction for all of us. At night, he'd watch television with us kids, shows like *Gunsmoke* or *The Honeymooners*. My mother would pass through the living room where we were congregated. "What's this world coming to? Everyone just sits in front of that boob tube. There are better ways to use your time," she'd say, and go off on a rant about how people were starving and struggling in the world and could use some help. The only thing she truly hated watching was football. She seemed to hate it as much as I hated *Captain Kangaroo*.

I discovered the show during fourth grade. I must have left a little later for school that morning. While Mom bustled about, Kathy and Walt, the only kids not yet school-aged, sat in front of the TV watching a show I had never seen. A man dressed like the captain of a ship was talking to a moose. I sat down to watch. That's when another man came on the scene, a tall, thin man with a plaid shirt and bib overalls. I froze. The resemblance to Raymond Bushey made me stop breathing. I went over and snapped off the television. Walt and Kathy took to fussing. Mom poked her head out of her bedroom. "Mary, what are you doing? Put that show back on, and get going to school." I turned it back on and glared at Mr. Green Jeans.

About the only other time we were allowed to watch television was on Friday nights, "fight nights," when the entire family watched boxing. Commercials advertising Band-Aids, Jell-O, Arm & Hammer, and Hamm's beer, with the cute little bear, aired between matches. Mom would pop corn and settle on the couch. She seemed to enjoy being in front of the TV then, her family surrounding her. I'd catch glimpses of her face when she thought no one was looking. I always marveled how happiness could feel sad.

That fall, my mother found a full-time job at McGregor Electronics. Every morning, she drove up the ridge to pick up my grandmother and bring her to our house to babysit. Then she carpooled across the Mississippi to the factory. When I arrived home from school, Grandma greeted me, her face close to mine, her hands cupping my face. "How was your day, Mary?" I'd share what happened, and in her quiet way she'd listen. Mom returned around suppertime, and either she or Dad would drive Grandma home. Occasionally, Grandma spent a night or two with us, especially if the weather was bad.

Snow covered the ground when Mom started getting sick. I heard her in the mornings throwing up in the little bathroom near the back door. I knew she was pregnant. She didn't announce it to the family—she never did—and no one brought it up, not even Grandma. Some months later, she was wearing a girdle. She tucked it into the back of her drawer after she took a leave from work. It was illegal for a woman to work while pregnant.

Charlotte Renae was born on September 2, 1956. The crib came out of the spare bedroom, and I commenced to change diapers again. Two years later, in February, Steven Joseph was born. Ten Mullikins now lived in the little house in Wauzeka. With each new year and new birth, the burden of childcare and household chores fell more and more on my shoulders.

I was excited to start high school and sick of summer. While

I loved the ball games across the street, July Fourth celebrations, and hanging with friends, the rest of it I could do without. Mom was working full time and had put me in charge of all the kids: Barbara, Kathy, Walt, Charlotte, Stevie, and baby Allan, born that past January. Breakfasts, lunches, laundry, vacuuming, dusting, gardening, and keeping tabs on everyone—I did it all. The only thing I refused to do was change Allan's diapers. I made Barbara or Kathy do that. And then there was Stevie, poor little Stevie with the wretched cough, who reminded me of Bonnie. I did my best to be patient with him and keep him comfortable. David was home but was too sick to help with much, and Bobby was now living with Father Cassidy in the rectory.

Bobby initially did odd jobs for the Father. Then he occasionally would have lunch or dinner with Father Cassidy. When he got his license, he drove Father Cassidy on vacations. Eventually, Bobby moved into the rectory. I'd see him at school and church and watch him play basketball at high-school games. I was jealous that Bobby got paid. Mom didn't pay me for babysitting like she paid other babysitters. When I turned sixteen, Father Cassidy asked me if I wanted to clean and iron for him. He paid me a decent wage. I overheard some parishioners grumble about our special treatment.

It was early August, one of those days where the air was so heavy you could almost lift it. Actually, I would have failed at lifting it. I'd been lifting one kid or another all day, it seemed. I also managed to clean the kitchen, pick up toys, and start boiling the potatoes for dinner before Mom arrived home. I had just folded the afghan on the couch and fluffed the pillows when she burst through the back door. A chorus of "Mommy's home" erupted. Mom threw her purse on the counter, walked into the living room, kicked off her shoes, and plopped down on the couch. Kids scrambled over her. The afghan fell to the floor, and Walt and Charlotte threw pillows at each other. As usual, Mom never said one word of thanks to me or acknowledged anything I had done.

I looked out the window and saw Mouse sitting on her porch. "I'll be back by supper," I yelled to my mother and ran out of the house before she could assign me another chore.

Mouse and I ended up walking to Helen & Bud's Kitty Korner Kafe, the restaurant bar about five blocks away. The place was a hangout for all ages. Helen Lindsey was about Mom's age and one of my favorite people. She had moved from Wauzeka to Florida and returned married to Bud. They ended up with four kids, two from Helen's first marriage and two of their own. Helen wasn't tall, but she was brawny. She wasn't afraid to cut someone off if they drank too much or boot them out on their butt, including her husband.

Mouse and I were sitting in a booth, a basket of French fries between us.

"I'm so sick of babies," I said, dunking a hot fry in ketchup. "I don't think I can handle my mom having another one."

Mouse's eyebrows arched. "Is she pregnant?"

"No, at least I hope not." I stuffed another fry in my mouth and chewed like it was the enemy. "She keeps having kids. It's embarrassing."

Helen was passing by, carrying dirty plates. She stopped. "Scoot over, young lady," she said. I slid over. Helen was pregnant and had to turn her body sideways in the booth. "Now, you listen to me. Every child is a precious gift from God. And it's another gift to take care of that child. You need to help your mother as much as you can." Helen's voice was stern but kind. She looked at me hard to make sure I understood. I nodded, my hand frozen in midair, holding a fry.

The mention of God by Helen, who could attend church but not receive sacraments of confession and communion because she had divorced her first husband, put me in my place. It would be some time before I truly understood the meaning of her words. At that moment, what I felt most was the red-faced guilt and shame that came with growing up Catholic.

Humidity had coated the day and was heightening my worry. I sat in the wooden rocking chair in the sewing room playing a 78 record on our old Victrola. I carefully set the needle on the edge of the record. Ruth Wallis launched into "The Dinghy Song." *Of all the dinghies that sail the sea, Davy's is the only one for me.* I saw Grandma walk into Mom's bedroom. I lifted the needle and strained my ears.

"How you doin', Illene?" Grandma said.

My mother groaned again, as she had been doing for the past few hours. Then silence. She hadn't been out of the bedroom all day. I had heard Grandma tell the carpool driver that Mom wouldn't be going in to work today, that she wasn't feeling well. I carefully set the needle back on the record. *Ever since we met my life has never been a bore, 'Cus when he leaves his ship, he brings his dinghy to the shore, And when we meet out on the sand and confidentially, His dinghy does more good upon the land than on the sea.* The song ended with a harsh yelp from the bedroom.

"Where's Bert?" my mother pleaded.

"He's still at work. I think you need to go to the hospital." Grandma's voice sounded worried.

A pit formed in my stomach. I abandoned my perch and walked over to the front window. Eighteen-month-old Allan was napping in his crib in the living room, and Stevie was asleep upstairs. Barbara, Kathy, Walt, and Charlotte were playing across the street. Last I had seen David, he was next door with his friend. I turned to go back to the sewing room. Grandma passed me on her way back into the kitchen, her hands stuffed in her apron pockets, her face drawn. I sat down on the rocking chair. I wasn't sure what to do.

Five minutes later, Grandma yelled, "Mary, come here." She never spoke sharply. Her voice echoed from the bathroom near the staircase and back door. I hurried back and peered into the bathroom. Mom was leaning against the sink, shaking and pale. Rivulets of blood ran down her leg. "Go into the bedroom and get your mother some clean underwear and clothes," said Grandma. "She needs to go to the hospital. We're going to have to find someone to drive her."

Grandma shut the bathroom door. I went in search of the clothing. If only Grandma could drive, but she couldn't, not a car or a tractor; even while she was married to Grandpa, she never learned to drive. I could run over to a neighbor's, but what if no one were home? Maybe, just maybe, I could drive Mom. Earlier in the summer, with a little help from Bobby and David, I taught myself to drive on a day Grandma had not come to town. Mom wasn't too happy when the neighbor tattled on me, but she didn't holler too much. She always maintained that she was driving a tractor by age six.

I knocked on the bathroom door. "I know how to drive," I said, handing the garments to Grandma. "Let me drive Mom to the hospital."

Grandma paused. "Oh my, I'm not sure," she said. "You

don't have a driver's license. If you get pulled over or something happens, you could get arrested."

Mom groaned. I could see her sitting on the toilet, head to knees. "Grandma, we shouldn't waste time trying to find someone. I'll be careful. I can do it." Grandma wavered for a moment, then nodded her head yes. I ran to find my mother's purse and the car keys.

As she walked to the car, Mom leaned heavily on Grandma. Per Grandma's instructions, I had placed an extra-thick towel on the car seat. Mom settled on it.

"Now, you drive carefully," said Grandma, her eyes locking with mine.

I put my foot on the brake, pushed in the clutch, and turned the ignition key, then shifted into first gear and nervously let out the clutch. I turned the corner, went down the hill, and merged onto the highway toward Boscobel. Mom pressed her cheek against the window, her moans coming in waves. I drove as fast as I dared.

I pulled into the hospital's emergency entrance. I was helping Mom inside when a nurse met us. "Is there anyone else with you?" she asked.

"No," I said. She looked at me skeptically, then told me that I should park the car and take a seat in the waiting room. I did as she said. No one else was in the waiting room except for a receptionist who answered an occasional phone call. I had no idea where my mother had been taken. The minute hand on the wall clock ticked.

At last the same nurse came out. I stood up, but she motioned me to sit down and took a chair next to mine. "We've admitted your mother," she said. "The doctor's taking care of her, and she's going to be fine, but she needs to stay with us overnight.

She should be okay to go home tomorrow." She put her hand on mine in a reassuring way. I waited for her to continue, but she didn't offer any more information. That was it. We were done.

I had no idea what had happened to my mother, though I had a sense it was somewhat serious. Not as serious as Bonnie's or Johnny's hospital stay, when they went in and never came back. This didn't feel like that black hole. Yet there was that familiar feeling of having questions that no one wished to answer, a nagging feeling of wanting a resolution but not being able to find one. I went out to the car, started it up, and turned toward Wauzeka.

During the drive, I replayed the time Bobby and I snuck into the loft of the birthing pen when we lived at the farm. After breakfast one day, Bobby and I overheard Mom and Dad discussing a cow. Before Dad left the house, he instructed Mom to check on the cow and to come get him when the cow was close to calving. Usually Mom would tell us to stay away from the barn when a cow was about to drop her calf, but after Dad left, she went right to stripping sheets off the beds to wash them and didn't pay us much attention.

"Come on. Let's go watch the cow," said Bobby.

We went outside, made sure Dad had driven out of sight, then ran over to the barn. We passed the milking stanchions on our way to the lean-to extension. Through the open doorway, we could see the cow in the pen of the lean-to. The safest place to watch would be from above in the hayloft. Bobby was up the ladder in no time. "Hurry up, Mary!" My heart pounded as I climbed.

I flopped down on the loose hay next to Bobby. The smell made my stomach flip. The cow bawled as if in pain. She got up, then lay down and got up again. Her bawls grew louder and more constant. I noticed something start to come out of her butt. It was the calf's front feet. Then the head appeared, and the entire calf slid out, covered in slime and bits of blood. The cow commenced to licking the calf. I wasn't sure I wanted to watch anymore, but Bobby wasn't ready to leave. Pretty soon, the cow popped out a bloody mass. After licking the calf some more, the cow turned and began to eat the mass. I thought I was going to throw up. The behavior scared me. I didn't understand it and wouldn't for years.

When I got home, Grandma quizzed me about what had happened at the hospital. After my brief report, she said, "It was a miscarriage" and went back to making dinner. I didn't know what she meant.

The next day, Dad brought Mom home from the hospital. No one mentioned the incident. Some months later at church, a new member was talking to Mom and asked how many children she had. I piped up and said eleven children and one miscarriage. Mom looked at me. For a moment, no words came out of her open mouth. Then, "No, that's not true. Elbert and I have had eleven children. Two have passed." I knew better than to argue. A number of other times, I had occasion to say the same thing, and each time Mom vehemently disagreed about the miscarriage until I began to second-guess myself. What had really happened? Had Grandma been right about the miscarriage?

Near the end of her life, my mother confirmed that she had had a miscarriage that summer. When she was hemorrhaging on the toilet in the little bathroom, she felt something pass. She stood up and looked in the toilet bowl. A fetus the size of a thimble was in there, surrounded by blood. She reached in and scooped up the mass, held it in her hand, and examined it. Whether or not she could tell the sex, she didn't say, but she decided to name the fetus Andrea after *The Christmas Box* character. She took water from the sink and baptized the baby in the name of the Father, the Son, and the Holy Ghost.

She was extremely upset at the nurse, who, while assisting the doctor during the D&C, had called the event a spontaneous abortion. My mother was as staunch an opponent of abortion as the Catholic Church. She even went to Washington, DC, to march against abortion. All those years later, Mom cried when she repeated the nurse's comment. "It was a miscarriage, not an abortion. I did not have an abortion!" she said. I explained the difference between a therapeutic and spontaneous abortion. Mom said she understood, but she looked sad and tired. "Still, she didn't need to say it was an abortion." I gave up.

Bobby and David, always the competent altar boys, had opened the church windows prior to the start of mass. The soft June breeze swirled through the sanctuary and choir loft as if floating on the doxology that our small but enthusiastic choir was singing. The choir director swooped her hands together as the hymn ended. I returned to the front pew of the loft. I had just finished my sophomore year of high school and was happy to be on summer break. I could see my parents below in their customary pew, two rows back from the altar. Mom held Stevie on her lap. Kathy, her head a mass of blond curls, leaned into Dad, and Charlotte sat next to her. Walt was kneeling on the pew, facing the back of the church. He looked up at the loft, saw me, and waved. I waved back. Barbara must have stayed home to babysit Allan.

After Father Cassidy finished the Eucharistic prayer, the congregation pulled down their kneelers. Mom shifted Stevie and pulled Walt around. I closed my eyes and listened to Father ask for forgiveness for our many daily sins. I silently added mine: getting mad at Barbara for wearing my can-can skirt the last day of school without asking; gossiping about a classmate; resenting Mom when she'd asked me to change Allan's diapers while I was watching *I Love Lucy*. Father Cassidy finished beseeching God before I could list all my transgressions.

When I opened my eyes, I happened to glance straight down. There, resting on the pew was a cowboy hat. Since most farmers wore a fedora to church or no hat at all, it seemed out of place. Then I noticed the young man sitting next to it. He had coal-black hair cut in a military crew, broad shoulders, and he sat ramrod straight. His neck was tanned and smooth. Though I couldn't see his face, I sensed it was a handsome one. My pew mate elbowed me to get off the kneeler. I sat and lost sight of the only person in church whose name I didn't know.

Father Cassidy finally arrived at the Eucharist. Bobby and David stood on either side of him in their black altar-boy robes and overlaying white smocks. The well-trained congregation filed out of their pews and approached the altar for communion. Back on the kneeler, I watched the dark-haired boy walk up the aisle, shoulders squared with self-assurance. He wore cowboy boots, jeans, and a long-sleeved shirt neatly buttoned at the wrists. He knelt down, received the host, stood, and turned to walk back to his pew. I felt my body flush. I was looking at one of the most handsome faces I had ever seen. The stranger tilted his face upward, as if knowing he was being watched. I swear our eyes momentarily met. Right then the thought hit me that I would go out with this boy. I had no idea who he was or where he came from, but somehow I knew, as well as I knew the Kickapoo River ran steadily behind the church, that I would date him. I would be sixteen in six weeks, and I had just fallen in love.

I swore the recessional we sang at the end of mass had extra measures and codas. I quickly stored my music book, then raced down the narrow stairs and out through the vestibule to the front sidewalk where parishioners gathered to greet each other and catch up on local news. My cowboy stood chatting with Mr. Doll. He looked up as I walked through the front doors, and this time, there was no question we looked directly at each other. His dark-brown eyes crinkled at the corners. He was so cute, certainly cuter than Mike Hubanks, the only other boy I had liked, and even cuter than James Dean, Buddy Holly, and the cutest of the cutest, Elvis Presley.

"Hi," I said.

"Hey," he said. I was about to step up to the conversation when Charlotte and Walt ran up to me. "Come on, Mary. Let's go," said Charlotte, pulling on my hand. I resisted until an inner knowing interceded and assured me that I didn't have to worry. I would meet my cowboy soon enough.

Later that afternoon when life at home settled into its quiet Sunday pace, with Dad sitting in his favorite chair reading the paper and Mom sneaking a nap, I carefully applied the makeup I had been too rushed to put on before mass and changed into shorts. "Going to Mouse's," I yelled to no one in particular. The kitchen door slammed behind me. Mouse was leaving her house at the same time. We had agreed to meet our friend Pat Borth at Helen & Bud's. I swung my bare arms through the air and listened to Mouse prattle on about how she had saved enough babysitting money to buy the Everly Brothers' 45 record of "Jezebel."

Pat was just getting out of her car when we arrived, and the three of us entered the café together. Sitting on a stool at the counter, visiting with Helen as if he were a regular in town, was my cowboy. My heart tumbled to my knees and made them shake.

"Hi, girls," said Helen, cheery as always. We walked up to the counter. "Have you met Johnny Payne?"

Johnny swiveled his stool toward us. "Howdy," he said.

"This here is Mary, Mouse, and Pat."

Johnny looked at me. "Didn't I see you in church today? You sing in the choir."

"That was me," I said, feeling my cheeks grow warm. Mouse and Pat looked as if they wished they could have been choir members belting out hymns.

We ordered a pop and asked Johnny Payne about himself. He had lived in upstate New York all his life and recently had hired on as a hand with Roy and Jean Kemerling, who fancied themselves cattle ranchers, though most folks considered them better at drinking than ranching. They rode their horses in the rodeo circuit. Johnny said he had grown up around horses and liked being on a farm. "Nothing like the smell of hay and horses." I flinched but smiled and nodded in agreement.

"The Kemerlings live near Bush Hollow. That's where these girls play softball," said Helen. "You oughta check out their games. It's a happening scene during the week and on Saturday nights."

Rube and Margy Mohr, a local couple, had turned a cow pasture into the Bush Hollow softball field. Rube recently had set up cinder-block and wood-plank benches to accommodate the ever-growing crowds and even grilled hotdogs. Eventually, he would get a beer license and add lights to the field. The games began around six and finished before it grew too dark to see. Helen coached our team.

"Think I might just do that," said Johnny. "Right now, I better be getting back. Got a barn to clean. Mary, girls, see you all later."

I watched him walk out the door, his back straight and broad. Johnny Payne, I thought. A movie star name.

Mouse leaned on the counter. "He has a crush on you, Mary."

My face heated up again. I couldn't believe I would ever be deserving of such a heartthrob.

True to his word, Johnny came to our softball game the following weekend. He arrived during the second inning. I was playing shortstop and saw him walk up and take a seat on the bleachers behind home plate. He looked handsome as ever in his hat, jeans, and ironed shirt. I stepped into a cloud of bliss. Happily, it didn't interfere with my game. I scored two runs and threw three players out at first. We won handily and exited the field to the applause of the local fans. Johnny made his way over to me.

"You've got some arm," he said. "Ever think about roping calves?" For a moment I thought he was serious, but then his eyes said he was kidding. Helen, Mouse, Pat, and other kids joined us, and we spent the rest of the night hanging out and talking. After it grew dark and the families with little kids left, someone brought out beer and built a bonfire. Johnny laughed, conversed, and joined in with an easygoing confidence. Even on that first night, I was pretty certain he had been accepted by our group and was equally certain everyone would soon know that Johnny Payne was mine. In a small town, new relationships are everybody's business.

By the end of July and my birthday, Johnny and I were a recognized couple. I couldn't legally drive yet, but that didn't seem to be a problem. He and I would meet at Helen's with the other kids, dance to the jukebox in the bar, then pile into cars and cruise around Crawford County to one or another of the many places to park and drink and make out. Johnny had the sweetest buttery-soft kisses. The way his hand wrapped around mine made me feel safe and strong all at once. We had enough time alone that we could share those deep parts of ourselves. I told him my dream of going to college to study journalism and eventually write. I told him how my baby brother, also named Johnny, died and how I felt him every time I walked into Sacred Heart Catholic Church, and how Bonnie had died too and how every fall I missed her terribly. He tenderly wiped the tears from my eyes. A part of me began to open up and feel lighter. Johnny listened and responded, shared and asked my opinion. I did the same with him. Even when he wasn't physically present, he stood by me as I mopped the kitchen floor, hung the wash, started dinner, or changed diapers.

It was a moonless night in mid-August. We sat on a log by the Kickapoo River. Fireflies blinked, and frogs told their stories. The river rippled through the darkness and cast its coolness into the air. I leaned against Johnny for warmth. He put his arms around me and pulled me close.

"I have a secret to tell you," he said, kissing my forehead.

"Oh really? I thought I was about ready to write the Johnny Payne biography." I ran my finger over one of the pearl buttons on his shirt.

"You'd have to call it something like *The Story of Johnny Payne, Formerly Known as Joseph Schaffhouser*."

I looked up at him, smiling, thinking he was goofing with me. "No really," he said, brushing my bangs out of my eyes. "My real name is Joseph Schaffhouser, though most of my family calls me Joe. When I got here and found the Kemerlings' ranch, I figured

I needed a Western name. I've seen every John Wayne movie, so I decided I'd be Johnny Payne."

I sat up, surprised. My Johnny was really Joseph? I thought about it for a moment. How incredibly daring and romantic. Johnny further disclosed that he was AWOL from the Marine Corps. Yes, he was from upstate New York and stationed at Camp Lejeune, North Carolina, for basic training—at least until his girlfriend mailed him a Dear John letter that sent him spiraling into desperate darkness. That's when he went AWOL.

"Mary, you need to know that it's just a matter of time before I have to go back and face the consequences."

"But you don't have to go right now, do you?" I said.

Johnny took my hand and kissed it. "No, not right now."

An owl hooted, and something jostled the undergrowth in the woods behind us. I picked up a stick and poked it into the soft earth. I knew going AWOL was a federal offense, one that could land Johnny in prison. If the authorities found out he had broken the law, they would whisk him away, and I might never see him again. I could feel the start of internal conflict. The law said one thing, and the law was made for us to follow. On the other hand, Johnny had shared his secret with me and trusted me not to tell. The church said it was a sin not to do the moral thing. Right then and there, I decided the moral highroad was to not betray Johnny. Not to Mouse. Not to Pat. Not to Father Cassidy. Johnny protected me, and I would as fiercely protect him.

"It's okay," I said. "I understand. I'll never rat you out."

He looked into me in that way he had, then kissed me, gently at first, then passionately. The river and the stars moved on, but Johnny and I remained on that log for a long time.

We continued to spend as much time together as possible, which amounted to every night and as much time as possible on the weekends. My parents met him at church, but I never invited him over to our house for supper or any type of family gathering. My mother simply said, "He's a nice boy. Hope he doesn't adopt the ways of Roy and Jean. They barely can take care of their kids with all the drinking they do. Imagine if they had to take care of twelve children." I didn't care. I had Johnny, and I was happy.

All too soon, Labor Day and the start of my junior year of high school arrived. It was Sunday. Johnny had asked me at church to come help him on the farm later in the day. I ended up hitching a ride with Pat, who I had spotted at Mouse's house. I found Johnny in the barn. As always, the smell of dry hay made my stomach somersault, but I had no intention of leaving Johnny's side. He was sweeping the barn floor. I located a broom and began helping him. Pretty soon, he flung his broom over his shoulder and marched around to a military cadence; I joined in. When we were near the ladder going up to the haymow, he paused.

"Come on," he said. "Let's go up."

He had asked me to go up with him in the past, but I always had an excuse. I knew what would happen if we climbed up there. But today felt different. Roy and Jean and the kids were gone. Johnny might be leaving soon. If I gave myself to him, maybe he would have to stay. Or maybe not. Either way, I felt more than ready to be with him completely—emotionally and physically. I loved him. Truly loved him. We climbed up the ladder, me leading the way, my heart pounding.

Johnny took my hand, led me to a pile of loose hay, and pulled me on top of him. We kissed, and his hands began to wander over me firmly but gently. He rolled me on my back and loosened the buttons on my blouse, slid off my pants. The hay prickled my bare legs, but I didn't object to anything. Together we unbuttoned his jeans and pushed them down to his ankles. I felt his hard penis. It was a split-second recognition. The disgusting image of Raymond Bushey besieged me. I sucked in my breath.

"You okay?" Johnny whispered in my ear.

"Yes," I said.

His penis pushed against me. Suddenly he stopped. "You've never done this, have you?" he said. He looked down at me, his eyes full of concern.

"No," I said. "But we can." My entire body wanted him.

"Mary, I had no idea." He slumped next to me, his arm across my stomach, his face buried in my neck. "I can't do this to you. I'm probably going to be leaving soon. What if you got pregnant? What kind of future would that be for either of us?"

We lay there half naked, not saying a word.

"I love you, Mary. But now isn't the time."

He proceeded to tell me that he had fessed up to Roy and Jean about being AWOL. They had encouraged him to come clean. He had contacted the authorities and soon would be going back to North Carolina. Most likely he would be court-martialed and have to spend time in the brig, but it was probably the best thing to do. He was tired of feeling guilty. He told me again that he loved me, and because he loved me, he couldn't take the chance of making a baby with me.

We never did make love that night, or any other night. I didn't understand at the time that Johnny truly was looking out for me. Maybe on some level I did, but it was hard to reach that level when my heart was breaking into a million tiny pieces, and a loneliness I had never experienced before, even after Bonnie died, was setting in. Part of me hoped I was pregnant. I doubted it was possible, based on what we had done. Still, I insinuated to Mouse and my other friends that I might be.

The day came for Johnny to leave. It was a Monday in mid-

September. I had seen him at church the day before. "Come to school before you leave," I said to him after the service. "I'd like to say good-bye." He knew when my lunch hour was. That night, as I fell asleep, I imagined the scene. Johnny coming into the schoolyard. Our embrace. Our tears.

The next day, I hung out with my girlfriends at school. I laughed and talked with one eye to the road. As the lunch hour dwindled, the pit in my stomach grew. Yet I never stopped hoping, even after the bell rang, that Johnny would show up. He didn't. He went AWOL from our relationship without that last good-bye my sixteen-year-old romantic heart had fantasized.

When I arrived home, my grandmother met me at the door. She gave me an extra-long hug. Then she pressed our foreheads together. "There are other boys in this world, honey. Someday you'll find the perfect match." I went upstairs and cried for a while. My mother, of course, never said a word about Johnny, though I knew she knew what had happened. Years later, when I read about Rube in her diary, I realized she knew more than the fact Johnny had left town. She knew what it felt like to feel loved and to love and then have it all stripped away in one moment. Had I not found her diary, I would never have known that we shared that experience.

That fall, I received two letters from Johnny. He wrote that when he returned to Camp Lejeune, he spent thirty days in the brig. He was sorry for what he had put me through and thought it best for me to move on and do well in school. Although I was happy to hear from him, it was not the letter I wanted. I felt hurt, betrayed, and confused. The letter was short. He didn't say he missed me. I wrote back a cheery letter, adding in a p.s. that I hoped he would continue to write. However, in his next letter, he asked if I would write to his friend Denny Blaney, a buddy from Camp LeJeune, who was going through a bout of loneliness.

Denny and I corresponded for almost a year. He kept me up to date on what Johnny was doing and where he was. It was a crushing blow when Denny informed me that Johnny and his girlfriend had reconciled. Denny and I kept our letters to general conversations about his military life and my school and family life. Occasionally, we exchanged photos. He participated in the Cuban Missile Crisis and wrote letters from the Caribbean. I didn't like the idea he was in a dangerous place. We planned to meet someday but never did. Between letters, I kept myself busy with cheerleading, marching band, dance band, choir, and weekend activities with friends.

Before I knew it, May had arrived, bringing with it the start of softball season. One day I arrived home close to supper, after having gone to Helen's with the rest of the team to discuss what T-shirts we wanted as uniforms.

"Hi," I said, walking into the kitchen. Mom was peeling carrots at the kitchen sink. Four-year-old Stevie sat on a chair at the table, and Allan, now two, was zooming a truck around the floor.

Stevie immediately stood up on his chair and threw his arms up in the air. "Mawy's home!" he yelled. It was our ritual. Whenever I arrived home from school, he came running to greet me and tell me about his day. I set my books on the counter and picked him up.

"Hey, big boy," I said. He put his arms around my neck and hugged me. We sat down at the table, and he poked his finger in a pile of wetted salt, then licked it. Mom brought carrots over to me to slice. She looked tired. Her morning sickness had stopped about a month before.

"We're moving back to the farm," she said abruptly. I almost dropped the knife. Mom's younger sister, Loretta, and her husband, Melvin, had been renting the farm for the past four years.

"Aunt Loretta said they purchased a farm and want to give it a go. Your dad and I are going back to farming." She picked up a potato. "We'll have to figure out the machinery and cows," she said, almost to herself. "We should move before school starts in September."

The peeler rhythmically clinked as it did its job. Allan reached out his hand, and I gave him a carrot. The farm? I didn't want to move back to the farm. It seemed like a lifetime ago that we had lived there. Horses, chores, hay. I loved living in town, especially in the summer, when I could walk across the street to baseball games or down by the Kickapoo or over to Helen's or anywhere I wanted. Sure, it was only a few miles away, but life would be different. I didn't respond. The decision had been made, though I almost blurted out, "Just make sure you don't hire Raymond Bushey." I had seen him walking on Main Street the other day. He crossed over when he saw me, like he always did, his head down.

I told Mouse we were moving. "Don't let any weirdos move in," she said trying to make light of it, but she looked about as bummed as I felt. "You better get your driver's license so you can haul down here to Helen's." Mouse's family didn't own a car.

A week after school ended, Mom walked in from work carrying an armful of packing boxes she had taken from McGregor. "We can start filling these with stuff in the junk room." I went over and picked them up. Might as well start now, I thought.

"You know," she said, dropping her purse on the counter and walking out of the kitchen, "you could stay here and keep an eye on things until we get everything moved."

I stopped. "You mean live in the house? By myself?"

"Yes," she called out from her bedroom. Had I heard her right? "The insurance policy we have isn't good if the house is empty," she said. "We need someone here, and I don't want to rent it out right now."

She continued talking, but the only thing I heard was the thought singing in my head: I don't have to move back to the farm, I don't have to move back to the farm. At least not until October or so. Mom said she wouldn't pay to heat the place during cold weather. It all sounded so exciting and a little intimidating. But I wasn't about to be a scaredy-cat. I had lived with a pile of people all my life. It would be an adventure. This was so out of character for my mother to give one of her children such independence. To do this day, I still can't explain what she was thinking.

Moving began in July. Mom ended up leaving a bunch of stuff in the house. I suspected she wanted an excuse to come check on me periodically. Mouse came over my first night alone, and we played Elvis Presley records and danced around the house. It didn't take long to adjust to having a place of my own. The dishes stayed in the cupboards, and the afghan stayed folded on the couch. It was quiet when I wanted it to be and noisy when I wanted it to be.

The neighbor next door, who had always liked David but not the rest of us, told my mother she didn't like me living alone. She peered out her window when my friends came over. One night we went to Helen's, got an empty beer case, and loudly toted it up the sidewalk past neighbors' windows and porches. Sure enough, someone reported us, and the police came over. They never found anything because we had brought the case through the front door, walked it out the back door, and returned it to Helen's. Frustrated, the cops checked every room while we reveled in our cleverness. Most of the summer was filled with softball, wild beer parties, and boys I didn't want to be with because they weren't Johnny.

Senior year began, and so did band practice. It was a Thursday, and the school and town were buzzing with excitement about playing our biggest conference rival the next day. The band teacher had let us out of practice early. I had all the windows open and was sitting in the living room on the couch doing homework and enjoying the breeze when I heard the kitchen screen door slam. I figured it was Mom stopping by to get something. She stopped by almost every other day with some excuse. I stood up to meet her. Much to my surprise, it was my Uncle Bud, my mom's younger brother by six years. He and his wife, Linda, and their two daughters lived on the other side of Wauzeka.

"Hello, Mary," he said. The words slurred out of his mouth. He stumbled a step toward me. The lopsided grin on his face didn't match the calculating look in his glazed eyes. "Living by yourself, are ya?"

I didn't know what to make of his presence. All the years we lived in town, he'd never been to our house. Mom never had much to do with him, though she never said why. I had a vague memory of him fondling me at the farm when I was five or six. It wasn't nearly as traumatic as Bushey. I often wondered if Mom had witnessed Bud's behavior and that's why she didn't like him.

"What's up, Bud?" I said warily.

"How you like living here without nobody botherin' ya?" He teetered and grabbed the kitchen chair, then walked into the living room. I followed him. "Bet all those boys you hang out with really like that, don't they now?" His crooked grin made my stomach convulse. "You can do anything you pretty well please with all those boys. I betcha they're lining up to get in there," he said, glancing at the open bedroom door. He took a few steps toward me and put his hand on my shoulder as if to steady himself, then pushed me. I twisted away from him, but in the wrong direction. I landed just inside the bedroom door.

"Get away from me!" I yelled. Panicked, I shoved his chest hard. He fell backward against the wall. I ducked around him and ran through the living room into the kitchen. He must have gathered himself quickly, because he was on my heels. I turned, ready to fight. His face flushed red, but the fire in his buggy eyes had died. He shook his head as if to clear it. "Guess I better go," he muttered and walked out the door.

I watched him get in his car and drive off. I wanted to throw up. I closed the kitchen door, wishing I knew where the key was to lock it, ran into the bedroom, and collapsed in the closet. I sat there shaking for who knows how long. The only thing I could see was Bushey, sitting over me, tobacco drool coming out of his mouth, his grin sickening. The smell of hay was everywhere. I started to sob.

A few hours later, my mother stopped by to pick up some things to bring back to the farm. By then, I was mad.

"Uncle Bud was here," I said. She looked up sharply from putting cake pans into a wicker basket. I proceeded to tell her what happened. Mom banged the last pan in the basket, her brow furrowed. She did nothing to console me or even give me a hint that she believed my story. She left abruptly, without the basket.

On Saturday, Mom returned. I was doing dishes. She leaned against the counter; arms folded, and in her brusque way said, "Linda's going to talk to Bud. If what you said is true, she's threatening divorce."

I was stunned. If it's true? Did my mother really think I made it up?

That was the extent of our conversation. Linda never talked to me about the incident, though whenever I was around her, I sensed she wanted to ask me about it. I didn't like thinking I might be responsible for her divorce. I liked Linda. I knew her marriage was troubled. From that point on, Bud and I avoided each other at family functions. Seeing him was like seeing Bushey walking the streets of Wauzeka. It gave me the creeps and made me nauseous.

At long last, I got my driver's license. On a crisp October day, Bobby drove me to Boscobel in our old '58 Ford, and I easily passed. He reminded me that Lyle took the test three times before he passed. A sense of accomplishment lifted my spirits. Afterward, we drove two blocks to the hospital, where, a few hours earlier Mom had delivered her twelfth baby, a little girl.

We weren't allowed to see Mom, but we could see our new sister, Sharon, through the nursery window. She was a pretty little baby with black hair framing a round face. Three years before, I had looked at baby Allan and my heart filled with resentment. But this baby felt like a gift, not a burden. Maybe Helen's words had sunk in, or maybe I was thinking about my love for Johnny and what the two of us could have brought into this world. I remained inexperienced with intimacy, but right at that moment, I knew on every level of my being that life was precious. The innocence and wonder living and breathing on the other side of the glass window confirmed it. Certainly, my mother felt something similar with the birth of each child. How could she not? But she never shared those feelings, even when I became a mother and she a grandmother.

On the way out of the hospital, Bobby and I ran into Dad. He pointed to a shiny-new blue Ford parked at the curb. With a funny grin on his face he said, "Think your ma will like it?" Turned out he had just bought the car. I've often wondered if he were celebrating the birth of another child or the birth of the twelfth child or the birth of the last child. At the time, it didn't matter a hill of beans. Another Mullikin had made it into the world, I had my driver's license, and our family had a new car. As I drove the old Ford back to Wauzeka, the blue sky seemed to kiss the tops of the maples and elms, making their leaves blush a deeper red, gold, and yellow. I rolled down the window and breathed in contentment.

I moved back to the farmhouse just before Thanksgiving. It was winter break when one of my girlfriends suggested that I go out with Butch Havens. I had been in the same class with Butch since eighth grade, when he and the other kids from the neighboring town of Steuben transferred to Wauzeka schools. A few years earlier, I had a crush on his older brother, Denny, two years Butch's senior and a cutie, but had never paid much attention to Butch. He was popular and always seemed to be dating someone. I knew he played catcher for the baseball team and had played running back and linebacker on our football team. I wasn't thrilled. I preferred older boys. Plus, Butch had blond hair and blue eyes, and I had dated only boys with dark hair and eyes. Besides, two of his front teeth were missing. But seeing as I didn't have anything better to do the week between Christmas and New Year's, I agreed to go out with him.

The plan was for Butch and two of his buddies to pick up Mouse and me. The girl who arranged the date wasn't able to join us. I was excited to wear my first store-bought coat; all my others had been second-hand. It was a deep red. Mom had splurged and bought it for me from the department store in

Boscobel and for Christmas gave me a matching plaid scarf, hat, and mittens. She also gave me a pair of vinyl boots with fake fur lining. They weren't the expensive leather kind that some girls wore, but they were pretty cool. Feeling stylish, I slid into the backseat between Butch and Mouse.

The snow looked like super-fine sugar crystals sparkling in the moonlight. It was so bright outside we could see the hills rolling into the distance and almost see into the woods. We drove around the county trunk roads, talking and joking, and ended up farther east than usual. We were flying along when all of a sudden there was a loud pop, and the car veered right. The tire had blown. Russell, the guy driving, said he wasn't surprised, the treads had been wearing thin. Back then, beer money trumped gas and new-tire money.

We limped along the side of the road. A farmhouse light splintered through trees. Russell stopped the car. In the moonlight, we could see a barn and silos. We whispered to avoid having a dog alert the farmer.

"I know this place. There should be an old car behind the barn. We can borrow a tire," said Russell.

"Hey, I always bring stuff back when I'm done using it," said Butch. Stifled giggles filled the car. The three guys discussed the matter and decided they could take a tire without being noticed. They got out of the car and headed toward the hedge of trees.

"Oh, man, I hope a cop doesn't drive by," I said to Mouse. Guilt surged through me. I wondered how many Hail Mary's Father Cassidy would assign if we got busted. We kept watch out the windows. A dog barked. I held my breath. The barking grew louder. No lights flicked on. Finally, the boys burst through the trees rolling a tire between them and laughing too loudly. They replaced the tire and got in the car, hysterical at their antics. We headed back to Wauzeka. Russell dropped me off. I told Butch

I'd see him at school. He was a nice guy and had a good sense of humor, but as far as boyfriend material, he didn't seem to have the right threads. The only other thing I learned that night was that vinyl boots with faux fur are not as warm as they look.

Butch must have felt differently because he asked me out. We met after basketball home games. Bobby played on the team, and I played in the pep band and attended every game. Butch and I sat next to each other on the bus going to away games. Weekends, we went to movies or school dances, or we'd hang out at Helen and Bud's before piling into a friend's car and cruising around the area. If Butch had access to a car, he'd pick me up, though I quickly learned not to depend on him.

On one of our first dates, we planned to see Elvis Presley's *Fun in Acapulco* at the Boscobel Theater. Butch said to be ready at 7:30 p.m. Forty-five minutes later the movie was rolling and I was still watching out the farmhouse kitchen window for the glare of his headlights. He finally pulled into the driveway with the excuse that his dad had the car and had run late.

The next weekend, Butch was late again. This time I didn't wait and went down to Bud and Helen's. I was in the bar dancing to "Jailhouse Rock" when Mouse nudged me. "Look who just walked in," she said. Butch was wearing his fake leather jacket and blue jeans and already attracting attention with his Donald Duck impression. Irritated, I turned my back to him but heard him launch into his imitation of Crazy Guggenheim. With his missing teeth, he was pretty good at it. Laughter erupted. Okay, so it softened my anger. I joined the crowd, but I was still pissed, and Butch knew it. He never did apologize.

It was the start of a cat-and-mouse game between Butch's irresponsibility and my need for his accountability that would continue far too long. My grandma was the only one who said a word about Butch. When I walked into the farmhouse kitchen one day, she took my face in her hands and leaned her forehead against mine. "I don't think that boy is good for you, Mary Mullikin," she said. "I don't like all the carousing that family does." I loved Grandma to pieces, but what did she know?

Then in February something happened. It was an unusually nice day with a shy sun high in a pale-blue sky, warm enough to unbutton your coat and let your bare fingers feel the fresh air. Butch's four-year-old brother, Timmy, had begged their mom to let him go play outside. She said no, but Timmy was a persistent little guy accustomed to running freely around the neighborhood. The Steuben townsfolk knew Timmy by name. She put his coat and hat on him and pushed him out the door.

The Havens lived next to Cecil and Dutch Miller's bar where Butch's dad, Cap, had a permanent stool. His dad had been the previous owner. Cap had a wooden leg from the knee down, and one of his eyes was cloudy from a past injury. Timmy went to look for Cap, who, sure enough, was camped out in the bar. The current owners had a shot glass and cigar reserved behind the bar for Timmy, a fact confirmed by a family photo of Timmy in his bib overalls holding the glass, a long cigar protruding from his mouth. That day, Cap told Timmy to scram and not bother him.

Timmy then went to the next place he knew—the gas station, where big brother Butch worked. Butch was supposed to be in school but had skipped out to earn a few bucks. The Havens were poor, even poorer than my family. Butch missed school about as often as Cap sat in the bar, though I think his truancy had more to do with his dislike of studying than it did with money. Timmy kept begging Butch for a treat. Irritated, Butch relented, gave him some candy, and told him to scram. Timmy then met up with his little friend Craig.

The boys decided to play on the ice rink near the Kickapoo

River. Timmy had been given explicit instructions never to go down by the river. In fact, the admonishments had made him afraid of the water to the extent that he never wanted to swim or even fish with his big brothers. But that day, his curiosity won, and he decided to explore the ice shelf that had formed when the ice rink was flooded. It hung over the river at such an angle that warm air could wheedle its way into the formation, creating a fragile honeycomb structure. When Timmy stepped onto it, it plummeted into the frigid river, and Timmy plummeted with it. Craig witnessed the fall. He took off running to the last place he had seen somebody—the gas station.

In a panic, Butch raced to the river and ran along the bank, screaming Timmy's name, his eyes peeled for the little boy. Within minutes, others joined him. Butch spotted his brother first. Timmy's jacket had caught on tree debris in a shallow part of the Kickapoo. Butch splashed into the freezing water and pulled Timmy to shore. The fire department arrived and began CPR, but it was too late. Hyperthermia had taken its toll, and with it, the life of the brown-eyed, much-loved little boy known to all of Steuben.

By the end of the school day, rumor had spread from Steuben to Wauzeka that Butch Havens' brother had died. I boarded the bus, my heart heavy with the Havens' loss. By the next day, Crawford County pretty much knew the chain of events. Upon hearing of Timmy's death, Cap made a beeline for the bridge and threatened to jump off into the Kickapoo. His sons and friends pulled him back, then kept a vigil around him the rest of the night. Betty, unable to forgive herself for sending Timmy outside, wept so loudly you could hear her from the street.

The wake was two days later. I asked Mom if I could borrow the car to drive to the funeral home in Boscobel. Her mouth sank at the corners, and a familiar sadness settled in her eyes. "Yes," she said. She and my grandma talked quietly at the kitchen table while Barbara and I carried wood in from outside and fetched water from the pump house near the barn. I was pretty sure they were discussing the Havens, though neither of them said anything to me or asked how the family was doing.

The wake was set to begin at four o'clock in the afternoon. I chose to arrive at the funeral home around seven so I could be present for the rosary. I hadn't talked to or seen Butch since the accident. When I walked in, he looked right at me. For a second I thought he didn't recognize me, because he had such a puzzled look on his face. I went over to him.

"Hi," I said. "I heard. I'm so, so sorry. Timmy was such a sweetheart." Butch looked as if he were going to cry, but he stood straighter, as if determined to swallow the tears. Behind me, a woman blew her nose and sniffled.

"I didn't expect to see you here," he said. Now it was my turn to be surprised. Of course I would be here, I thought. It was my duty. "I'm glad you came, though," he added.

I noticed his brothers Denny and Terry milling behind him; his other brother Gary sat off to the side alone. They bore equally lost expressions. Butch's sisters, Theresa and Susan, looking confused, sat near Betty. Betty stifled her cries and kept pressing a worn handkerchief to her face. A couple from Steuben who I vaguely recognized came up to Butch. I excused myself and went to pay my respects to Cap and Betty. Cap squeezed my hand and seemed to stare through me with his good eye; his cloudy eye seemed to be crying of its own accord.

I moved on to Timmy's casket. His head rested on a pillow, every brown hair in place. He wore a white button-down shirt. He was about the same size as Bonnie when she died. He laid there, another sleeping angel. I wasn't sure how I was supposed to feel. Death and grief were right next to me, and yet I didn't want to let either get too close. Death dredged up a curiosity planted oh so long ago, when I looked at baby Johnny in his white basket. Part of me understood it, but another part felt overwhelmed by the thought of someone being alive one moment and gone the next. I thought if I started to cry, I wouldn't stop. So I opted for the other choice, which was to bury my grief and be strong for the Havens family, especially Butch.

After the rosary, everyone began to leave. I offered to drive Butch to Steuben. We walked out without saying a word to anyone. Cars lined both sides of the street. Someone had salted the sidewalk in front of the funeral home, but farther up the sidewalk, the snow squeaked under our boots. We climbed in, and I turned the key in the ignition.

"Never been to a wake before," said Butch. "Who would have thought it would be for little Timmy?" His voice cracked. Then sobbed. "I-I-I can't believe he's gone." The words sputtered out between gulps of air.

A lump formed in my throat. Keep it together, Mary, I lectured myself. Butch needs you now. For the next twenty minutes, he cried and talked and talked and cried. We pulled up to the curb across from his house, and I turned off the engine. Another car pulled into the Havens' driveway. Butch dragged his sleeve across his face. "You'll be okay," I said, taking his hand in mine. "I know it's really hard, but it will be okay." I felt at a loss for words. Butch looked at me and nodded.

"Thanks for being here," he said.

"I'll come to the funeral, too," I said.

He leaned over and gave me a quick kiss, took a deep breath, exited the car, and headed toward his house. Another half-dozen cars were pulling up as I drove away.

The next day, after the funeral, everyone gathered at Cecil and Dutch Miller's bar in Steuben for food and drink. And was there drink. Bonnie's funeral had been a solemn, whispered event at our farmhouse. Johnny's had been a mysterious experience at the church. The light filtering through the dirty bar windows highlighted the cigarette smoke wafting through the air. The jukebox played The Beatles' "I Feel Fine." Someone laughed loudly. An unease settled about me. I drank a Coke while Stan talked football with his brothers and uncle. I didn't hear Timmy's name mentioned the rest of the night. Maybe I was in familiar territory after all.

Butch and I become a recognized couple. His grief sat like a rock on his shoulders. I had a feeling I was one of the few who could see it weighing him down. Around our friends, he acted more macho than he had in the past, but when he wasn't entertaining in a loud voice or goofing around, I'd see sadness flash across his face.

"How you doin'?" I asked one day in the hallway after classes had ended. Butch had just slammed his books into his locker and kicked it shut with his foot. He had skipped school the past three days.

"Eh, I'm okay." His voice moped through the words.

"Want to go for a walk? It's not too bad outside." Big, lazy snowflakes had been falling since noon. We went outside and ambled up the street. The white houses and streets looked like they had new life. Butch zipped his letterman's jacket, and I hooked my arm through his.

"So how's your mom?"

"She cries all the time," said Butch. There was a hint of anger in his voice. "And my dad, he's still not right. Goes over to the bar in the morning and doesn't come home until late at night. Seems nobody's gettin' much sleep."

"You can't keep beating yourself up over this," I said. "Everyone has regrets about what happened." If anyone knew guilt, it was me.

"God, I miss the little shit," Butch said. His voice wavered. We had arrived at the park across the street from our empty house. Mom still hadn't rented it out, nor had she sold it.

"Let's go this way," I said, pulling Butch in the direction of the house.

As I suspected, the back door was open. Since all the furniture had been moved to the farmhouse or given away, the only place to sit was on an old mattress that for some unknown reason remained in the middle of the living room. We perched on its edge, our coats warding off the cold. I held Butch's hand. The simple gesture loosened his defenses, and he opened up about the discord between his parents and how his mother struggled to fix meals and clean house, while his two sisters seemed lost and his twin brothers ran rampant. If people weren't yelling at each other, they were listening to their mother cry. Butch sounded so bewildered, confused, and hurt. He put his head in his hands. The next moment, tears were wetting his face and his shoulders shook. I put my arms around him and held him for a long time.

We returned to the house later that week and the next week and the week after that. Not every day, but enough to make it a safe place for Butch to talk and cry. We lay on the mattress and held each other. One thing led to another during those weeks. Clothes loosened. Hands explored. He needs this, I thought, this intimacy. It's consoling him. We fumbled through lovemaking, but make love we did, with me well aware that by doing so I was committing myself to Butch. My mother said it and the church said it: once you had sexual intercourse with a man, you were committed to him. I would have no other choice but to marry Butch and stick by him for life. I was okay with that commitment because I loved Butch and Butch loved me. Maybe not in the same way Johnny and I loved each other. I had seen Elizabeth Taylor and Richard Burton in *Cleopatra*. That's us, I kept telling myself.

Life, however, doesn't always trudge along the path you expect it to. Sometimes the path that seems as stable as a thick block of ice in subzero temperatures is really a thin, honey-combed shelf. If you step on it too hard, you get dumped into the icy waters. My vinyl boots were thin enough to tell me I was treading on some slippery, cold ice, but like poor sweet Timmy, I had no idea how thin that ice really was.

PART THREE

After Butch's tears dried up, or were dammed up, he pulled jackass stunts. He taunted the principal. He cursed like a drunken sailor. He took his parents' car without permission. When Cap confronted him, Butch refused to back down. Betty screamed at them to stop arguing. Cap swung at Butch and missed. Later, Betty told me she knew the ironclad fist of Cap and feared if he were sober and connected with Butch's face, he might kill him. On top of all that, Butch couldn't graduate high school because of his absences and dismal grades. The principal, a former military man, told Butch if he enlisted, he would give him his diploma. So Butch joined the navy.

After graduation, he reported to Great Lakes Naval Training Station in North Chicago, Illinois. He'd hitchhike to Wauzeka on his days off. Mom found a position for me at McGregor Electronics. She insisted I pay rent to live at home and contribute to her carpool, which I had no option but to join. Every day seven people, sometimes eight, piled into her car, and for thirty minutes smoked, laughed, and complained. I just wanted out from all of it.

"Sure would be nice if you could be closer," Butch said in September

"Sure would do Butch a world of good to have you nearby," said Betty.

"It'd be okay if you moved near Butch," said Mom.

"You stay here with your folks and let things take a better course," said Grandma.

"A woman must stay with the man she has sexual relations with," preached Father Cassidy.

That fall, I managed to extract myself and move closer to Butch. One of my aunts was moving to Norfolk, Virginia, to be with her husband, who had been called up from the naval reserves. They owned a mobile home in the town of Bristol, Wisconsin, less than ten miles north of Butch's base. Bobby and two of my uncles also needed a place to stay, so the four of us rented it. I found a job at a nearby manufacturing facility, and everything seemed to be in place. Butch started spending nights at the trailer. The guys knew he was there, a source of constant embarrassment and shame for me. I always intended to send him home, but his persistence for sex won out every time.

A few weeks after I moved, Butch said, "Hawk and I are going to buy a car." Hawk was his new navy buddy. "But we need you to go in on it with us, Mary."

He and Hawk had discovered that banks weren't keen on lending money to transient navy personnel earning meager wages. My income and job could anchor the ship in the bank-loan harbor. "You could drive the car to work," said Stan. Since I left for work before the sun rose, I readily agreed.

Butch and Hawk found a sleek 1960 Ford Fairlane Sunliner. It was lavender with white vinyl seats. "Oh, baby!" said Butch when he drove the car out of the lot. I was just as excited. Butch stayed over at the trailer that night. I fell asleep in his arms, the proud owner of a new car. The next morning, Butch drove me to work. He pulled up in front of the building. "I'll be back by three," he said. We kissed, and off he went. What a relief not to have to think about how I was going to get home from work.

A few minutes after three, I walked into the parking lot expecting to see a lavender car and Butch. I knew he had finished guard duty at noon, plenty of time to shower and get to me. It was a cloudy, gray day, and chilly gusts pushed their way through my jacket. I waited for a while, watching fellow employees drive away. The low sky let loose a fine mist. I dug a headscarf from my purse and tied it on. Frustrated, I went back inside to call Butch at the base. No answer. I couldn't believe it. I could feel heat rising in me. An hour and a half later, Butch arrived. He said he had gone out with his buddies and lost track of time. He wouldn't do it again, he promised.

But he did do it again. More than once. Enough for me to start making rules and setting consequences, like a mother to a child. On the surface, we had fun adventures in a world that was new to both of us. But below, I sensed an undercurrent of problems, one that I chose to ignore; I didn't believe it was strong enough to pull me under. We bumped along, occasionally arguing, yet always ending up snuggled together under the covers, Butch sweet and full of apologies. I'd bring out my checkbook and make the next car payment.

We were sitting in the Fairlane on a crisp fall night down near Lake Michigan. Butch reached over and opened the glove compartment.

"I figured you'd never marry me without a ring, so I gotcha this," he said, pulling out a small box and handing it to me. Oh no, I thought. I opened the box. Inside was a thin yellow gold band with a small diamond in the middle and two smaller diamonds on either side. "Costs me ten dollars a month," said Butch proudly. He slipped the ring on my finger. How was I going to tell him I didn't want to get married right now? I couldn't depend on him. I couldn't trust him. Military life was unstable, especially with a war going on. On the other hand, I didn't want to break his heart, especially before he shipped out. The thought of him going off to war without my commitment played on my heart.

My dad, grandma, and siblings offered subdued congratulations. My mother looked rather grim, as did Cap. Betty was the only enthusiastic one. She still held out hopes that Butch would grow up. Butch and I didn't set a date. We thought it better to wait to see where he'd be stationed. That was perfectly fine by me.

Being engaged didn't make Butch any more responsible. One night, after waiting and waiting and waiting for him, I called the guard shack at the base and asked if he were still on the grounds. They said he had signed out three hours earlier. I hung up, found the engagement ring box, and jammed the ring in it. When Butch finally arrived and walked into the trailer, I lit into him like I had never done before. He insisted nothing was his fault. I insisted it was. Fuming mad, he walked out the door, got into my car, and began backing out. I went after him, ring box in hand. He stopped when he saw me and rolled down the window. Without a word, I fired the box through the window. He tore off, spraying gravel all over. Some days later, my guilt surged, and Butch and I made up, though by then he had returned the ring to the store. He hadn't kept up with payments, and the store owner had been hot on his trail to repossess the merchandise.

Just before Christmas, I found a better job at a new Montgomery Wards in Kenosha, a town along Lake Michigan, which Butch could easily reach by train. Bobby had taken a job at American Motors and had just married Carol, so I moved in with them.

"You can't stay overnight anymore," I said to Butch. He

pouted; relief flooded through me. I still physically desired him, but I was more than happy to keep the guilt and shame of a mortal sin at a distance, though we ferreted out places, like the backseat of the Fairlane, to satisfy our raging hormones.

Butch continued to whine that he wanted to get married. "You'll only marry me if you get pregnant," he said. Secretly, I suspected he wanted me to get pregnant. He occasionally would say the navy would release him if he were married and his wife got pregnant. I had heard otherwise.

I fended him off. "Why don't you get your teeth fixed instead?" I said. When Butch enlisted, the recruiting officer had said the navy would replace his missing teeth. I couldn't convince him to take advantage of the opportunity. The one thing he wanted to do was change his name from Butch to Stan. His parents had named him Stanley after the baseball player Stan Musial. That seemed easier than getting married, so I started calling him Stan.

It was February 1965. Stan and I and two navy buddies were in the Fairlane, flying along the highway from Kenosha toward Wauzeka. The guys had a free weekend, and I was heading home to celebrate Mom's fortieth birthday. It was nearing dusk when Stan turned into the farmhouse driveway. Snow crunched under the tires. Everything looked white and gray except for the cozy glow of light in the farmhouse windows. Stan opened the trunk and handed me my bag.

"See you Saturday night at Helen's. Seven o'clock," I said.

"Yep, we'll be there." He kissed me.

"Make sure you're on time."

He peeled out of the driveway. I noticed Walt heading to the barn. We exchanged a wave. The rickety screen door was wrapped in plastic to fend off the cold. I pushed it open and stepped into the kitchen. Warm air gushed over me, smelling like pork roast and onions. An apple pie sat on the counter. Grandma was putting a log in the stove. Before I could set my bag down or take off my coat, seven-year-old Stevie came running in from the living room.

"Mawy!" he yelled, his little arms wide open like he was going to launch himself into the air. He looked so cute in his bib overalls and striped shirt. "Mawy's herrreeeee!"

I scooped him up, tickled him, and kissed his neck. He doubled over, laughed, then gave a hard cough. I gingerly set him down before he coughed again. I peeked in the living room. The other kids were watching TV, sitting close to the oil-burning stove. Kathy looked up and waved. Sharon was sucking her thumb, snuggled on Kathy's lap.

"Hi, honey," said Grandma, coming over to give me a hug. I gave her a one-armed hug, since Stevie had my other arm and hand in a tight grip. He pulled me into the living room.

"Where's Barbara?" I asked over my shoulder.

"She stayed at school. There's a game tonight."

"Oh really?" Maybe I'd go. Most likely Mouse and other friends would be there. I sat in Dad's chair. Stevie climbed onto my lap.

Later, after the supper dishes were done and Dad had settled in his chair to watch TV, Mom and I bundled up in our coats and boots, and she drove me down to the basketball game. She was whizzing along at her usual fast pace and was about to crest a knoll when a brilliant light exploded over the horizon. We both saw it. The car slowed as if Mom had forgotten to press the gas pedal.

"Something bad is going to happen," she said, almost to herself. "Something bad is going to happen soon."

Three weeks later, on a Monday, Mom called me. Phone calls between us were rare because of the long-distance charges. She wanted to tell me that Stevie was in the hospital in Boscobel. He had developed a tooth infection and high fever the previous night. His body was having a hard time fighting the infection, and his doctor wanted to administer a stronger dose of antibiotics and keep an eye on him.

"It's nothing to worry about," Mom said. "He was asking if you'd be home this weekend." I told her to reassure him I would see him Friday after work. I hung up. It's nothing to worry about, I reminded myself. Nothing to worry about.

On Thursday, Mom called again. Stevie was still in the hospital, his fever high and his breathing labored. I tossed and turned that night. The next day, work dragged by. Stan had duty at the base and couldn't break free, so I drove alone to the farm.

It was well after ten o'clock when I pulled into the driveway. Everyone was in bed. I tiptoed into Mom and Dad's bedroom. The yard light near the pump house cast shadows in the room. I shook Mom awake.

"How's Stevie doing?" I asked.

"The doctor doesn't think he's going to make it," she said, her voice shaky.

Mom lay there looking up at the ceiling, tears starting to leak from her eyes. I saw a tear roll down Dad's cheek. I knew he had to get up for chores in the morning. I couldn't process the thought of losing another sibling. How were my parents going to handle losing a third child? A part of me felt I needed to be tough, to be strong. If I fell apart, who would pick me up? I hoped it would be Stan, but I wasn't so sure he was capable. It had been only a year since he lost Timmy. I went upstairs to the girls' bedroom and shoved in beside Barbara.

"He wanted tomato soup on Sunday night," whispered Barbara. "But I wouldn't give him any. I was tired of taking care of kids and sent him to bed. When he woke up so hot, Mom and Dad took him to the hospital. I should've given him the soup."

"It wouldn't have mattered," I said. "He still would've gotten sick. Don't blame yourself." I thought of Bonnie and bouncing on the bed in this very room.

Early the next morning after chores, Mom and Dad left for the hospital. I stayed behind to help care for the kids. I was vaguely aware of some men walking around the barn in the late afternoon, presumably to milk cows and do chores. Mom called to report that Stevie hadn't gotten any better. I fed the kids, put them to bed, and tried to watch TV, anxiously praying for a miracle, yet in my heart doubting one would happen.

The next morning, Mom and Dad still weren't home, so David and I drove everyone to church in our cars. Before mass began, Father Gerum approached the pulpit. "I was called to the hospital last night in Boscobel," he said, "to give Steven Joseph Mullikin his last rites."

Last rites? Barbara, David, and I looked at each other in alarm.

"He passed into the arms of our Lord shortly after," said Father.

My chest tightened, and I could hardly breathe. Barbara and I grabbed the others and, with David, hurriedly left the church and drove to the hospital in Boscobel.

The day before the wake, a huge snowstorm moved in and all but buried us at home. The county plows came up the ridge as far as our farm in order to open the road for us. Only a few people attended the wake. The day of the funeral, the sun shone, the roads were clear, and the church was packed to overflowing.

Come warmer weather, another young Mullikin would be buried in the graveyard behind the Sacred Heart Catholic Church. In private, I cried my eyes out.

Johnny. Bonnie. Stevie. Gone forever. I tried to push the thought away while washing the dishes, dressing for work, laying out merchandise at Montgomery Ward, driving the Fairlane, drinking a beer, kissing Stan. I could hear Stevie happily yelling my name and snuggling close on my lap. I was making my bed one morning when it hit me that the one thing I missed about him was that feeling he always gave me of being appreciated, of being wanted. That little guy with the protruding tummy, the big round eyes, and the pale blue lips had unconditionally loved me. I had been around children and babies all my life, but somehow Stevie's death changed something in me. It was almost as if his absence awakened a taproot of nurturing. I needed someone to love, someone who would love me, someone my future husband and I could love. I needed a baby.

By the end of April, I was pregnant, though didn't yet know it. I had been laid off at Montgomery Ward and decided to move to Milwaukee, where I'd taken a manufacturing job and had found a room to rent. Mouse, unemployed, decided to join me. We rented an upstairs room in an old house managed by a nosy woman who peered through the crack of her door and watched our comings and goings. When Stan was with me, the crack expanded enough for me to see beady eyes and a disapproving face. I found a job at an industrial manufacturing plant. Stan once again finagled the car, leaving me to take the bus to work.

I suspected I was pregnant after consecutive days of feeling nauseous the moment I awoke. I refused to puke because I didn't want the neighbor lady hearing me. The smell of bus fumes only intensified the nausea, as did the sharp odors of oil and paint at work. I wasn't supposed to leave my station until break time, but one morning I felt so sick I had to rush to the bathroom. A coworker came in while I was wiping my face at the sink. I could tell she knew I had been throwing up. About that time, Mouse, still unemployed and running out of money, decided to move back to Wauzeka. I wasn't keen on living by myself with a snarly old snoopy nose, so I packed up too. I dreaded having to call my mother and ask her if I could move back home, but I did. I didn't mention my morning sickness or that my diet consisted mainly of soda crackers. As usual, she sighed through the phone, then took control and found me a job back at McGregor Electronics. Sadly, I had to sell the Fairlane because the payments were too expensive and Stan could never cough up a contribution. There I was, back to paying rent at the farmhouse and riding in a cramped carpool. The whole situation was enough to roil my stomach.

I'm sure Mom grew suspicious when she caught me throwing up off the back porch before going to work. She didn't say anything. I knew it would be a matter of time before she figured out the state of affairs. She had been a love child, a status she despised. After Bobby and Carol married, they got pregnant right away. Mom fretted and fretted that the baby would be born before they had been married nine months, but the baby arrived in the clear. "Your ma is sure happy that baby didn't come sooner," said Dad, chuckling.

When I overheard her muttering to no one in particular, but within my earshot, "I made damn sure I wasn't pregnant when I got married," I decided it was time to move out. Mouse, Diane, and another girl had just rented an apartment above a drugstore in Prairie and were looking for another roommate. The place had two beds; I shared one with Mouse.

It was a Saturday in July, and for some reason, just Mom and I had to work overtime at McGregor, so she picked me up. After we finished, she drove me back to the apartment. It was a hot, humid day, and neither the car nor my apartment had air-conditioning. I was tired and planned on taking a nap, maybe until the next morning.

Mom pulled the car over to the curb. As I was about to get out, she looked at me and said, "You're pregnant, aren't you?" My heart skipped a beat. I felt faint.

"Yes, I am," I said, hoping she would show at least an ounce of excitement.

She simply said, "I'm not going to tell your father about this. You'll have to do it." And off she sped before I had barely shut the door. I went upstairs into the stifling apartment, lay on the bed, and cried and cried. I missed Stevie so much and always missed Bonnie, and now I was a disgrace to my family. Here was my chance to have someone to love and to be loved back. I knew I would make a good mother, but all I felt at the moment was tremendous shame. By the time Mouse came home, my eyes were puffed-up slits. She asked me what was wrong. Her sister had been pregnant, so she had kind of figured. Later, we shared the news with Diane, and the three of us got excited and proceeded to talk wedding plans.

When I told Stan, he was thrilled. "Now we can get married!" he said. I wondered if he still thought my pregnancy would get him discharged. Neither of us broached the subject. Betty hoped a baby would help Stan grow up. Cap scowled and walked over to the bar. By the time I got around to telling Dad, he already knew. Maybe after twelve kids, he recognized the signs, or maybe in a moment of frustration my mother confided in him. My Grandma pulled me close and didn't say anything. My brothers and sisters probably talked among themselves but never said anything to me, and I never said anything to them, my feelings of guilt flaring when I visited the farm and keeping me quiet.

"We need to go see the priest," Mom said a few weeks later, just before my nineteenth birthday. She had scheduled an appointment with Father Gerum for that evening after work. I presumed it was to discuss wedding plans.

It was still light out when we parked in front of the parish rectory. I was tired and hadn't eaten much since lunch. Father Gerum directed us into the front office. Not much had changed over the years. The desk, bookcase, and wooden armchairs were the same ones I had carefully dusted. Father Gerum had replaced Father Cassidy right before Stevie died, and I hadn't yet had a private conversation with him. All I knew about him was that he had been a chaplain in the military.

The second after we were all seated, Mom said, "Father, Mary's pregnant, and I don't know what to do. She wants to get married."

I almost gasped.

Father Gerum folded his hands on the blotter. "Yes, I've heard rumors to that effect," he said, his stern face hinting disapproval. I looked down at my lap.

"Butch Havens will not make a good father," said my mother. "He's irresponsible and immature. And he doesn't attend church." She paused. "What do you think about her giving the baby up for adoption, Father?"

It was as if I had gotten socked in the middle of my stomach. I couldn't look at Mom for trying to get my breath back. She marched right on. "If Butch gets called over to Viet Nam, who knows what might happen? Being a single mother without a husband is terribly hard."

Father Gerum nodded knowingly. "I've seen this many times in the military. Young soldiers come into the service no more than boys. They think before shipping out, they need to get married, but they have little idea, if any, what marriage is really about." He continued lecturing about young men and the military, then paused and looked at me as if to give me a chance to say something, but I couldn't. I was still in a state of shock. "I won't marry you and Butch, Mary. I've seen enough of bad marriages."

I glanced at my mother. For a moment, she looked completely surprised. Her shoulders slumped, and she leaned back in her chair.

"I think you should seriously consider giving your baby up for adoption," Father Gerum said. "There are many husbands and wives looking to have children. This child could have a good home, a very good home."

Mom piped up again. "Mary could go to an unwed mother's home in California. My Aunt Hattie lives there, and I know there's one not too far from her. They would take care of placing the baby."

Do I have a say in any of this? They were talking as if I weren't in the room. My stomach burned and I willed myself to stay seated. I looked squarely at Father Gerum. "I'm not giving this baby up," I said. "I'll have it without getting married."

Silence filled the room. Father Gerum shifted his gaze to the window. A squirrel chattered outside. Maybe it was berating the two people who knew best.

"You're not getting married by a justice of the peace," said Mom, though her voice had lost some of its steam.

The Father pressed his palms against the blotter, then folded his hands again. "I suppose Butch could talk to the chaplain at the base. Perhaps he would agree to marry you."

"You mean Stan," I said, icily.

"If he would take responsibility and talk to him," Mom said, almost under her breath.

There wasn't much else to say, so we left. Mom and I didn't exchange a word on the way home. I was exhausted from having been paraded around. I was raised to respect a priest's authority and my parents' authority, but both had just laid me lower than I had felt in a long time.

Much to my surprise, Stan immediately followed up. He was hopping mad at Father Gerum and was going to show him. The Havens were Catholic, but only Betty attended church. Stan always claimed that during catechism class in third grade, some kid threw a pencil at his head, and it stuck in his scalp. He turned around and said "you sonofabitch" and promptly was booted out of class. He never returned. Stan went directly to Father Rooney, the base chaplain, and asked if he would marry us. The kind father said yes, he would.

We set the date for September 11, 1965. Time was closing in on us, since Stan had received orders to report aboard the USS *Boyd* (DD-544) navy destroyer. As soon as we were married, he would head out to Long Beach, where the ship was docked. I planned to follow in early November.

I looked at wedding dresses in the Sears, J. C. Penney, and Montgomery Ward catalogues. They were so pretty. Floor length. White. Some with lace, some all satin. The bridesmaid dresses came in an array of colors. Mouse and I debated whether bright yellow or light blue would be better. Or maybe a shade of green. I drafted a guest list and mulled over where to have the reception.

Mom was standing at the kitchen counter kneading bread

dough in her metal mixing bowl when I shared my plans with her. She looked up from the white flour glob she held in her hands. Her lips pursed. "You're not getting married in a white dress," she said. "You'll wear a black dress. And you'll get married in front of the priest. No big wedding. No reception."

Trapped in shame again. I looked out the window and tried not to let her see me wipe my tears. Thankfully, Virginia Kelly, Mom's boss at McGregor Electronics and a good friend, intervened and told her she needed to let me wear a white dress.

A few weeks later, Mom handed me a package that had arrived in the mail. It contained a sleeveless knee-length dress made of white brocade. The scooped neck and cut covered my growing tummy. A matching long-sleeved coat with silver buttons added to the pretense. Mom also ordered long navy-blue gloves and a pillbox hat with a short veil. The entire ensemble had been purchased with not one word of input from me.

"I suggest you wear a girdle," said Mom after Labor Day. She handed me a Sunday missal she had purchased. It was covered in mother-of-pearl inlay. "You can carry that instead of flowers."

Sometime later, Mom told me that if Stan and I weren't getting married at home, Dad refused to attend the wedding. I was so beaten down by then, I didn't have the energy to talk to him. Years later, I wondered if she ordered him to stay home, or strongly suggested it. Stan's brother Denny offered to walk me down the aisle in Dad's absence. Stan's cousin and her husband were matron of honor and best man. I just wanted to get the whole thing over and done with and move to California.

Our wedding day arrived. Had I not been feeling so unsure about marrying Stan and devastated that Dad was back at the farm, I might have ended the day chuckling at the sequence of events. Stan and I drove to the chapel with the matron of honor and best man. Mom, Grandma, Betty, and Denny followed in another car. Somehow our small convoy separated. We arrived at the chapel on time, but the others were tootling around who-knew-where.

Stan and I met Father Rooney inside the compact chapel. For weeks, Stan had boasted that for all naval base weddings, a red carpet would be rolled down the aisle and a naval honor guard would march in ahead of us and raise their sabers. It sounded glamorous and would make up for the lack of attendees, flowers, music, and long, lacy wedding dress. As it turned out, of course, only Stan wore a uniform, and there was no red carpet. In fact, there wasn't even one bouquet of flowers. It was yet another one of Stan Havens' tall tales that I had been gullible enough to believe.

The first thing Father Rooney said was that the wedding couldn't take place because he didn't have Stan's baptismal records. The wedding was scheduled for ten o'clock; by that time, it was quarter to ten. Stan was flying out to Los Angeles on Monday. If the wedding didn't happen that day, it most likely wasn't going to for months, if not longer.

At two minutes before ten, the lost car arrived bearing Betty, the one person who knew where Stan had been baptized. Father Rooney made a call to the appropriate church and obtained what he needed. At eleven in the morning, the sun having burned off the fog and shining hopefully through the narrow chapel windows, Mom, Grandma, Betty, and Denny watched as Stan and I exchanged vows. I plastered a smile on my face and reassured the baby growing inside me that we would be okay.

Our entourage returned to Stan's parents' house, where all Stan's brothers and sisters, my sister Barbara, and one of my uncles showed up. Stan and I opened a few presents and had cake and ice cream. Later in the afternoon, after Mom and Grandma left, Stan, his brothers, cousin, Barbara, and Kenny hiked around the lake while I sat at the house, physically and emotionally worn out, waiting for my husband. I had waited for him before and would wait for him again. For better or for worse. In sickness and in health. Till death do us part.

I shifted on the wooden bench, trying to ease my lower-back pain. I had been sitting for two hours but didn't dare walk around the terminal for fear of missing Stan. Besides, my feet still hurt. I had removed my shoes just before the train crossed from Arizona into California. Big mistake. By the time it pulled into Los Angeles' Union Station, my feet were so swollen that I was forced to hobble with my shoes half on, my heels squashing the back of my pumps. I shouldn't have listened to Aunt Hattie when she advised me not to spend money on a sleeper car. I was seven months pregnant. Trying to get comfortable while lying across two passenger seats proved nearly impossible.

It had been over forty hours since Mom and I said good-bye at the Prairie du Chien train station. "Look for Uncle Clarence and Aunt Florence. They'll meet you at the station in Chicago and help you find the Santa Fe train," Mom said.

Excited and a bit anxious, I took a window seat. I had never traveled beyond Wisconsin, Iowa, and northern Illinois. Here I was going cross-country, on the same trip my mother had taken as a teenager. I waved at her through the window. I had a feeling she exhaled relief as the train pulled my very round body away from the wagging tongues and watchful eyes of Wauzeka. The day before had been my last day at McGregor Electronics. I had made enough money to pay for my trip, plus had a small savings to supplement Stan's paltry military income. At least I wasn't heading to California to a home for wayward mothers.

I had visions of getting off the train and running into Stan's arms and hugging and kissing him and he being amazed at how much our baby was growing. Instead, a sea of unfamiliar faces greeted me. The terminal was gigantic, with a high, vaulted ceiling and people coming, going, and connecting. As it emptied, it became obvious that Stan hadn't arrived. I looked around for a seat and half-dragged, half-carried my two suitcases. Fortunately, a stranger asked if he could help and got me settled on the bench. A big clock hung on one wall. I had now seen its second hand, minute hand, and hour hand move. I thought about lifting one of the suitcases at my feet onto the bench and resting my head on it, but I was so exhausted that I feared falling sound asleep and missing Stan, and Stan missing me.

I watched a janitor wring his mop, dip it in a bucket, and swish it across the tiled floor. I felt him looking at me from a distance. When he moved closer, I glanced up, and for a moment our eyes locked. Embarrassed, I looked down at my lap. He continued mopping. I could see his feet moving in my direction.

"Your ride's a bit late, huh?"

I looked up at the janitor. He had a kind face and sympathetic eyes. "Yes," I said, "my husband's traveling from the San Diego navy base." I could feel tears start to well. "Something must have detained him. Maybe the bus is late."

"I doubt it," he said. "Those buses, they keep on schedule. I noticed you been sittin' here for some time. I'll be around for another couple of hours. If you need any help, just let me know."

The janitor resumed mopping. I was starving and hadn't eaten since breakfast. How much longer should I wait? I had no idea how much a taxi to Aunt Hattie's would cost. Surely a bus would be less, but how would I maneuver everything? I had an address but didn't know how far away she lived. Just as my thoughts were beginning to overwhelm me, I noticed Stan lumbering toward me in his navy uniform. I didn't move. He bent down, kissed me. "Sorry I'm late. The bus from San Diego took longer than I thought."

"I'm glad you're here," I said, thoroughly relieved. I didn't have the energy to be mad or ask why he hadn't checked the bus's arrival time.

The janitor walked over to us. "She's a very patient woman," he said to Stan. "I'd keep her if I were you."

"You bet I'll keep her," said Stan. I stood up. He didn't offer to pick up my suitcases right away, so I grabbed one.

"You gonna let your woman carry that?" said the janitor.

Stan's face flushed. He grabbed the suitcase from my hand, picked up the other one, mumbled, "Thanks for your help," and set off. I couldn't look the janitor in the face.

The first thing out of Aunt Hattie's mouth after she kissed me was, "My god, you're as big as a mountain." Her beef stew, clean bathroom, and comfortable bed soon made me feel as if I could tackle any mountain. Well, at least an Ocooch Mountain. Aunt Hattie introduced us to her son, Warren. Later, while she and I washed dishes in the kitchen, she warned me not to be alone with him. "As big as you are, you'll never be able to get away from him." She didn't elaborate, and I didn't ask. Maybe it was the way he looked at me or shook my hand, but he had given me the willies when we met. He had big hands and long, thick fingernails.

The next day, her grandson Robert came over, toting his pool cue in an elegant leather case. While he and Stan ventured to the pool hall, Aunt Hattie and I sat in her backyard basking in a California sun. We picked oranges and grapefruits from the trees surrounding the patio. I peeled an orange right there, not minding in the least when the juice from a slice squirted on me like fresh perfume. Next to the trees was a garage with an apartment above it. A young couple with a baby had just moved out, leaving many baby items behind. Aunt Hattie let me rummage through them and take what I wanted. I felt as if I had just won the ring toss three times over at a local carnival. Infant clothing, blankets, toys. Aunt Hattie suggested taking the car seat to the hardware store to get it fixed.

That night I showed Stan the lucky finds. He held a pair of booties in his hands, and we giggled at how tiny they looked. I cuddled next to him in bed and was just about asleep when he said, "After your operation, we can have decent sex again." What an odd comment, I thought, but was too tired to say anything. The next morning, he hitchhiked back to San Diego.

For the next two weeks, late morning breakfasts and early evening suppers became the norm. Aunt Hattie was a sweet but very frugal woman. We usually took a walk every day. Aunt Hattie clipped right along and would order me to pick up glass bottles lying in the street so she could turn them in for refunds. I didn't mind, even though the bending over was getting to be a challenge. We made meals together. She asked me how I was feeling and seemed truly interested in what I had to say. She never uttered a single word of disapproval.

One of the most wonderful days we had was driving down to San Diego. She commissioned Warren to drive and of course insisted on going with us. The ocean showed off its glistening whitecaps as we sped along the freeway. A salty breeze flowed through the window and lifted my spirits. Aunt Hattie pointed out where migrating whales swam near the shore. She talked about California's Spanish culture and the Catholic priests who founded many of the cities. At her insistence, Warren reluctantly exited the freeway and wound through downtown San Juan Capistrano. I imagined the legendary swallows swooping over the Great Stone Mission every March when they arrived to build their mud nests, lay their eggs, and raise their young. In Oceanside, we stopped for lunch, and I tasted my first shrimp cocktail.

Stan had rented an efficiency apartment for sixty-five dollars a month. It was furnished with a hide-a-bed couch, end table and coffee table, a radio, one dresser, kitchen appliances, and table and chairs. Stan was shipping out end of April, and we could only live there for ninety days. Aunt Hattie helped me carry in the linens, blankets, pillows, dishes, and pots and pans she gave us. We made up the bed. Before leaving, she filled a bowl with the oranges and grapefruits from her trees and set it on the table.

"Okay, Mary, dear. You and Stan be good, and let me know if you need anything." She hugged and kissed me and was out the door. I waved at Warren. He had been told to wait in the car. I watched them drive away. I couldn't recall the last time I had felt so pampered. I wondered if the baby kicking inside me could feel the sense of adventure that swelled through me. I sat on the hide-a-bed couch and allowed my eyes to close. Rest overcame me. Had I known what adventure lay ahead, I might not have felt so relaxed. Maybe I would have even migrated with the whales or taken flight with the swallows.

Stan and I slipped into a routine. In the morning, he and his shipmate buddy Jim took the bus to the port, then ferried to the destroyer. Sometimes they shoved out to sea for several days. Jim's wife Beth and I occasionally hung out together, but they had a very hyperactive, annoying little girl, and I preferred to be alone. We barely had enough money to pay our rent, so our refrigerator and cupboards had next to no food. It was a good day when Stan snuck food from the ship, mostly stuff he easily could hide beneath his uniform—lunch meat, a sandwich, or square of starchy cold casserole wrapped in a napkin. It satiated the hunger that constantly gnawed at me. He ate breakfast and lunch on the ship and continued smoking two packs of cigarettes a day. I never told him just how hungry I felt.

My mother's words looped through my head. She was right; I deserved whatever I got for marrying Stan in the first place. One time I was so desperate for food, I knocked on the doors of the local Catholic Church hoping to get something to eat. No one answered. I ducked around the side of the church and cried. Fortunately, I discovered the local library. I read *Gone with the Wind* sitting on the couch in the apartment. Sustenance for the soul.

I discovered that I wouldn't be able to deliver our baby at the naval base because I was too far along in my pregnancy, so I located a civilian doctor and hospital. On Thursday, January 27, the doctor told me it would be at least another week. The next day, Jim and Beth invited us over for dinner. We pooled what little food we each had and made a dinner out of it. We hung out and played cards until quite late. Beth suggested we spend the night. I wasn't comfortable saying yes, but Stan readily agreed. They graciously let us sleep in their bed.

Stan turned off the lights and crawled under the covers. "How long after your operation do we have to wait to have sex?" he asked me again. I had figured out he didn't know how babies were born, so I had explained the birthing process, but out of habit he continued to use the word operation.

"I'm not sure," I said, adjusting my pillows. "Maybe six or eight weeks. Depends how I feel."

He rubbed his hand over my belly and breasts. "That's so long. How 'bout we try now?"

Good Lord, I thought, of all nights. But as usual, I didn't say no. We tried, but it hurt too much, so I sat up and turned on the light. That's when I noticed blood. Stan turned white.

"Go get Beth," I said.

"Mary, I think you're in labor," Beth said. Intermittent pains had made me shift in my chair all during dinner, but now the pains were worse. She timed ten minutes between contractions. None of us had a vehicle, so we called the police department. They sent a squad car, and by ten o'clock Stan and I were in the delivery wing of the hospital.

"I feel sick," I said to a nurse. Before she could get a pan, my supper flew across the room. Little pieces of hotdog.

The nurses prepped and monitored and at the appropriate times allowed Stan in the labor room, but all he did was ask when the baby was coming and why was everything going so slow. I had no information to give him. Childbirth classes didn't exist at the time; fathers weren't allowed to be in the delivery room during the birth. All I felt was scared, and his questions only fed my fear about what was happening. Maybe the nurses were getting as weary of him as I was because they told him to go home and get some sleep.

The next morning at nine o'clock, they phoned him and said it was time. The anesthesiologist had just finished administering a spinal when a nurse came in and squeezed my hand. "Your husband's here," she said. Thank God he's not two hours late, I thought. Mirrors were set in place, and I watched my baby being born. A girl. Shannon. I finally understood what Helen was talking about all those years ago. The miracle of life.

A nurse wheeled Shannon and me to a window. On the other side stood Stan, grinning, his tongue sticking out the gap in his front teeth. For a moment I was embarrassed at how goofy he looked. My own Crazy Guggenheim. Then I noticed tears streaming down his cheeks, and shame surged through me. I had never seen him look so proud. Tears tumbled down my cheeks. The hospital awarded him a diploma, Magna Cum Laude for Having Survived the Hardships and Perils of the Ancient Craft of Fatherhood, a certificate he frequently and proudly showed off. The next day, he left for a week at sea.

On one hand, I loved the hospital stay. I could choose anything and everything I wanted on the menu. Sometimes I wondered if the doctor knew I didn't have much food and told them to let me have whatever I wanted. I attended classes on how to bathe and care for Shannon. Everyone was kind and friendly, and yet Shannon and I were alone. We had no visitors, no cards, no flowers. No one to share in the excitement and joy of the moment. My hospital roommate had a continuous stream of visitors. While I was at class, she placed some of her flowers on my side of the room.

Stan returned home excited to see Shannon. He didn't want to do anything but hold her. If he didn't want to do that, he handed her back to me. He would lean over and watch her while I nursed her. Shannon was a good baby and slept through the night almost right away. On the rare occasion that she awoke, I brought her to bed with me and let her nurse. Stan hated having her in bed with us.

Two weeks later, the first of the navy's monthly baby allowance arrived. I felt as if we hit the jackpot when a large package from my mother followed. It was a baby buggy that doubled as a bassinet. Shannon would no longer have to sleep in the dresser drawer. Mom had held a coin baby shower by proxy for us and also sent the cards and money. We could afford groceries again. I even splurged on a box of cocoa and baked a chocolate cake.

As expected, Stan received orders to ship out in April to the Gulf of Tonkin. I wanted to remain in California and wait for him, but he wouldn't hear of it. "I don't want any military guys around you or my daughter," he said. "You can't trust those sons of bitches for a damn minute." But we had no money for travel expenses, which meant that I'd have to ask my family for help, something that appealed to me even less than dining on crusted noodle casseroles. I knew we needed to go back to Wisconsin, if for no other reason than to give Betty and Cap a chance to see their son before he shipped off to war and to meet their first granddaughter. So I bucked up, asked my mother for travel money, and started scraping some savings together.

It was a warm spring day. We would be leaving for Wisconsin in a few weeks. Stan had the day off and had just gotten paid. I was weary of scrubbing diapers and baby clothes by hand, so I gave myself permission to pay for the communal washer and dryer next to the pool. The sky was bright blue, and the sweet scent of orange blossoms infused the air. Stan put on his swim trunks, and we settled Shannon in the infant seat by his chair at the pool. As I headed back into the apartment to sort clothes, I could hear him talking to her, explaining how he would get her swimming lessons someday. We might not have much money, I thought, but we have a beautiful daughter. We're a family now.

I checked the pockets of Stan's pants before throwing them in the washer. In one was an envelope addressed to him. It was postmarked Long Beach, where he had been stationed before I arrived. The name on the return address was Rebecca Lyons. My hands shook. Should I read it? What right did I have to invade my husband's privacy? Dang it! I wanted to know what it said. I listened for approaching sounds. Nothing. I pulled out the letter. Neat, cursive handwriting filled the page. "Dear Stan, I got my 'friend,' so you don't have to worry about a thing. Be safe over in

Nam. I hope to see you again. Love Rebecca." Bile rose into my throat. I reread it. I wasn't stupid. I knew what she was talking about.

Later, after Shannon had nursed and fallen asleep, I shoved the letter in front of Stan. "What in the hell is this all about?"

Stan didn't say a word, just stood staring at the letter. Then he grabbed my arm and tried pulling me to him. I resisted.

"What is this?" I said, fighting to keep my voice quiet.

"It isn't what you think," said Stan. "A bunch of us went to the USO, where I met her. I played pool with her a few times, and that was it."

"Really, Stan?" I said. "You want me to believe that? And who's her 'friend'?" I used as much sarcasm as I could muster.

"Her friend?" He grabbed his cigarette pack from his shirt pocket, lit one, and watched the smoke curl to the ceiling. "She was lonely, and I had offered to get her a puppy. You know, go to the shelter, get a free one. She said she'd let me know if she wanted one. So she let me know. Guess I don't have to go up to Long Beach to the animal shelter." He shrugged and walked into the bathroom.

I stood fuming and debating what to do. What a bunch of bullshit. But he would be leaving for war. Did it matter what had happened between him and this woman? Perhaps not. Still, I felt my trust in him dwindling. And that made me even angrier. I was still standing there when he emerged dressed in civilian clothes.

Scowling, he picked up the letter and ripped it into pieces. "If you don't want to believe me," he said, "then don't believe me." He stormed out of the apartment, but not without stuffing the torn letter in his pants pocket. The next time I checked, the pocket was empty.

Stan's fourteen-day furlough began in fog. Visibility was so limited that the San Diego airport bussed us to Los Angeles, where we caught a direct flight to Chicago. On the bus, Shannon cried and fretted. I discreetly tried to nurse her, which sent Stan into a fit of condescending comments about how it wasn't right to do that in public. When we arrived at LAX, we ran to catch the plane and just barely made it. I collapsed in my seat, a still-fussing Shannon on my lap, sweat trickling down my back. A kind flight attendant accidentally overheated Shannon's bottle, and Shannon screamed her displeasure, which drew glares and more rude comments from Stan. Then, to top it off, Shannon's baby blanket deposited fuzz on Stan's required dress blues. By the time we arrived in Chicago, I was ready to wipe out his rude mouth with that fuzzy blanket. But I didn't. He would soon be going to war. We exited the plane with me lugging Shannon in the baby carrier, diaper bag and purse slung over my shoulder, and Stan handling himself.

Our first stop was in Milton for a week's stay with Cap and Betty. They couldn't get enough of their granddaughter. They oohed and aahed, held her, changed her diapers, tickled her, commented on her good nature, and argued over who she looked like. Especially Cap. He took to calling her George, as he did his grandsons. On the day we left for Wauzeka, I had to take Shannon from his arms in order to get her into the car. As he planted a big kiss on her head, sadness flashed across his face and lingered in his good eye. It was still there after he and Stan shook hands good-bye.

Neither Stan nor I said much during the two-hour drive to the farm. He pushed the accelerator to the floorboard, shifted as he rounded curves, raced to the bottom of dips and floored it at hilltops, making the car lift off the road. He liked scaring me. When the odometer neared ninety, I told him to slow down. Otherwise, I gazed at the barren fields, the dark soil wet and heavy in the afternoon sun. On the surface the day appeared fresh and promising, but beneath its spring veneer, I felt a clump of dark anxiety.

I had no idea what the future would hold for me. My husband was going off to war. We had no money. I didn't like being dependent on my parents, but once again I was. I had an idea of what constituted a normal family. Stan, Shannon, and me. We were a family. Then why didn't things feel normal? When Stan turned the car into the farmhouse driveway, I hadn't shared any of my thoughts. I noticed the big elm tree buds had not yet sprouted, though bright green grass poked up around its trunk. Little reminders to keep hoping for the best.

When we walked into the kitchen, a big family commotion erupted. Mom and Grandma set down their dishtowels. They hugged me and looked at Shannon, already in Barbara's arms. I had dressed Shannon in the lacy pink dress with a white Peter Pan collar that Betty had bought her.

"Shannon," Mom said. "What an interesting name." Sharon toddled up to Mom and leaned her mass of unkempt hair against Mom's leg. I wondered what my mother was thinking. Was she glad I had kept this baby? What would she have thought if someone asked her to give up her baby? Stop thinking about the past, I chastised myself. Enjoy the moment.

The other kids clamored around us, eager to meet their new niece. I glanced at Stan, standing behind everyone. He looked proud but also relieved. He didn't have to hold Shannon. The back door opened, and in came Dad, eyes twinkling, a big grin on his face.

"Well, who do we have here?" Kathy had confiscated Shannon from Barbara. "Aren't you a cutie?" he said, leaning over Kathy's shoulder. "Look at those blue eyes." A warmth filled me, and I felt myself beaming.

After the initial excitement died down, I noticed that David had returned to the rocker in the living room. "Would you like to meet your Uncle David?" I said to Shannon. Her eyes were alert, and her cheeks had turned a rosy pink. I carefully set her in David's arms. He smiled and rocked her for a few minutes, then was besieged by coughs. I lifted her up. Grandma came out and wanted to hold her. "She looks like her dad," she whispered.

Mom never held Shannon that day. As more babies were born into our family over the years, I would see a sad look cross her face when she was around them. She would smile, but it never seemed to be a genuinely happy smile. Maybe it was the way she tilted her head or never extended her arms to hold the baby. She couldn't seem to share the enthusiasm and excitement that my sisters, sisters-in-law, cousins, aunts, and nieces exhibited when in the presence of a newborn or a plump eight-month-old or even a toddler.

The next seven days flew by. In addition to helping around the house, caring for Shannon, and showing her off to family and friends, Stan and I had sex every chance we could, and always without protection. I prayed it wasn't a fallacy that nursing mothers don't get pregnant. Each time, I wondered if it would be our last lovemaking. Would he return from Viet Nam in a year? Would he be the same? Would I be the same? Whatever thoughts rumbled in our minds remained tucked in there, not privy for the other person to know.

On the day of Stan's departure, our anxiety was as thick as San Diego fog. We didn't talk much during the car ride to O'Hare Airport. I wanted to tell Stan that I believed he didn't have anything to do with the girl in Long Beach, but I couldn't bring myself to say it. What did it matter anyway? In less than seventy-two hours, he would be aboard the USS *Boyd*, the bow pointed toward Viet Nam, the engines laboring. I might never see him again.

All too soon, we were standing at the gate. "I promise I'll write every day," I said. "I'll send Polaroids of Shannon too, so you can see how she's growing." I forced a smile. "And you'll write me every day?"

Stan looked uncomfortable. "I'll try, but I'm not sure what I'll have to say. Besides, it makes me lonesome thinking about writing you."

We stood at the gate until the last possible moment. Our embrace spoke all the words we didn't say in the car. I watched him walk down the ramp to the plane, then stood at the window until the speck of plane disappeared into the overcast sky.

Once again, Mom found a job for me at McGregor Electronics. Just thinking about the factory odors almost made me sick to my stomach. Being a desperate single mother, I needed the job, so I was grateful to have it, though I took it with the unspoken goal of finding a new position elsewhere. Mom also arranged for Shannon and me to move in with Grandma, who now lived in town and wasn't fond of being alone in her house. Grandma was still babysitting for Sharon and didn't mind taking care of Shannon too. Besides, Grandma was such an easy soul to be around and felt more like a mother to me than a grandma. Then there was the added bonus of being out of the farmhouse hubbub.

One night Grandma and I were sitting in her living room. She was busy crocheting. Stan's letter was addressed, stamped, and ready to be mailed. Shannon had finished nursing and had fallen asleep in my arms as I rocked her. The rocking chair squeaked a comforting rhythm on the wooden floor.

"Grandma," I said, "what was it like when you were first married to Grandpa?"

Grandma set the doily she was working on in her lap and looked at the ceiling. "Well, now. After we got married, your grandpa was determined to make a living on the farm. He rolled up his sleeves and got to it. Back then, he was a lusty fellow. Lusty for life. Lusty for me." She giggled. The lamplight accentuated her dark eyes and the dark hair framing her face. Grandpa must have seen her beauty. "So it wasn't but seven months before your mom was born, but that never bothered either of us. Some things just don't matter when you're young and in love."

I wondered if my mother knew that Grandma had been in love and had shrugged off any shame she should have felt about her premarital pregnancy. Grandma continued. "It wasn't until after we had several kids and the war hit that things changed. Money got real scarce. Your grandfather worried about how to pay for the farm and how to get the crops harvested. But everyone was pretty much in the same straights. So everyone chipped in."

I knew how much time and effort it took to put up crops. "That's when the threshing crews traveled from place to place?"

"Yes, that's how it worked." She paused. "About then, things went a different way. I'll never know for sure, but I think something snapped in your grandpa. Maybe it was the stress. Maybe it was the whiskey he drank every night during harvest. It was the only time of year that he drank until he passed out." She leaned toward me, a conspirator uncovering the secrets of the past. Her voice was low. "Your grandfather had a nasty temper and could be downright mean. When he got liquored up, he'd start cussing me out for one thing or another. Mainly it was for having so many kids. He would say all the babies weren't his and accuse me of sleeping with the hired hands. Then he'd wallop me or shove me. Sometimes he forced me to have sex. Not nice sex. Mean sex." Her cheeks flushed.

I sat there, stunned. Poor Grandma. One of the sweetest and kindest people on earth. My heart hurt. Stan might have been with another woman, but at least he never physically harmed me or anyone else.

"Did the kids ever see anything?"

"You know how it is with lots of bodies under one roof. When he'd start, I'd try to get into the bedroom and shut the door, but I didn't always get there."

My mouth felt dry. What had my mother witnessed during her childhood? Part of me wanted more details, but another part didn't want to know any more. Maybe this was a story better left untold. Grandma picked up her doily and needles, and I went to settle Shannon in her crib. We never discussed the subject again.

The following March, Stan sent a letter saying he was injured. He was in Da Nang goofing around with some of his buddies playing John Wayne and Kirk Douglas action heroes when the Viet Cong decided to let loose some sniper fire. A forklift operator, unable to hear the shooting, drove the forklift right over Stan's foot and crushed it. Stan ended up on the naval hospital ship in the Philippines and was almost sent home due to the initial severity of his injury. The good docs, however, patched him up and shipped him back to Da Nang to finish out his tour.

His tour couldn't be over soon enough for me. Shannon was walking and talking. She and I had moved out of grandma's house because the navy had unexpectedly sent Stan back for two months of special training in Virginia. Shannon and I accompanied him. After he was sent back to Viet Nam for a one-year tour of duty on land, Shannon and I lived in Madison with my good friend and her husband. When her husband proved to be a drunk, I decided to accept a secretarial position at the Crawford County University Extension Office in Prairie du Chien. It made the most sense to move back to Wauzeka. Eleven people now lived in the three-bedroom farmhouse. It was crowded, with people coming and going. And on top of it, poor David was declining.

David had been living on his own in Bristol, Wisconsin, but declining health had forced him to quit his work and move to the farm. A couple of truck drivers in Wauzeka who knew him hired him to do easy jobs. The owner of the local gas station also paid him to pump gas and do odd jobs around the station. David had applied for disability benefits but was denied them because he now lived with Mom and Dad. It irked me that the government was willing to give him money to set up his own apartment but could offer him nothing if he lived with his parents. David had asked Mom and Dad if they would install indoor plumbing at the farmhouse. They agreed. It was time to remodel. They wouldn't be able to start, though, until after the ground thawed in spring, and they could dig a new basement. So remodeling began with the barn. Dad hired a local contractor to build the new barn in the cow yard. Unfortunately, they didn't raze the old barn that I still despised.

David noticeably declined after Stevie died. It was as if he knew the cystic fibrosis eventually would catch up with him. Instead of trying to sprint ahead of it, he began to give up. My heart broke at times when watching him. More than once, I saw him attempt to connect with Shannon, then saw the hurt look in his eyes when she refused to go near him. His coughing fits scared her. He would break into uncontrollable, loud coughs that shook his entire body. Sometimes just walking across the room triggered them. His lips turned even a darker blue than normal. The noise was so heart-wrenching that I could feel my own lungs fill with panic. All I could do was pray and wish air into his lungs. When he could muster the energy, he went down to the gas station in Wauzeka to get a Baby Ruth bar and hang out. He was well liked and respected. I'm sure others noticed his decline and worried.

At the beginning of June, David was admitted into the hospital in Madison. The first chance I had, I drove the one hundred miles to visit him. His eyes smiled when I walked into the room. He couldn't speak a word because of the tracheotomy tube inserted into his windpipe. It suctioned the thick mucus from his lungs periodically throughout the day, while the tubes running into his nose delivered sacred oxygen. While I was there, a cheery nurse came in to suction his lungs. She inclined his bed, put a tube down the port located at the base of his throat, and hit the pump button. She vibrated his chest to help remove the secretions that ended up in a jar next to his bed. After she left, I asked him if it hurt, and he shook his head no. Our conversation was limited to my asking questions that required a yes or no answer, though sometimes he wrote on a little chalkboard. The only question he wrote out for me was, "Are the tomatoes ripe yet?" It took all my energy not to cry.

Grandma Mullikin lived in Wauzeka with my Aunt Hazel, and on my way home I stopped to see her. She asked about David. "I wish God would take both of us," she said. She was ninety-six.

God obliged. David Lee Mullikin died on June 14, 1967. The kind and gentle brother who loved trucks, especially semi tractors and trailers, who salted everything he ate, who watched life mostly from the sidelines, and who was loved by everyone he met, left our family. He was my parents' eldest child and their fourth child to die from cystic fibrosis. Thirteen days later, Grandma Mullikin died.

Family and friends gathered for David's funeral inside Sacred Heart Catholic Church on a warm, sunny day, the kind that ripens tomatoes. After the service, we funneled out of the church behind the pallbearers. As I stood holding Shannon, listening to the priest, I glanced over at my parents. Dad stood looking straight ahead, his arm around my mother's waist. Mom looked fragile and broken, her head cocked to one side, her eyes staring blankly at the casket. The priest droned on. Across from me, David's best friend Cliff looked ashen even in the sunlight. The rest of my family seemed caught up in their own thoughts, compressing their heartache in their chest, barely able to breathe lest the release of air give way to sobbing. The priest sprinkled holy water on the grave, then passed the aspergillum to my parents. They passed it along the front row. I watched the water droplets tumble through the rays of sun onto the casket.

Suddenly, a stricken wail filled the air, startling the crowd. I looked over at my sister Barbara. Her mouth was open. The pain on her face was almost unbearable to see, the sound even more so to hear. Uncle Larry grabbed her around the waist with one hand and with the other, grabbed her hand that held the aspergillum, shook it, and quickly passed the aspergillum on to the next person. We all stood there dumbfounded, even the priest. I hugged Shannon tightly, my only source of comfort. She put her head on my shoulder, too young to comprehend the pain around her, but aware that something was amiss.

Several months after the funerals, I happened to be alone with my father in the kitchen, the one that was being built so David could enjoy indoor plumbing. We were examining the progress of the construction. He had stopped talking, and I assumed he was going to leave. But he just stood there, his hands shoved in his bib overalls. Then his shoulders shook, and tears streamed down his cheeks.

"Dad, it's okay," I said. I was standing on the other side of the room. He continued to weep. I walked over to him and put my arms around his stooped shoulders. He pulled out his bandana from his pocket and wiped his eyes.

"I think this damn place is cursed," he said.

Maybe, I thought. Maybe.

It was November, and everyone living in the farmhouse was crowded together in the cozy old living room watching TV. I could feel the draft around the doorway of the new part of the house still under construction. Mom was ironing clothes near the phone in the living room. A sharp cramp seized my stomach, as it had been doing off and on for the past months. I nearly fainted when I stood up. Mom watched with a concerned look as I passed her on the way to the bathroom. "It's just nerves," she said softly. I was grateful for the new indoor plumbing. I was still in the bathroom when the phone rang. I heard my mother say, "Yes, I'll accept the call." Seven-year-old Allan ran to the bathroom door shouting, "Stan is on the phone, Mary. It's Stan!"

When I got to the phone, my blood was pumping with anticipation. Then I heard my husband. "I'm in San Francisco, ready to board a plane to Chicago," said Stan, his voice hoarse. "Come get me!" He laughed. I laughed. My heart and spirit laughed.

The next thing I knew, I was backing out of the driveway and pointing my Mustang toward the Windy City. Stan and I estimated the drive and flight would take about the same amount of time. I had left Shannon in the care of my parents. Stan would see his daughter soon enough. Thankfully, it wasn't snowing. I arrived at the terminal at two o'clock in the morning. The plane had arrived first. Sailors were collecting loved ones and luggage. I wandered through the crowd but couldn't find Stan. Perhaps he had been reassigned to a different flight. As disappointment and panic threatened to take hold, I screwed up my courage and asked a sailor if he knew Stan Havens and had he seen him.

"Oh yeah, Havens. He should be around. Saw him on the plane."

On cue, Stan emerged through the doorway near me. I couldn't move. He looked so handsome in his dress blues, standing tall and straight. He spotted me, paused for a moment, then walked slowly toward me, his eyes never leaving mine, took me in his arms, held me tightly, and kissed me ever so passionately. It was my movie moment. My husband was home.

We decided to check into a hotel and make love until morning. Once in the room, Stan didn't want to remove his shirt with the lights on because he had a disgusting jungle rot infection on his back, exacerbated by Viet Nam's high humidity. He was embarrassed.

"I can handle it," I said, my care-giving instincts kicking in. "Remember, I was raised on a farm." I finally convinced him to take off his shirt. My stomach turned. Pus-filled sacs covered his skin and emitted a horrific stench. I was afraid to touch his back, mainly because it looked so painful. I helped him get his shirt back on. We turned off the lights, then made gentle love until the pale day announced itself behind the curtains, and we sank into a deep sleep for a few hours. Too soon it was time to leave for home. Part of me wanted to stay another night, but a much larger part was eager for Stan to be reunited with his daughter.

Stan wanted to stop in Milton to see his parents. Betty came running out of the house first, with Cap and Stan's brothers and sisters not far behind. We sat in the kitchen eating cookies and drinking coffee and caught up on everybody's activities.

"You ready to do some hunting?" said Cap. "If you get your license, we can get out there and get some deer."

Stan shifted in his chair "Nah. Too cold for me." He looked wistful. "Remember when I was a kid and you took me hunting? When it was too cold and I went to the car? You never asked me to go again."

"Huh," said Cap. "Don't remember. Anyway, you probably want to spend time with Shannon. She is one cutie-pie." Cap, typically a man of few words, prattled on about Shannon and how much she had changed over the past year. I noticed Betty eyeing Stan over the end of her cigarette. No one mentioned Viet Nam, including Stan.

We arrived in Wauzeka close to suppertime. "New barn looks good," said Stan, pulling his duffel bag from the trunk. He waved at Dad and Walt, who were herding the cows into the barn. I was so excited for Stan to see Shannon that I had to stop myself from running into the house and grabbing her. We walked up the steps to the side door. The minute we entered the kitchen, there was an eruption of hugs and smiles and how-are-you's. Shannon was in her highchair viewing the commotion with wide eyes. I went over and picked her up.

"Look who's here," I said. "That's Daddy." Every day for the past year I had shown her different photos of Stan and talked about him.

Stan extracted himself from the crowd and walked toward us. Shannon buried her head in my neck and wouldn't look at him. When he tried to take her, she screamed and held on to me as if her life depended on it. The hurt in Stan's eyes was worse to witness than the sores on his back. "She just needs time," I said, but he had already turned away.

Though Stan did not have to return to Viet Nam, he did have to complete the last six months of his four-year tour of duty. He received orders to report to the USS *Oklahoma City* in San Francisco. The navy gave him a month leave including travel time. We planned to take a week to drive out to California, where we would live until the following May. I was excited to be going back to California.

For the next three weeks, Stan dropped me off at work, took the car, and visited family and friends in the area. Grandma continued to watch Sharon and Shannon during the day. Stan had taken a dislike to my sister Sharon. When he was overseas, I had mailed him a photo of Shannon with her bangs cut at an angle, the handiwork of Sharon and her scissors. Stan was appalled that Sharon would do that. He called Sharon spoiled and pointed out how she dominated Shannon when they played together.

One day Stan picked me up from work and immediately launched into a tirade about how Shannon wouldn't listen to him, and how Sharon had told him in a sassy voice that Shannon didn't have to do what he said. Something didn't sound right. The girls had never interacted like that before. I didn't want to believe that Stan had spun such a story about his own daughter. I asked Grandma about it in the car while driving her home.

Grandma gave me a confused look. "Shannon and Sharon were fine all day. I don't know what Stan is talking about."

"I'm sure Stan misunderstood what Sharon said. Or maybe I misunderstood what he was saying."

Grandma smiled in a sad way, then climbed out of the car. As

I waited for her to unlock the front door, I pushed away my own feeling of sadness. Maybe Stan truly had misunderstood whatever he witnessed, but something niggling inside me said that wasn't possible. It had been two weeks since he had returned home from Viet Nam, and he had yet to really connect with Shannon. If she were in the room with me and he walked in, she would grab my leg and look at him as if he were a stranger, even when he called to her. He watched her run happily to my dad or my sister Barbara, or worse yet, to Cap and Betty. I kept reassuring Stan that she just needed time to adjust to his presence, but he would get a disgusted look and storm out of the room, causing Shannon to tighten her grip on my leg.

He showed his frustration in a particularly disconcerting way. More than once, I had seen Stan grab Shannon by the arm and watch her cry as she tried to break free of him. The more she twisted and turned, the harder he held her. Horrified, I would intercede, but he would throw such a tantrum that I'd step back. He mostly acted like this when he had an audience. Others would watch, a look of shock and disapproval on their faces, but oddly, no one said a word.

That night, I climbed into bed next to Stan with a new game plan in mind. In less than a week, we would be leaving for California.

"Maybe we should leave Shannon with your parents in Milton and ask Barbara to fly out with her once we're settled," I said. Stan didn't respond. "It's going to take us at least four full days of driving to get to San Francisco, plus time to settle in. It could be our time together."

Stan turned off the light. He didn't say a word. Well, I'd try again in the morning. I let my head sink into the feather pillow and felt exhaustion consume me, exhaustion from a full day of work, from helping with dinner preparation and cleanup, from bathing Shannon and getting her ready for bed. Stan hadn't changed her diapers since arriving home. I was drifting to sleep when he said, "Barbara can bring Shannon." He rolled over and was snoring before I found my way back to the brink of sleep, the decision to leave Shannon already gnawing at my conscience.

Barbara agreed to fly with Shannon to California, then stay with us until we returned in May. I carefully choreographed our departure. Stan would drive me to my last day of work, then return to the farmhouse to load the car. Then he and Shannon would pick me up at noon and we all would drive to Milton, where we would leave Shannon with his parents. I was grateful to Barbara for agreeing to bring Shannon, but I dreaded being without my daughter. I knew I would hurt with missing her, and I wasn't looking forward to saying good-bye. Before I left for work, I stuffed a wad of tissues in my purse.

Stan was waiting curbside in the Mustang when I walked out of work. I opened the passenger side door and glanced at the back seat. It was empty.

"Where's Shannon?" I said to Stan.

"I dropped her off at my parents'," he said.

I sat down in the front seat, confused. "What do you mean she's at your parents'?"

He shifted the car into first gear and squealed away from the curb.

"Wanted to save some time, so I dropped her off. We can stop at the farmhouse now, then get out of here today rather than tomorrow. Betcha we can hit Kansas City tonight." Stan sounded happy. He did a sharp U-turn, away from where Shannon was, sending my stomach into somersaults.

I couldn't believe my husband had not let me say good-bye to my daughter! I wouldn't see her for at least two, maybe three weeks. I'd never been away from her for more than a day. The low-hanging gray sky seemed to sink into me, to weigh me down. It tasted sour. I could feel it trying to split my heart. One side of me seethed at Stan's lack of empathy; the other side wanted desperately for him to take on the role and responsibility of being a father. He had taken Shannon by himself to his parents. He had made a decision. But what a self-centered decision. I wanted to rip the blinders from the sides of his head and scream, what about me, what about my feelings? I leaned against the car door, wallowing in anger, and watched leafless trees and rounded hills blur by. Even back then, I knew I was playing a role—the role of the good wife who sits back and lets her husband take control without criticizing him.

It was well after midnight by the time we checked into a motel on the outskirts of Kansas City. I flopped into bed wearier than usual. The last image from the day that crossed the screen of my mind was of my mother asking why we had a change in plans, then shaking her head, her patented look of disgust appearing when I said Stan had decided to drop off Shannon first. I never would know what she mumbled under her breath. But I probably could have guessed.

The world transformed while we slept. When I awoke, Stan was standing at the window smoking a cigarette. All I could see was white on the other side of the glass.

"Damn it all," he said, pushing his head closer toward the windowpane. "Looks like we got a flat."

Why I was surprised he didn't want to go out in the snow and change it, I don't know, but I was determined not to show disgust like my mother, even though I was feeling it. I picked up the telephone book, located the AAA service station listings, and phoned for assistance. When the truck arrived, Stan laid back down on the bed. I slipped on my coat and boots and trudged into the winter wonderland to greet the attendant, then returned a second time with his payment. When I handed him the money, his mustache now white and frozen, I spotted Stan peering out between the long drapes. So did the attendant, who waved at him. Stan quickly pulled the drapes closed. Only five days and two thousand miles to San Francisco.

I missed Shannon every minute, but I was determined to make the best of sightseeing and spending time with Stan. Plus, it was my chance to ask about Viet Nam. What happened there? Who did he hang around with? Was it scary? Pretty? I had so many questions, few of which had been answered in his letters, and as it turned out, few of which were now answered beyond a few terse sentences. Sometimes he would be driving down the interstate, his hand on the wheel, smoking a cigarette, the look on his face indicating he was somewhere else. If his face had been a map, maybe I could have pinpointed the exact longitude and latitude. Sometimes he returned from his mental voyage with a smile. He'd crank the radio, and we'd belt out the lyrics to our favorite songs. Other times, he'd abruptly pull into a rest stop. "You drive," he'd say, then fall asleep for the next two hours. He's just tired, I'd tell myself, squirming over the germ of a feeling that something about him had changed.

One of the strangest things he said was that he shot at kids in the water. "We sat up on the LCU boat and shot at little bastard gooks when they got close to us. You never knew if they had a hand grenade to blow you up, so we shot them, and the water turned red from their blood."

I almost blurted out, "Oh my God!" But intuition took control. I knew Stan wasn't telling the truth; it was just one of those things I instinctively knew. I looked out the window and didn't say a word.

When we arrived in San Francisco, we discovered the navy goofed. Stan's ship, which hadn't been docked in the bay for the past six months, was actually in San Diego. So off we headed down the coast of California, content to be returning to a place we knew and one we could afford. Before Shannon and Barbara arrived, we found an apartment to rent in World War II row housing. We had to leave the Mustang on the outside of the surrounding fence, enter through a gate, then cross an open yard to our front door. Eventually I got to joking that I didn't know if I would make it from the car to our apartment before someone grabbed me. It wasn't exactly the friendliest-looking neighborhood, with sagging buildings long overdue for a coat of paint, potholed streets, and a homeless population. But I was so happy to be there. Shannon would soon join us, we would be a family, and I would feel whole again.

That day finally arrived. I barely slept the night before. Brimming with anticipation, I left for the airport earlier than necessary. It was a few days before Christmas, and people were coming and going, embracing and laughing. I couldn't wait to get my arms around my daughter. The plane landed, and an attendant finally opened the door to the jetway. Adrenaline pumped through me. I didn't have to wait long. Shannon came walking out, dressed in a brown plaid dress, ribboned pigtails on each side of her head. Barbara was right behind her, carrying the diaper bag and Shannon's favorite blanket and pillow. I squatted down and held out my arms. Shannon's expression barely changed. She looked me in the eye, looked unsure whether she should smile or not, and walked right past me. My daughter no longer knew me! I forced my tears to stay put.

Barbara looked at me sympathetically. "Shannon was an angel," she said. "Everyone loved her. The couple across the aisle couldn't believe her vocabulary. We ended up in first class and got the royal treatment."

Shannon let me pick her up, and I kissed her once, twice,

enough to make her start giggling. I felt better. I half-listened to Barbara's details. I had my daughter back.

Stan arrived home just before supper. Shannon was sitting in my lap on the studio couch. "There's my big girl!" he said. She gave him one look and burrowed against me. His pained expression must have mimicked mine from earlier in the day. "She's still adjusting," I said. "Give her a little time."

Stan laughed cruelly. "Look at the little baby. Such a mama's girl."

I wrapped my arms around her tightly and let her bury her face in my chest. "It's okay, honey, he really doesn't mean it."

Barbara walked past us, a surprised look on her face; she was about to say something, seemed to think better of it, then walked up the steps to the bedroom she would be sharing with Shannon.

Before Shannon went to bed, Stan tried to pick her up. She screamed so loudly I thought the neighbors might knock on the front door to see if everything was okay. I couldn't get her into her bed, she clung to me so tightly. That's when I knew she had been tormented by our separation. A heavy new layer of guilt piled on top of the existing layers. I settled her next to me in bed.

"What the hell?" said Stan. "This is ridiculous. Get her the hell out of here. I don't want her touching me."

I moved Shannon over to my other side, so she was away from her unreasonable father. She snuggled close the entire night. If only I could have stayed the protective barrier between them.

PART FOUR

The following May, the navy released Stan. He had finished his tour of duty. I was three months pregnant and had no desire to return to Wisconsin. I liked the sun, the ocean, the big-city feel of San Diego and wanted to stay, but Stan was hell-bent on returning to Steuben. I wasn't sure why, since his parents and siblings lived in Milton. I proposed that we live in Prairie du Chien, thinking that a town of five thousand would be more exciting than a town of two hundred. Stan said he hated Prairie. So I packed up the apartment, bracing myself for Steuben. I was still in the stupid mind-set that a woman follows her man and his dreams.

Fortunately, Stan landed a job with his brother Denny working for a semitrailer manufacturing company near Milton. His parents still rented the two-bedroom lake cottage on Charley Bluff where we had our wedding reception. Charley Bluff abuts Lake Koshkonong, an expansive reservoir. It wasn't exactly the Pacific Ocean, but it had a beachfront and paths for Shannon and me to walk. Stan's two younger sisters, Theresa and Suzie, and his brother Terry also lived in the house. At least we weren't in Steuben, I told myself as I unpacked in Terry's bedroom. He graciously had agreed to sleep on the sofa; the girls had long been sleeping on a bed set up in the living room. I reassured Terry that we soon would be in our own place. That was my goal, anyway.

Since the law prohibited pregnant women from working,

I spent my time caring for Shannon and helping Betty around the house. She worked at a nearby nursing home on rotating shifts. Every morning around eight, Cap took Shannon with him to the local tavern to show her off to the regulars. Having horrible morning sickness, I appreciated the chance to rest in bed. Shannon always returned holding a stick of Juicy Fruit gum, which I didn't think was good for her teeth, but I hated to tell Cap no. Stan worked from three o'clock to eleven at night. It was pretty typical for the crew to head to the bar after work for a few hours. I didn't mind too much, because Stan wasn't a big drinker. Still, I didn't sleep soundly until he arrived home.

It was the end of June, and the night air was hot and thick. I couldn't find one cool spot on the sheets and dragged myself out of bed to adjust the floor fan yet again. I considered lying on the tile floor, but moisture beaded on it and it always felt slimy. I was exhausted. It was two o'clock in the morning. Where was Stan? Frustration surged, making me toss and turn. Finally I dozed but woke with a start at five. Still no Stan. I punched my pillow into a ball, propped my head on it, and stared at a crack in the ceiling. An hour later, Stan sauntered in.

I bolted upright. "Where have you been?" I demanded.

He peeled off his work clothes. "A bunch of the guys and I drove over to the Oasis. Got something to eat and sat around shootin' the shit."

"You should have called me. I was worried something had happened to you."

"Didn't realize the time," he said.

Next thing I knew, he crawled into bed, turned his back toward me, and within minutes was snoring. I wasn't sure if I was boiling from humidity or anger.

Stan's absences increased. When I asked him where he had been, he would say he had hung out with the guys or fallen asleep in his car or would snap at me to quit hounding him. Each time I suggested we go look at an apartment or house to rent, he'd come up with one reason or another not to go. He was tired. The place was too far from his parents. We didn't need to rush into a move. I wanted to believe his excuses, believe in him, but I couldn't find it in me to completely trust him, not after California. Denny's wife, Jean, fueled my suspicions. She often stopped by Cap and Betty's for coffee and cookies.

"You know, Mary," Jean said one day, leaning close to me at the kitchen sink where I was washing coffee cups, "Denny said Stan's been shooting pool with some gal at the bar. They play almost every night and are still hanging around when Denny leaves." She didn't say much beyond that, but I knew what she was insinuating.

I willed myself to ignore her. I was convinced Stan and I were having the son he always wanted and began telling myself that once this baby was born, Stan would finally settle down and become a father. We were saving money and soon would have our own place. I wouldn't be so sick anymore, something Stan greatly resented, and he would be happier, nicer, and less restless. We would be a family. The thoughts reeled through my mind like ticker tape.

A week later, Stan walked out of the bedroom late morning. For once, he had come home at a reasonable hour. He had slept in. I was sitting on the couch watching a game show, wondering how I was going to keep my breakfast down and, for Shannon's sake, get through another day. Cap was in the kitchen drinking coffee and feeding her cookies.

"I found an apartment for us to look at," I said to Stan. "Maybe we can go see it today. It's about twenty minutes from your work."

Stan stopped in the middle of the room and looked at me

as if I were asking him to go back to Nam or care for Shannon while I toured Europe.

"I'm not looking at an apartment with you," he said, his voice flat. "In fact, we're not getting an apartment. I don't love you, and I don't want to be with you." His eyes held something I had never seen.

Acid pooled in my stomach and crept up my throat. "What?" I managed to say.

He erupted. "Just get out! Leave. I don't want to be with you." He flung his arms around like a madman.

"What are you talking about, Stan?" My voice rose in volume to match his.

I heard Cap's chair slide back and a moment later the kitchen door slam. Through the bank of living-room windows, I saw him hobble to his car. I ran into the kitchen, lifted Shannon from her chair, and returned to the living room. Stan looked at Shannon, frowned, and stormed into the bedroom.

"For God's sake, tell me what's going on," I said, following him. "You have a daughter and a pregnant wife. What are you thinking?"

Stan slammed a dresser drawer.

"We're done, Mary. That's it."

He stalked out, holding a fistful of clothes.

I shifted Shannon to my other hip and hurried after him. "We haven't even talked about this. You need to tell me what's going on. I don't want to move out."

He didn't say another word, just shoved his free hand in his pocket for the car keys. The next thing I knew, he peeled out the driveway, spraying gravel against the house.

I stood at the kitchen door holding Shannon—or maybe Shannon was holding me. An earthquake I had experienced back in California had rocked the world, displacing items on shelves and leaving me momentarily disoriented, but nothing like this. I felt dazed, dizzy, and numb. I couldn't move.

"Mommy?" Shannon had her little hands on my cheeks. Her eyebrows were raised and eyes filled with curiosity.

"Mommy and Daddy are having a fight," I whispered. "Daddy's upset."

"Daddy," she said, as if still testing the word. "Daddy come back?"

I couldn't rein in my tears. They ran over Shannon's knuckles and dripped onto the floor. I let them flow. Hot, angry tears. Sad tears. Self-pitying tears. Tears of dread. I had no car, no money, no job, and now no husband.

Over the next few days, we all tried talking to Stan during the few times he came back to the house for this or that item. I begged him to give us a chance to work things out. Cap ranted so loudly at his son, I worried the neighbors would think a brawl was underway and call the police. None of us could pry information from him, and the more we tried, the less he said.

I reached my breaking point one night just before midnight. Worry, grief, and failure seemed to cling together in the humidity and settle on my skin. In the darkness, I couldn't see options. How would I support Shannon and this new baby? Was I destined to move back to the farm? I could barely stomach the thought of living with a crowd of people in my mother's domain. How she would disapprove! A deep hopelessness engulfed me. I got up and dressed, found a pad of paper, and scribbled a note.

Dear Cap and Betty, I'm leaving. Stan isn't going to change his mind. I'm not able to care for Shannon. She loves you and you'll take good care of her. Don't come looking for me. Mary

I left the note on the kitchen table, grabbed my purse, and

crept out the kitchen door. A full moon hung high in the sky. Maybe it knew before I did that I would be leaving and made sure to shine extra bright. Cool air brushed against my bare arms, my neck, ankles, trying to soothe me. I trudged along Charley Bluff Road, regretting that I didn't think to bring tissues. I thought I didn't have any more tears in me, but here they came, pouring out again. I sobbed and walked, trying to see the road through my blurry vision. I arrived at road construction with no vehicle access, a new byway into town. I'd follow it to Milton, find a pay phone, and call Barbara. She lived near Madison and would come pick me up. I pulled out my wallet to make sure I had change. Walking across soft clay rutted from heavy machinery proved slow going. Without warning, the moonlight seemed to grow brighter. I turned around. A car was bouncing over the dirt. When the headlights reached my feet, it stopped and a door opened.

"Mary!" It was Cap. "Mary, wait!" He ran toward me with his wooden-leg limp. He didn't stop until his arms grabbed me and pulled me close. "Mary, don't leave. I love you. Betty loves you."

I sobbed into his shirt. He didn't care. He just stood there holding me.

"Shannon needs her mother. You're a wonderful mother. Stan may not see it, but Betty and I see it every day." He didn't let go, and I didn't stop crying.

"We'll work something out. Even if Stan doesn't come back, we'll work it out."

My sobs gradually retreated, and my breathing calmed.

"Come on, now. Let's go home. We'll figure out what to do in the morning." Cap had worked on road construction and knew how to drive without getting stuck.

I later learned that Shannon had awakened and went to look

for me. Maybe she sensed something was wrong, or maybe she heard me. At any rate, she woke up her grandpa and kept telling him Mommy was gone. Finally, Cap got up to show her that I was fine, but instead discovered an empty bed and my note. Back at home, I found her snuggled between Theresa and Suzie. She reached for me, and I broke down again, thinking what a precious child she was and how her idiot father couldn't see it.

The next morning, after the waves of nausea had passed, I picked up the phone and placed the dreaded SOS call to my mother.

"Stan came home and said he doesn't want to be married anymore. He wants me and Shannon gone," I said into the phone. "I don't know what to do." It felt like my stomach had climbed into my throat, and I was having trouble swallowing it.

She sighed. "Do you want me to come and get you?"

"Yes," I said. "Please."

I heard her sigh again. "I would have thought the military would have made him grow up," she said, but to me it sounded like "I told you he was a problem. You shouldn't have married him."

I lived at the farm for six weeks. Grandma came in the morning to babysit Allan, Sharon, and Shannon. Mom assigned Charlotte, Kathy, and me chores, then rushed off to work. Walt and Dad spent their days in the fields. No one asked me what happened, not even Grandma. I'm sure she heard whatever story Mom fed her. I spent much time weeding and hoeing Mom's vegetable garden. It had to be three times the size of Cap and Betty's living room. I pulled weeds from between plants: tomatoes, potatoes, corn, radishes, carrots, rutabagas, wax beans, squash, pumpkins, and sweet peas. The feel of the moist earth in my hands and the warm sun pressing against my back eased my anxiety and anger. I sank the hoe into the soil, pushed and pulled it around the plants, all the while imagining what life would be like without Stan. No one to call me a liar or explode into tantrums.

What really had been getting to me was when he criticized or condemned me in front of his parents or my family. It seemed to happen when the topic turned to parenting or jobs. I became his target. And the worst of it was, no one defended me. I occasionally caught Betty or Cap or one of my sisters shaking their head as if in disbelief that Stan was going off on me, his wife. But that was it. No one told him to shut up or quit or leave the room. I silently took his abuse while burning inside. Like me, they were afraid to challenge him. There was something about his presence. He wasn't tall, but the way he held himself always looked threatening. Because he was so muscular, no one wanted to provoke a fight. I had never seen him hit anyone, but when he was angry he looked like he could take a swing any second. People actually backed away from him.

I wondered if the navy had instilled that presence in him. I had stopped bringing up Viet Nam. It was like throwing a grenade into the middle of our discussion. But I remember the special training he had back in 1966, before leaving for his year-long tour in Viet Nam. The navy sent him to Virginia for Survival, Evasion, Resistance, and Escape (SERE) training. If a soldier fell into enemy hands, rather than sitting and twiddling his thumbs in enemy territory, he would possess the skills to try to escape and survive, or stay and survive, or resist and survive. Stan later claimed the skills came in handy when he supposedly was captured and tortured in Laos. I could never find any records of that capture in the files that the navy gave him. I always had the sense that he was pulling maneuvers on me.

My mother heard me talking on the phone. "Was that Stan?" she asked after I hung up. "What's happening?"

"Cap and Betty are bringing him here this weekend," I said, sitting on the red velvet fainting couch she recently purchased. It was beautiful, even if it looked like it belonged in a brothel. She walked over to the shelves and adjusted a porcelain robin, mumbling something I couldn't hear. She bobbed around the room like a bird at the feeder. The tilt of her head, the straight line of her mouth, and the downward angle of her chin loudly spoke her disapproval. I leaned back on the couch and closed my eyes. The horsehair stuffing poked at my legs. As she passed me, I heard, "Your dad's not happy about this." She could hit her target as precisely as Stan.

Shame rattled through me. I peeked at her out of one eye. I could almost see the cogs moving in her mind, sifting through ways of taking charge of the situation and fixing it for me. I went into survival mode and tuned her out. I knew what she didn't want to admit: that the only way out of my mess was to commit the sin of divorce. I could think or say the word "divorce," but putting it into action would further shame my family. I already felt like a failure. I had vowed, promised, and agreed to stand by my husband. I felt as trapped as a fox up a tree.

When Stan arrived at the farm on Saturday, I met him at the car. For privacy, we walked into the fields behind the old barn. He hung his head, apologized, and promised to take care of the kids and me. Part of me felt like a parent reprimanding a child; the other part refused to admit that his promises might be nothing more than bubbles of hot air. I yearned to have somebody take care of me. Since he was offering to do so, I took him back.

Stan agreed to move out of his parents' house. I found an apartment above a tavern in a town near his family. We even bought a few pieces of new furniture and planned to investigate getting a VA loan to buy a home. I let myself feel hopeful that things would work out between us, and this new baby would settle Stan into fatherhood. We had chosen the name Shayne.

Shayne was born on November 27, 1968. The weather was miserable, but not as miserable as my labor. He had a round head with a touch of blond fuzz, big eyes, and protruding red lips. At first I thought he was ugly, which made me feel incredibly guilty. Stan miraculously arrived just before Shayne was born. The hospitals still didn't allow fathers into the delivery room, so I didn't get to see Stan until I returned to my room. He already was there, a big grin on his face.

Seven months later, we moved again. This time we rented a cute, little two-bedroom house with an unattached garage and nice lawn. It was located on Charley's Bluff, close to Stan's family. In exchange for the first month's rent, we painted it and fixed it up. Just as I began to think we were getting onto the normal family track, Stan started to pull shit. I couldn't count on him to come home as planned, do things around the house, or play with the kids. I'd fuss and holler. He'd take a break from his escapades, then get right back to them. He knew exactly how far he could push me before he needed to reel me back.

When a summer job opened in a seafood factory near us, I decided to apply. Stan was now working at General Motors and making a decent wage, but he had no sense of money management. His theory was that money in the bank account should be spent, especially on cars. Thus, we owned the newest '69 Mach I Mustang hatchback. He reluctantly agreed to take care of the kids when I announced that I got the job. The extra cash was nice, but just as satisfying was the sense of independence I felt at having my own paycheck.

The only home improvement we hadn't done was lay linoleum

on the bathroom floor. I pestered Stan to please put it down. The old stuff was peeling off, and Shayne kept crawling in there and putting little pieces in his mouth. I feared he would choke like a cousin of mine, who ended up brain damaged as a result.

Then one day that very thing happened. Shayne scooted out of sight for only seconds, but by the time I caught up with him, he had stuffed a piece of linoleum in his mouth and was sputtering. I dug it out, incensed that Stan hadn't taken care of the problem. It was a Saturday, and he had gone out fishing. I loaded Shannon and Shayne in the car, drove to the hardware store, purchased a sheet of linoleum, glue, and the proper tools, and went back home. I pulled the toilet up and laid the linoleum myself. With juggling the kids, it took most of the day.

"Come see the bathroom," I said when Stan returned home late that afternoon.

We stepped into the small space. He looked at the clean, shiny floor, then looked at me.

"Did you do this?"

I nodded my head yes.

"Jesus. I wouldn't even know where to begin." He turned and walked out. I could have sworn I glimpsed embarrassment on his face.

Having gone through such a traumatic pregnancy and birth with Shayne, I decided I didn't want to have any more children. I broached the subject of birth control with Stan. He didn't want another baby either and suggested I do whatever was necessary. We fought over who should do what. I wanted to go on the pill, even though the Catholic church forbade it. He wasn't in favor of that because then I could freely have sex with someone else if I wanted. Like that was going to happen. I didn't want him to have the vasectomy for the same reason, an event far more likely to happen. So, we did nothing.

On my birthday, strongly suspecting that I was ovulating, I succumbed to his pressuring for sex, and we made passionate love in the dark, humid night. God, I prayed more than once, please don't let me be pregnant. But God had something else in mind for Stan and me and the little soul he gifted to us that night.

I dropped the scrub brush in the bathroom and ran to answer the phone, ringing insistently in the kitchen. It was my mother. She knew I had the day off.

"Sharon wants to stay with you before school starts," she said. "She keeps asking me. She's afraid to ask you."

I doubted Sharon had pestered Mom at all about visiting, especially since Grandma Krachey was still babysitting. More than likely, Mom didn't want Sharon underfoot, any more than I wanted Sharon underfoot. But I knew Shannon would love having a playmate. Oh, what the heck, I thought. I suspected I was pregnant, though didn't know for sure, and had yet to deal with morning sickness.

"Why don't you bring her this weekend?" I said. "Then we'll bring her back on Labor Day. That's about two weeks."

While making supper, I shared the news with Stan.

"Why do we have to take care of Sharon? She's a conniving, self-centered brat," he said, leaning against the counter and lighting a cigarette.

I hefted the pot of boiling potatoes and carried it to the sink. Sharon was the youngest of twelve children and yes, she was spoiled, but she wasn't naughty or unruly. She certainly was willing to help when asked. I knew part of Stan's annoyance stemmed from being on kid-care duty more frequently now that I worked. Cap still pitched in by taking Shannon every morning for a pop at the bar. He liked Sharon and probably would be happy to take her too.

"She'll be fine," I said. "You probably won't even notice she's here."

Sharon had been with us for over a week. I needed to do some laundry, so I gathered up the clothes and put Stan in charge of the three kids. He was sitting on the couch watching television. "Your dad's going to stop by while I'm gone." I reminded him. "I asked him to bring the lawn mower. He's going to watch the kids so you can mow the lawn."

When I returned toting clean laundry, Cap and Betty were at the kitchen table drinking coffee and smoking. Stan was pushing the mower across the backyard. I said hello, then went to peek in on Shayne, who was taking his morning nap in his crib. After I put the clothes away, I returned to the kitchen, poured a cup of coffee, and sat down to visit. The girls giggled in the living room.

Betty was telling me about Barbara and Terry's wedding plans when Sharon ran up to me. She put her hand on my leg.

"Mary," she said, looking up at me, "Stan put his hands down my pants and touched my butt."

An eerie shock zinged through me. Betty stopped talking midsentence. The grinding lawn mower whirred close to the house, then journeyed away. I set my coffee cup on the table and looked into Sharon's face. Innocence mingled with confusion. It was as if her eyes were asking me questions, ones I knew all too well. What was he doing, Mary? Why did he do it? I could see Raymond Bushey kneeling between my legs, his sickening smile exposing brown teeth, the smell of chewing tobacco too close. Everything too close. Cap caught my eye and looked down at his coffee cup, shaking his head. Part of me didn't want to believe Sharon. It would be so much easier just to pat her hand and tell her it was okay and go on believing Stan wasn't capable of doing such a thing. But I couldn't. Raymond Bushey wouldn't let me.

I found my voice. "Can you tell me what happened?"

Sharon hung her head and repeated her statement. The embarrassment. The shame. I could tell she felt them. I didn't want those feelings stuck in my five-year-old sister the way they were stuck in me. I needed to open the door and let them out. Damn that Stan! What was he thinking? Fury bubbled up thick and oily and inflammable. I told Sharon to go play with Shannon, I'd talk to Stan.

Cap and Betty didn't move. I walked out the back door. Stan's back was to me. He was wearing shorts and had shed his shirt. His well-tanned skin glistened with sweat. I could see each muscle move. The body of an athlete. He turned the mower and headed toward the house. I waited for him to get closer, then waved at him to come inside. He idled the motor and walked across the grass, calm, as if unknowing and innocent. I stood on the back stoop, holding the screen door open to the kitchen.

"Sharon just told me you stuck your hand down her pants and touched her butt," I said, my voice low and surprisingly steady.

Surprise registered on Stan's face. Then it turned red, and the muscles in his jaw tightened. "What? I didn't touch her except to pull her off that damn jumping horse so Shannon could ride it."

"Why would she say something like that?" I said, moving closer.

"She's a little liar. You know she is. Makes up stuff just like your mother." Stan's voice grew louder. "I should go in there right now and give her a good swat. Right on her butt, which I did not touch!"

Out of the corner of my eye, I saw the girls run toward the bedroom. "Stan, if Sharon's going to make something up, it's not going to be that!" I was hoping Cap and Betty might chime in, but they remained stone still.

"This is fucking ridiculous! She's a spoiled brat who gets off making stuff up, and you know it. How can you believe her?" He glared at me, then went back to the lawn mower, turned it off, marched into the kitchen, grabbed the car keys from the counter, and stormed out the door.

My knees felt wobbly. I wilted into a chair. The car tore out of the driveway, and the tires squealed up the street.

Cap shook his head again. "I can't believe it. I just can't believe he'd do something like this." He got up from the table and limped out the door. Betty picked her purse up from the floor and without a word followed him, her shoulders slumped. The screen door bounced shut. I sat alone at the kitchen table with three cups of coffee, three children, and a giant, miserable problem staring me in the face.

The wind blowing through the open car window swept Sharon's mass of hair away from her face. Freckles covered the bridge of her nose and her pale cheeks. A slight frown had settled between her eyebrows. She occasionally glanced at me, her blue eyes filled with lingering confusion. The drive from Charley Bluff to the nearest hospital was taking forever. I had explained to Sharon that we needed to go to the hospital for a quick checkup, just to make sure she was okay. Back in California, I had taken to reading *Psychology Today*. Stan hated the magazine, but I found it fascinating. I recalled an article about sexual abuse recommending that a doctor examine a victim. Before leaving the house, I had called work to say that I was sick and wouldn't be in. Next, I called Betty to see if she would watch Shannon and Shayne and if I could borrow their car. Cap picked us up.

I dropped him off at the tavern and dropped the kids off with Betty. "An exam will prove that Stan didn't really do anything," I said to Betty, feeling as if I were lying.

At the hospital, Sharon and I were ushered into an examining room. Sharon didn't want to leave my side, but the empathetic nurse persuaded her to undress, then covered her with a sheet. I remained in the room while the doctor examined her. He asked me to step into the hallway while the nurse helped Sharon dress.

"There's no evidence that Sharon has been harmed," he said. Thank God, I thought, feeling cautious relief. "But a five-year-old doesn't make up a story like this. I would wager your husband did touch her." His anger snuffed out my relief. "You say you have two children? For your safety and theirs, I suggest you get yourself and your children away from that man. I've been in practice long enough to know these patterns don't change easily."

My mind reeled. The doctor was certain Sharon was telling the truth, yet he couldn't hand me evidence I could use to confront Stan. My anger swelled. I wanted to lash out at Stan. What in God's name was he thinking? I thanked the doctor and gathered Sharon. He told me to call Rock County Social Services.

When I drove up to the house, our car was nowhere to be seen. I noticed Stan's work clothes were gone from the bedroom. I was still enraged, but an intense sadness overwhelmed me. I pushed it into my gut and called social services. The intake receptionist agreed that an appointment was in order. She put me on hold, then offered a date two weeks out, an eternity, but I scribbled it on the calendar. Before we hung up, she connected me with a counselor, who advised me to take Sharon home.

Cap and Betty agreed to my request to continue babysitting. I called Mom and said I was bringing Sharon home and needed to talk to her and Dad. Sharon and I packed up her bag and climbed back into the car. The day's trauma must have exhausted her, because she immediately fell asleep. For one hundred and twenty-five miles, I contended with my thoughts. Though I dreaded telling my parents about what happened, I envisioned their support. I rehashed Stan's Jekyll-and-Hyde behavior since returning from Viet Nam. His manipulations. His extended absences after work and the rumors I overheard about his affairs that seemed to start after Shayne was born. And now Sharon's accusation. No proof of anything, just a belief he was guilty. And if he were, would I leave him? The question hovered, casting its dark shadow on me. I thought about the unprotected sex we had on my birthday. I was almost certain I was pregnant, but hadn't said a word to anyone. How could I leave if that were the case? I wouldn't be able to find a job; I'd have to rely on Stan for support. My mind looped and relooped through the dismaying thoughts.

I pulled into the farmhouse driveway feeling as though I had driven ten thousand miles. Everything was summer-green and lush. The black-and-white cows. The cool shade from the elm tree. It looked so idyllic, so peaceful. Only the old barn loomed against the blue sky. I opened the car door and shivered. My parents greeted us at the kitchen door. I was glad Grandma wasn't there. I didn't want to witness her heartbreak.

"Let's go talk in the red room," I said. My mother had wall-papered the new living room in deep red, and we all called it the red room. Sharon dragged her bag upstairs to her room, her head hanging. I wanted to tell her it was okay, but didn't say anything. I closed the door. Dad settled in his mother's old rocking chair, Mom chose the piano bench, and I pulled up an old wooden straight-back chair. In halting sentences, I told them what had happened. Mom kept her eyes on her lap.

Then Mom said, "I don't know how Sharon could come up with such a story!"

I looked at her, wondering if I had heard her correctly. Had she just convoluted my story?

"Would Stan really do something like that?" said my father, his eyes never leaving mine.

My mother jumped in before I could speak. "No, of course he wouldn't!"

I felt as though I was on trial. Maybe it was not being believed enough in the past. Maybe it was not being heard enough over the years. Maybe it was the chair keeping my back straight, refusing to let me slump or cower or hide from that which had been hidden far too long. But something snapped in me. It was time to expose the truth.

"You need to know why I know Sharon isn't making this up," I said. "First of all, she's too young to understand this type of behavior. Captain Kangaroo doesn't talk about it. Nobody talks about it. I'm speaking from experience." Anger pushed me forward. "The same thing happened to me when I was five. Only it was worse."

I proceeded to tell my parents what Raymond Bushey did to me in the barn nineteen years earlier. For the first time in my life, I described out loud what had happened. My mother folded her hands on her lap and looked down. Her voice shook. "Why didn't you ever tell us?" she said softly. Dad didn't say anything. Tears filled his eyes. They had heard me.

Shame filled me, as if I were the one who had done something wrong all those years ago. I hated that shame. It didn't make sense to my logical mind. I hadn't been in the wrong. Bushey was the creep, the culprit. Yet, I had done what I shouldn't have: I had acquiesced.

"I still can't believe Stan did anything to Sharon," my mother said.

I jerked up in the chair. Instead of flinging me a life preserver of acknowledgement, of saying yes, Stan abused Sharon, her response was to doubt her daughter. Did that mean she didn't believe my story about Bushey? I thought of the photo my mother had taken of Dad and Bushey kneeling in front of the Christmas tree, Bushey holding a quart of booze. Why would I fabricate something so horrid and heinous? I wouldn't lie about such a thing any more than my sister would. I felt defeated and alone.

As I drove back to Charley's Bluff, the same thought replayed: I know he did it, I know he did it. I rolled down the window. Hot air rushed into the car and into my head. "I know he did it," I screamed out the window. A car passed me. I screamed it again. "I know he did it." I screamed at every driver, every trucker, every bird, every road sign. Tears ran down my cheeks. The doctor had believed Sharon in a second. Why wouldn't the people who mattered most to her, to me, believe what happened?

By the time I arrived home, I was exhausted. Betty took one look at me and offered to take Shannon and Shayne for the night, but I said it wasn't necessary. I didn't add that I needed to be with them. They were my anchors. Without them, I would have exited the freeway, would have kept driving somewhere, anywhere away from the fray I had been living in for too long.

It was midmorning the next day when I heard a car crunch over the gravel driveway. I peeked out the window. Stan was getting out of the car. As usual, he wore his driving gloves. I had no idea where he had been, and I didn't really care. During the time it took him to walk from the car to the door, I let myself hate him. Before he even opened his mouth, I launched into what the doctor and social services had said.

"I didn't do a thing," he growled, flexing his leather-gloved fist. We glared at each other. Stan walked into the bedroom and shut the door.

A few days later, the phone rang. It was Mom. "I spoke with

Sharon," she said. "Things didn't happen the way she told you. She said she was playing doctor and nurse with her cousins next door and made it sound like, you know, typical child exploration. She said Stan never touched her." Mom sounded proud, as if she had investigated and uncovered the truth. I felt the pain of an all-too familiar punch.

I phoned social services and spoke with the same social worker. "I don't know what to do next," I said.

The voice on the other end went quiet for a moment. "Probably best to close the case at this point," she said gently. I hung up the phone, deflated once again, but also defeated. I ran into the bathroom and threw up. Morning sickness had set in with a vengeance.

It was a pretty Sunday morning in mid-September. The first hint of fall played in the air, and everything had a golden touch. I had just returned home from having attended church with Betty. Stan had the day off, and I thought we could take a walk around Charley Bluff, get some fresh air, let the kids run around, and reconnect as a family before another busy workweek began. Stan was still working at GM full time but also had taken a part-time job at the local gas station. I walked into the kitchen. I barely had set my purse down when Stan came charging in, his face blustery.

"What in the hell took so long? I've been watching these kids while you run off to the goddamn church." He grabbed the car keys from the rack where I had hung them. "Shayne hasn't stopped crying. He's hungry, and his diaper is full of shit." He stalked to the door.

"Where are you going?" I said, bracing myself against his sudden explosion.

"To the bar to watch football with my dad and brothers," he yelled over his shoulder.

My heart sank. There goes our nice Sunday afternoon, I thought. I tamped down my rising frustration. What was the use? Stan needed to blow off steam, and it was my job to give him the space to do that away from the kids and me. I went into the bedroom to change my clothes. I peeked in the bedroom where Shannon and Shayne were playing. Well, the three of us would just have to take a walk.

I was tying my tennies when Shannon came in. "What did you and Daddy do while I was gone?" I asked.

"We ate Fruit Loops," she said. "Then Daddy watched TV."

That figures, I thought. At least he could have taken them outside and tossed the ball around. Shayne was only ten months old but loved to run after a ball, any ball. I had a feeling he was going to be as coordinated and athletic as Stan.

Shannon leaned against the bed and looked at me. In an almost cheerful yet questioning voice, she said, "Daddy tickled my butt."

My body stiffened. I felt my stomach lurch. "What do you mean he tickled your butt?"

Shannon jumped back as if I had done something to startle her. Had I? Maybe I was losing my mind. How could this be happening again, only two weeks after the incident with Sharon? The same words. "Tickled my butt." I asked her for details. She ducked her head as if embarrassed and said no more. Maybe she saw the hurt in my eyes, or maybe Stan had told her not to tell, or maybe she'd overheard the conversation when Sharon told and didn't want to alarm me any more. I asked Shannon to lie on the bed and let me see her bottom. I examined each fold. No evidence of trauma anywhere. I didn't have proof Stan had touched Sharon, nor proof he had touched Shannon. But some creepy-crawly feeling deep inside me said he was guilty.

I told Shannon to go play with Shayne. My mind buzzed. What to do? Who to tell? I needed to tell someone, had to tell someone. I was terrified. Who was this crazy person I was married to? Or was I the crazy person and imagining all this? No. That couldn't be. Insanity wormed through me. My mind flipped through family and friends and finally landed on Cap and Betty. I could walk to Cap and Betty's house. They knew about Stan's behavior, not just *this* behavior, but his explosiveness, his immaturity. Betty had said more than once to me, "What did I do that my boys turned out this way?" She would be empathetic. And so would Cap, for that matter. They loved their grandchildren. They loved me. They would be the parents, the support I needed.

"Let's go see Grandpa Cap and Granny," I said to Shannon, trying to maintain calm.

When we arrived at the Havens' house, Cap was sitting at the kitchen table playing solitaire. I set Shayne on the floor, and he immediately crawled after Peppy, their dog.

"You're going to have to move faster than that to catch that old girl," said Cap, chuckling.

"Why aren't you at the bar with the boys?" I asked.

"Not in the mood to sit up in that smoky, noisy place," he said. Then he scooped up Shannon. "How's my pretty, big girl today?" Cap made Shannon guess which hand held the stick of gum. She got it right, and he tickled her, making her squeal. I told her to take Shayne into the other room and play with the basket of toys Betty kept in the corner. Betty came in from the bedroom and joined us.

My heart thumped. There was no easy way to say what I needed to say. "When I got home from church," I said, "Shannon said the craziest thing to me." Cap and Betty looked up, curious. "She said Stan had tickled her butt. I don't know what it means or why she would say it."

Cap's good eye grew large, then he slammed his fist on the table. I flinched in my chair, totally unprepared for his reaction. "What the hell are you trying to do to this family?" His face scrunched in anger, giving his bad eye an ominous glow. "I don't ever want to hear you accuse Stan of such nonsense again. Never again. Understand?"

I was dumbfounded.

"Cap!" Betty yelled. "Stop it." The family matriarch looked fierce and ready to fight.

"Damn it all to hell, Betty!" He pounded the table again. "Where does Mary get off coming up with these lies? Stan may not be perfect, but my son is no pervert."

Cap seldom swore. His words sliced into me. I ran from the assault into the other room, picked up Shayne, grabbed Shannon's hand, and fled out the kitchen door. I didn't even bother to put Shayne in the stroller, just pushed it across the rough asphalt, crying the entire way home. Shannon jogged to keep up with my pace. Another piece of my world had fallen off and shattered. My parents didn't believe me. And now Stan's parents, a main artery of support, questioned my veracity. But they knew their son! Knew how crazy he could be. There was so much I had wanted to say, like maybe Stan has a problem, maybe we should get help, but with Cap glaring at me, poised as if to hit me, I became afraid to utter another word.

At home, I forced a calm facade. I made lunch for the kids, we played, they napped, I vacuumed and dusted. All the while I could feel anger turning to rage, an acidic rage. In my stomach. My throat. My head. By the time Stan returned late that evening after the kids were in bed, I was the crazy one. I demanded to know what Shannon meant.

He laughed. "Aw heck, I was just tickling her belly." But he never looked me in the eye. All afternoon I had wondered why he ran out the door so quickly. That night, however, I never asked the question. It was late, and my weary, overwrought brain began to think that perhaps I was the one overreacting. I crawled into bed and tried to find the door to sleep, but for too many hours all I could find was the aluminum front door to the Havens' house, and all I could hear was Cap's raised voice and his accusations, followed by the doctor's advice to get out, to get away from a man who does those kinds of things.

Darkness was descending earlier. I looked out the kitchen window at the thin line of orange sky hanging above the horizon, the last gasp of day. Soon, snow would start falling. The draft slipping through the window frame already held a chill. The fuel tank for our heater needed refilling. I tried to squelch the panic that had been rising since the previous day when Stan returned home without a bank-deposit slip. It was payday, and on payday Stan always handed me a deposit slip. I was the household accountant who paid the bills on time, balanced the checkbook, and knew how much money we had or didn't have. Right now, we had none. Zero. I looked at the bill holder on the kitchen counter. Among the envelopes calling for immediate attention was the bill for our Mustang. For weeks now, I had been trying to talk to Stan about our finances, but he either shrugged his shoulders and walked out of the room or blew up and thundered out of the house. I never knew which Stan I'd get. The day before, when I asked about the check, he snarled and left.

I tamped down the panic again. I added salt and rice to the water boiling in a pot. If Stan came home, he'd have to find something else to eat. But then again, Stan might not come home. Last night he never returned, and this morning he offered no explanation of where he had been.

A month or so after the blowup over Shannon's accusation, Stan called out a name while sleeping. Rebecca. I didn't know a Rebecca. Rather than dig into him, I teased him about it. He grew agitated. "Why do you make up such fucking lies?" he yelled.

He knew I backed down when he swore. Such language hadn't been a part of my childhood, and I didn't want it to be a part of my children's. The next thing I knew, he was going AWOL at night, and I wasn't sleeping. Now here I was with bare cupboards, an empty checkbook, and no car.

When the rice was done, I spooned some on plates. One of the rice kernels looked different. What the heck? I looked closely and gasped. I hadn't washed the rice before I cooked it. They were cooked rice weevils. I quickly searched through the rest of the dish. Another bug. Another. And another. It was all I could do not to throw up. I poured what little milk was left into two glasses, made a peanut butter and jelly sandwich out of a piece of folded bread for each kid, and served it with the rice. I felt like the worst mother on earth.

I crept out of Shayne and Shannon's bedroom. They were sleeping soundly after having been bathed, read to, and tucked in. I kissed each one on the forehead again. My precious babies. God, how I loved them. They deserved a better life than this. They deserved a better mother. Surely they would be better off with someone who could give them a sane home. And here I was, bringing a third child into the world. I choked back sobs and tiptoed out of the room.

I crumpled to my knees next to the living room couch and laid my head on the coffee table. My shoulders shook. Maybe God would be merciful and abort this child. My heart instantly filled with shame at such a sinful thought. Helen's words came back to me. This child has every right to live. These problems aren't her fault!

I pulled myself up, turned on the TV, and collapsed on the couch. Lawrence Welk was introducing his next guest. I dozed to the music, then awoke with a start in the middle of a Bayer aspirin commercial. I looked at the bottle on the screen. We had the same one in our medicine cabinet. I could do it, I thought. I could swallow the tablets. All of them. Stan would come home and find me dead, and he'd be sorrier than he'd ever been. But I was too tired to move my body. Mr. Welk returned, smiled encouragingly, and tapped his baton for the next singer to begin.

The next thing I knew, Stan was shaking me.

"Why aren't you in the bedroom?" he said.

For a moment, I was confused. The TV station had gone off the air. "What time is it?" I said.

"I dunno. Late."

The clock on the wall said five o'clock. "Where have you been?" I asked, feeling tired and irritated.

"Working," Stan said, turning off the television.

"No you weren't," I said, now fully awake. "I called the station, and they said you had left. Did you and Rebecca go somewhere?"

Stan pointed his finger at me. "No! I did not go anywhere with anyone named Rebecca. Now just get that out of your messed-up mind."

"Lower your voice, Stan. You'll wake the kids."

He looked at me as if I was the crazy one. "I'm going to bed."

Ten minutes later, he was in bed with the light turned off. I was so sick of his games. I went into the bathroom, filled a glass with water, and opened the medicine cabinet. My hands shook as I poured out every single aspirin and gulped them down. I went into the bedroom and threw the empty bottle at my husband. "I hope you're happy. I'll be gone, and you can do whatever you want."

I went back to the couch. It didn't take long for the aspirin to take hold. I could feel my body relax. I started to float. So easy. So quiet. Peaceful floating into the purples and pinks of a sunset and never having to step out of it again . . .

I felt something push me. Then sounds. A voice. The word ambulance. In the distance a siren. Then the words in my ear, "Now everyone will know just how fucking crazy you are. Only crazies do something as stupid as this."

Dr. Tom was sitting on the edge of my hospital bed. He had delivered Shayne and he was a doctor I liked and trusted. He informed me that I had arrived at the hospital barely conscious and they had pumped my stomach in the emergency room. I had a vague memory of it.

"You know, you could have harmed your baby," he said. "I know you haven't been happy, but at least get through this pregnancy." His concern, empathy, and gentle way of speaking set me to crying. "Maybe you should ask your priest for help," he suggested.

I was released that afternoon. Cap and Betty came to pick me up. Betty looked sad and helpless, and Cap looked confused and helpless. None of us said a word about what had happened. When I got home, Stan was nowhere to be found. I wasn't about to call my parents. Attempted suicide was a sin. I couldn't endure my mother's reaction.

The next day, my self-pity boiled into anger. I borrowed tools and nails from Cap. Stan and I had bought window coverings, but for all my badgering, he had never put them up. While Shannon and Shayne napped, I cut sheets of plastic, wrapped them around wooden laths, climbed the stepladder, and nailed the sheets over each window and screen door. It was awkward work, but I finished the project. That's it, I thought. I'm better off without a husband. After this baby is born, it's time to leave. One way or another, I'd make it without him.

I made an appointment with Father McEnery in Milton. He wore a black patch over one eye. He didn't know me well but saw me with Betty in church and had baptized Shayne. I told him everything that had happened, from Sharon to Shannon to my aspirin overdose. He just shook his head.

"You seem like a strong woman. You'll get through this," was all he said.

We could no longer afford our rent; Stan unexpectedly had quit his job at GM, though he never admitted why he quit. One of my cousins, who also worked at GM, later told me that Stan had mouthed off to his supervisor and was fired. I made the dreaded phone call to my mother, who asked *what* did he do *now* and said we could all stay in the upstairs of the old log cabin part of the farmhouse. Mom was planning to turn it into a separate rental apartment but hadn't yet started renovations. On a blustery March day that might have blown me over had I not been eight months pregnant, we loaded the kids into our Mustang, our stuff into a friend's pickup, and moved from Milton to the farm. "We can move to Steuben after the baby's born," Stan said, during the drive. He sounded almost cheery.

I didn't respond. By the time we pulled in the driveway, it was biting cold and raining. Even the elm tree, with its bare, exposed limbs, looked miserable.

Fortunately, Stan soon found work with a state-funded juvenile delinquent program near Prairie. He was tasked with setting up and managing a gas station, complete with a bay for minor car repairs, and teaching troubled youth the mechanic's trade. Being a kid himself, he fit in well and seemed content.

I wanted Dr. Tom to deliver this baby, so two weeks before my due date I returned to Milton and stayed with Cap and Betty. I took the kids with me and left Stan at the farm. That week, Stan and I talked every night on the phone. The next week, Stan wasn't always around when I called. I could hear the disapproval in my mother's voice when she said he hadn't come home and didn't know where he was. He refused to leave a number for her. I could only imagine their looks and comments to one another. My mother pushing Stan for accountability, Stan pulling her in with his tactical defenses and then punching her with his defiance. Both strong-willed. Both hitting below the belt. Push. Pull. Punch. And there I was, over one hundred miles away, about to give birth, helpless to intercede. I had heartburn so bad, I was chewing gum constantly to ease it, loving the snap, crackle, and pop that drove others batty. Juicy Fruit. My only sense of control and joy.

When I hadn't heard from Stan in three days, I called the center where he worked.

"How did you get this number?" said Stan, sounding surprised to hear my voice, when he answered the gas station phone.

"The operator. Why didn't you give it to my mother when she asked you for it?"

"It's none of her business!"

He could piss me off in an instant. "How did you expect me to get a hold of you if I go into labor? And, why haven't you been going to the farm at night? Where have you been staying? You promised to call every night," I said, snapping my gum.

"I crash on a cot here."

I finally got him to promise he would be at the hospital for the baby's delivery *if* he didn't have to work. After we hung up, I unwrapped a fresh piece of gum. Yeah, right, I thought. A cot.

Only a few days later, contractions kept me up most of the night. In the morning, I called the farm before Stan was to leave for work only to learn he hadn't been home all night. I asked my mother to try to find him and let him know I was in labor. I spent the day counting and timing my contractions while calling around, frantically trying to locate Stan. It was after eight at night when I called Barbara and asked her to take me to the hospital. Now married to Stan's brother Terry, Barbara lived in Janesville. Terry was serving in the military overseas.

Once we were at the hospital, the labor became intense. Dear sweet Barbara sat next to the bed and massaged my back with each contraction. I tried not to cry from the pain of labor and from once again being abandoned by my husband. Barbara stayed as long as possible but had worked all day. I knew she was weary. At four in the morning, I told her to go home. At 8:22 AM, with not one family member or friend present, I delivered a pretty, eight-pound-six-ounce girl, my first baby with dark hair. Happiness fought against exhaustion and disappointment.

It was late afternoon when Stan walked into my room.

"Man, am I sore from playing basketball last night," he whined. He leaned against the windowsill away from me.

Basketball, I thought. You missed the birth of your daughter and you're talking about basketball? I was too tired to get into it with him. Instead I said, "Did you see our Shawntel?"

"No."

I swung my legs over the edge of the bed. "Let's walk to the nursery."

"Nah. I'll look at her on my way out. She's just a baby. All babies are ugly."

His comment knocked me flat against the pillow. He rambled on about his job and boasted how he took charge of the juveniles, and on and on. I sank into an abyss of invisibility. I could only stare at him as he ranted for the next thirty minutes, at last concluding that he needed to go back to Wauzeka to work. Thank God he left.

Shawntel and I moved back to the farm, but Stan didn't. Days merged into nights, and I barely slept. My hormones surged out of control. Bills mounted. I needed to get a job, get some money, and get on my own. If I worked, I knew Grandma would help take care of the kids, as would two of my sisters, Kathy, now a senior, and Charlotte, when they arrived home from high school.

Every day when my mother came home from work, she asked me about Stan. Where is he? What's he up to? I have no idea, I'd tell her. She'd give me a condescending look and abruptly march out of the room, leaving me feeling like a failure. I felt that she wanted me out of her sight, while all I wanted was someone to hold me and let me cry. The thought of suicide again crossed my mind, but I just couldn't do that to my babies. I focused on getting a job.

When Shawntel was three weeks old, I went to Transformer, a local company, and lied about how old my baby was. At the time, an infant had to be at least one month old before a mother could go to work. They hired me. The day before I started, Stan showed up at the farm and met his daughter for the first time. He looked at her with a mixture of guilt and awe, then handed her back to me and drove off into the sunset. My mother watched him through the kitchen window but didn't utter a word to me.

The local rumor mill had been grinding out hearsay about an older woman, a guidance counselor at Wyalusing Academy where Stan worked, who had a teenage son. She and Stan had been spotted together more than once in our sporty red-and-gold Mach 1 Mustang. Thinking about them practically drove me crazy. Well, if I were going to suffer, so was Stan.

I decided to go to Stan's supervisor and unload the sordid affair between Stan and the woman, whose name I discovered was Katherine. How could a married man with three children, one less than a month old, be a fit mentor to teens, I asked. And how could the woman with whom he was shacked up with be a fit guidance counselor? When I left, I felt smug, empowered even. It was the first time I had gone against my husband. After Stan's boss confronted him with my allegations, Stan called me.

"I will kill you if you ever try to destroy me again," he screamed into the phone. Then he handed the receiver to Katherine, who lit into me, threatening to file slander charges and a full-fledged lawsuit if I continued to implicate her. My face burned as I fought to contain the rage building in my stomach. My hand clutched the telephone, unable to hang up on her. She slammed the phone down, disconnecting us. Humiliated, I imagined how they must be sitting there, snuggled on some sofa, laughing at me for being so naive, for thinking I could go to a professional who would actually help me.

Somehow I worked through the uproar. By then, I was an expert on masking my feelings. No one at the farm said much to me. Every night I felt so alone in the darkened bedroom, the kids sleeping. I buried my face in my pillow and cried. If anyone heard me, they never came to console me. They saw me caring for a new baby and two small children, but that was the norm in a household brimming with bodies. It wasn't until later, in counseling, that I learned this behavior of being distant is common among family members who haven't bonded. I managed to buy a cheap old car from a friend in town. When I could, I saved money. I desperately wanted a place of my own.

Shortly after the Katherine incident, Stan was fired. He had not been making payments on the Mustang, and the bank repossessed it. He called me at the farm.

"Will you take me to Iowa and drop me off so I can hitchhike to California? I don't want anyone from around here to see me."

I had heard that Katherine had moved to California. "Why are you going there?" I said, playing stupid.

"I think I can get a job there. When I do, you and the kids can join me. You always liked California."

I thought of Katherine, of Rebecca One and Two. Secretly, I hoped he would make it there and shack up with one of those bimbos. When he called for the kids and me to join him, I would say no. He was an adulterer, and the Church did not condone adultery. I would soon have enough money to move out. Maybe I was closer than I thought to finding a way out of my marriage. Other than him dying or a woman taking him away, two things I secretly hoped would happen, I could never discern a way out. I blamed Church doctrine for holding me hostage.

The day Stan left, I asked my sister Charlotte to keep an eye on the kids for me. Stan loaded his military duffel bag in the car, and we drove west over the ridge, through Prairie du Chien, and into Iowa. I dropped him off at a truck stop. He pecked me on the cheek and said he would call as soon as he got to California. I quickly left.

For the first time in years, relief flooded over me. I drove along enjoying the bright greens of summer and the blue sky. A hawk swooped in the distance as I crossed the mighty Mississippi. I felt free, cautiously free. I imagined telling my mother and sisters that Stan had left. I didn't even mind that I would have to explain his absence to the kids. "Daddy went away. We'll be fine," I'd say. "We'll be just fine." I'd wait a day or two, maybe a week, before saying anything, just to make sure he was in California. And wouldn't he be surprised when I refused to follow him? I pulled into the farmhouse driveway and parked in the sunshine.

The next night, after I had tucked Shannon and Shayne in bed, nursed and settled Shawntel, the phone rang. I happened to answer. The operator asked if I would accept a collect call from Stan Havens. For a second I wavered, but then acquiesced. Stan was at a restaurant in Winona, Minnesota. Would I come get him, he pleaded. He wanted to be with me, with the kids. My heart plummeted and I thought I might throw up. I wanted to tell him to follow Katherine, to make a new life for himself in California, but I couldn't. He was a father and a husband, and he wanted his family back. Guilt made me say that I'd be there soon. Once again, I allowed life to throw me back into a dank, dark cell. I cried all the way to the restaurant.

I looked out the window and watched the gray-haired woman head up the sidewalk toward our front door. Leaves littered the cement. I had asked Stan to rake them off the front lawn, but he said not unless we received a discount on the rent. I didn't think our landlady would agree. Rent already was rock bottom, which it should have been given the condition of our side of the duplex and the fact we shared a hallway and bathroom with another renter. We were lucky to have the place in Prairie du Chien, especially since we had been forced to declare bankruptcy before moving. I was relieved Stan had found the job assembling and constructing mobile homes, which allowed us to escape from the farm. My former boss at the Crawford County University Extension Office had called and asked me to come back. Preferring office to factory work, I agreed.

The doorbell rang. Shannon raced to answer it. "Hi, Mrs. Walker," she said. Since waking up, she had been asking when Mrs. Walker would arrive. Today was Mrs. Walker's first day of work. I previously had given Mrs. Walker instructions, so I kissed my babies good-bye and set off for the two-block walk to work.

It was a pretty Indian summer day. Warm air lifted the scent of decaying leaves and white clouds drifted overhead, not in a rush to get anywhere in particular. The sidewalk reminded me of living in Wauzeka. Funny how I was about as close to work as my dad had been from the cheese-box factory. I crossed the street thinking of Bonnie. Fall was her season, the time I seemed to remember her most. It was like another lifetime, but I still held her close to my heart. The office was located in the basement of the post office and across the street from the pizza parlor I used to frequent in high school. It was where my Aunt Alice took me for my very first pizza, a delicious shrimp pizza. I could still taste it.

Life actually remained calm until right before Thanksgiving. I had just given the kids a bath when the phone rang. It was Betty. I was surprised to hear from her. Usually she would be just waking up to get ready for work at this time.

"Cap went to see the doctor today," she said. "Those test results came in." She paused, and then her voice cracked. "Turns out a brain tumor is causing all them headaches."

Shock punched me mid-center and left me breathless. I could hear Betty sniffling. "Is there any treatment?" I asked.

"Not much," she said. "The tumor is in a hard-to-get-to place. The doctor wants us to see a surgeon in Madison next week."

I told her I'd call her later and hung up the phone. Shannon and Shayne had picked out books to read and had climbed into their beds. Shannon was reading to Shayne, or at least telling the story in her words. Poor Cap. He loved the kids so. When he refused to discuss the possibility that his son abused my sister and daughter, I lost some respect for him, but I still loved him. I wanted to believe he would be okay, that some brilliant doctor would be able to fix him and keep him limping around and drinking coffee for years to come, but the reality of the situation kept trampling those hopes.

Cap had surgery in mid-January. The doctors had located the tumor but weren't certain they had removed it all. Every time I mentioned Cap, Stan abruptly changed the subject or walked out of the room. I regularly checked in with Barbara, who had moved in with Cap and Betty to help. Terry had been deployed to Iceland for a year with the air force. At the beginning of February, she called me to say that Cap was returning to the hospital with severe symptoms. Things didn't look good, she said.

I told Stan we needed to go see his father. This time he agreed. On a Saturday, we dropped the kids off with my mom and drove the ninety miles to Madison. Betty, along with Stan's brothers Denny and Gary, were already in the room when we arrived. Cap looked pale and shrunken, his good eye now cloudy. He asked after Shannon and Shayne, and I relayed as many details as I could. Stan and his brothers drifted into the hallway. Soon their voices escalated.

"Goddamnit, I'll get you for that one." Stan's voice, then a herd of racing footsteps across the linoleum floor and a thud against the wall. Laughter erupted. More swear words in Gary's voice, then Stan's. I sat in my chair, horrified, certain that other patients and visitors could hear them. The sorrow in Betty's eyes had increased every time I saw her. Now they also held embarrassment. Finally Cap looked over at her.

"Tell those boys to stop swearing," he said, sounding like a father weary of trying to discipline rambunctious teenagers.

I said I would do it. I walked into the hallway in time to see the three of them racing down it. Stan turned the corner, and Gary followed, yelling "you son of a bitch."

"You guys, keep it quiet," I said when I caught up with them. "This is a hospital. People are sick."

"People are sick," said Stan, mimicking me.

Betty rounded the corner. "That's enough. Your father asked you to be quiet." Tears filled her eyes.

Denny put his hands on his hips. "Now boys, look what you've done. I told you to stop." The three of them burst out laughing.

By the time we all returned to Cap's room, they had settled down somewhat.

"It embarrasses me to see you act like this," said Cap, trying to sit up. It was too much of a strain, and he slumped back onto his pillow.

That deflated the lot. They hung their heads and shuffled around, until Denny said, "We better go. We'll see you, Dad."

"See ya," said Gary. No apology. No embrace.

I looked at Stan, and he jerked his head toward the door. I gave Betty a big hug, wishing I could ease her many pains. Then I hugged and kissed Cap and told him I loved him. "I'll see you soon," I said, smiling.

"Give those kids a big kiss from their grandpa. And a piece of gum," said Cap. His good eye had lost its twinkle.

Stan drove over one hundred miles per hour back to Prairie du Chien. I watched the snow-covered hills whip by, their outlines blending into the gray sky.

It was the last time I saw my father-in-law. Cap Franklin Havens died February 12, 1971. In the very last moments of his life, when he remembered few people, he asked for Stan and me. The decision was made not to call us. It was the middle of the night, and we were ninety miles away. Once again, I felt cheated by death for not providing that last opportunity to say good-bye and tell him he was a loving grandfather and a good man.

"Mommy, how many days before school starts?" Shannon had been asking me this question every day for the past week. I pulled a hair tie around her ponytail.

"Let's see. It's still two weeks until Labor Day," I said. "That's fourteen days. And then, the next day you start!" Shannon's blue eyes lit with contagious excitement. Since we lived only a few blocks from school, I wanted to ensure that she was comfortable walking to school and crossing the street. Many evenings after supper, we walked to the stoplight and practiced going across the street.

"I hear Mrs. Walker at the front door. Can you let her in?" Shannon scampered out of the bedroom. I finished getting ready and set off to work. Stan left before I did, so he rarely saw Mrs.

Walker. Thankfully, he was more even-keeled since his father's death.

Late that afternoon my phone rang at work. It was Mrs. Walker.

"Mary, I don't know where Shannon is. She was out back playing and I called for her, but she didn't answer, and now I can't find her anywhere." So much panic filled her voice I thought she might have a heart attack.

"Did you check with the neighbor kids?" I said, not yet alarmed.

"They aren't out there!"

"Well, she couldn't have gone far. Walk over and see if she's at the neighbors. I'll be home soon."

Shannon was a very responsible child, and it was not like her to take off. When she was on the farm, she had so many places to run and play. Maybe she had slipped into that mode. I rehearsed my lecture. She mustn't frighten Mrs. Walker like that.

Mrs. Walker called a short while later and said that Shannon had come home. I relaxed and finished work. I walked home through the sticky air, a sheen of sweat quickly covering me. Mrs. Walker looked pale and pulled me into the other room so as not to speak in front of the children. Maybe she was having a heart attack, I thought. She proceeded to tell me that Shannon had been picked up by a stranger, taken somewhere, and was dropped off again. She didn't have any more details than that, she said.

My heart beat faster. Raymond Bushey leapt from the memory box where I stashed him. With him came that acid rage I knew too well, the one that settled in my throat and turned my stomach more sour than tobacco juice.

"Shannon's safe now," I said, forcing on a mask of calm.

"That's the important thing. But I'll call the police and let them know." The words seemed to calm Mrs. Walker, and she left.

The kids were playing in the backyard. I called Shannon inside and with a steady voice asked her to explain to me what happened.

"I was practicing walking to the stoplight when this man stopped and asked me to get into his car. He said he would give me some money to buy candy."

"Where did he take you, Shannon?"

"Down by the river."

"Where by the river?" As she described the place, I realized he had taken her to French Town Road where weekend cabins bordered the Mississippi River, near the Winneshiek Tavern, a dingy old bar. My imagination went wild. This perp could have killed her and thrown her into the river, and we might never have found her. My voice quavered. "What did he do to you?"

"He made me lay down on the seat, took some lotion and rubbed my butt. When he was done, he drove me back, and he let me out by the store. He gave me a quarter and said I could buy some candy there." Shannon looked at me, her eyes big, innocent. "I found my way home, Mommy."

I wanted to cry, scream, accuse, lash out at this horrid person who had dared to touch my daughter, who had dared to mar her childhood in this way. I had been there. I knew what this was like. But this wasn't the time or place. Somehow I muscled my way past those feelings.

"Yes, you did," I said. "You did such a good job, and I'm glad you're home safe and sound." I pulled her onto my lap and wrapped my arms around her.

I sent Shannon back outside and called the police. Almost immediately, I could see two officers leave the station and walk across the street. They asked if they could question her. The officers were professional and kind. Shannon seemed confused but answered their questions. Memories and sensations of what had been done to me years before squirmed in my head. While the police tried to piece the evidence together from Shannon's statement, I berated myself for once again failing to protect my child. My child!

After the police finished their report, they informed me that Shannon was one of several girls who had reported such an incident. They asked Shannon if she thought she could identify the person. She said maybe. They said they would put a patrol car out near the Winneshiek resort area. The newspaper had not reported any previous incidents, leaving the public clueless about what was happening in the community.

When Stan came home and learned what had happened, he went ballistic. "I'll cut that bastard's head off," he yelled. His violent reaction alarmed me. I believed he was capable of killing.

We agreed to bring Shannon to the station whenever the police arrested a suspect. Stan insisted on taking her there. Late one night, they asked us to bring her to the nearby town of Lancaster, where they were sure they had the man. Stan and I stood with Shannon behind the mirrored wall looking at four men. I watched Shannon's face turn pale. She shook her head no. That was it. I couldn't take any more. This routine had to be at least as damaging as what had been done to her. On the way home, Stan and I discussed the scene and for once agreed. All of us were asking too much of a five-year-old child.

The next morning I called the police department and told them we had decided to end it, but that certainly we did want the man caught and punished. It took several weeks, but an eight-year-old girl finally identified him. The perp had been in a mental hospital in Iowa for molesting children, then released. His punishment this time? He was banned from ever stepping foot in the state of Wisconsin. End of subject.

The late July breeze had found its way through the window and was collaborating with some cheerful birds to nudge me awake. Sunday. Another day off. I just wanted to sleep but had promised myself I would go to church, then unpack boxes. Once again we had moved. Our landlady had put the duplex up for sale, forcing us to pack our bags. I found a quaint house close by and only blocks from Mrs. Walker. The day before, Stan had disappeared. He took the car in the morning and returned just in time to drive the kids and me to my late afternoon softball tournament. Helen had asked me to substitute in a softball game. I initially declined because I didn't want to drag the kids, and I didn't trust Stan to take care of them at home. She wore me down until I agreed. I insisted we all go. Stan had arrived at the last possible minute to pick us up and keep me on time.

I pulled the sheet up to my chin. Ten more minutes, I thought. That's all I want. Yuck! What was that smell? Puke? I sat up, fully awake. I looked at Stan sleeping next to me, looked at the sheets, the floor. Everything was clean. Stan stirred.

"Do you smell that?" I said.

"Smell what?" he said, still groggy.

I climbed out of bed and followed the smell down the hallway and into the kids' bedroom. The room smelled to high heaven— not just of puke, but something else. I opened the window and looked about. Shayne had kicked off all his covers, and Shannon had her usual rosy glow. I walked over to Shawntel's crib and almost wilted. She was lying on her back, her face pale, or at least the half that wasn't covered in dried puke. Her pajamas, baby blanket, and sheets were a mess. Then it hit me. The other smell was beer. Shawntel woke up and began to cry. I grabbed a clean towel and picked her up.

"What in the world is going on here?" I yelled. "It stinks like beer."

I heard Stan start laughing in the bathroom.

"Pete thought she was so cute drinking beer and stumbling and falling all over."

I stopped wiping Shawntel's face. "You watched him give her beer and thought it was funny?" I didn't know if it was the sickening thought or the sickening smell that was making me queasy.

"Yeah, it was funny, so funny," said Stan. The toilet flushed, and he appeared in the doorway. "She kept going back to him and taking the plastic cup and downing it. It reminded me of Timmy when he was little, sittin' on that stool at Miller's Bar drinking out of a shot glass."

I was fuming. I walked past Stan into the bathroom and flipped on the tub faucet. Shawntel whimpered. Stan tagged along, needling me with more details. "You should have seen her. She couldn't stand up and kept falling on the grass. Everyone was cracking up."

"What in the hell were you thinking? Is that what a father does?" I said, my anger gushing faster than the water. "Look at her! She could have suffocated. I can't believe you let Pete give her beer." I didn't think Pete even liked Stan, but when beer was involved, everyone became best friends.

Stan's face clouded, and he tossed out his favorite comeback lines. "You don't know what the hell you're talking about. You think you're so innocent and never do anything wrong."

"If you don't think it was wrong, then here, you get down on your knees, right here and give your daughter a bath," I said, pointing to the floor.

Stan glared at me, then slumped away. He had never once given the kids a bath. All I could think was, "What an asinine move."

"There you go," I said to Shawntel, lifting her out of the tub. "All fresh and clean." I gently toweled her hair dry. She took off for the bedroom. She had walked at nine months and now seemed to be on track to be as athletic as her father and brother. I heard her struggle with a dresser drawer. I quickly cleaned up and followed her. The room still stunk. At least Stan could have stripped the crib sheets. He probably didn't know how.

Through the GI Bill, Stan applied for and was accepted at a community college, where he would earn an associate's degree in business administration accounting. He wouldn't start until January. He wanted to live closer to the town of Fennimore, where the school was located. I didn't want to move from Prairie du Chien, but he was making an effort and we only had one car, so I agreed to remain on the trail of Stan's dreams. We moved into my parents' house in Wauzeka. My mother was remodeling it into two three-bedroom apartments, one upstairs, the other downstairs. She agreed to let us rent from her.

On an unusually cool day in late August, I carried a box up the steps to the front door. For a moment, I could see twelve-year-old David perched there, watching the tomatoes ripen on the vine, determined to take the first bite of the fruit. I stepped inside. Goodness. I had come full circle, back to where Stan and I began our relationship, back to where we first made love. My heart didn't exactly sing.

In September, Shayne died. But only for a minute. Stan and I had gone on vacation before school started to visit my sister

Kathy in Columbus, Ohio, and left the kids with my parents. When I called to check in, my mother told me that one of Shayne's testicles had swollen. As soon as we returned, I took him to the doctor, who diagnosed a hydrocele and hernia, common with little boys. Surgery was scheduled for mid-September.

The day of the surgery, I dropped Stan off at work, then drove Shayne to the hospital. I knew the surgery was common, but I couldn't help but feel a knot or two or ten in my stomach. I picked up a magazine from the waiting-room table. The operation was estimated to be an hour long. Another woman came in and we chatted a bit, then she left and I sat alone. All of a sudden, commotion erupted. Nurses scurried in the direction of the operating room. I silently prayed this didn't have anything to do with Shayne, even though I didn't think any other patient was in there. Finally the doctor came out, his mask hanging below his chin.

In a trembling voice, he said, "We lost him on the table, but he's fine now. He was given nitrous oxide, and he may have had a reaction to it. I'd like to keep him for a few extra days to make sure." I felt faint and sat down.

"Do you want to call someone, maybe your husband?" he said, sounding calmer.

I shook my head no. "When can I see my son?"

"He's on his way to his room, so it should be soon."

A few days of undivided attention from the nurses taught Shayne how to play for sympathy. When he complained that he couldn't walk, I questioned the doctor, concerned. He assured me Shayne was just fine. Saturday afternoon, Stan and I sat with our son in the solarium. Shayne was whining to be picked up. Stan took out his cigarette lighter and tossed it across the room. "Go get it, Shayne," he said. Shayne ran halfway across the room before he realized he had just been busted. He turned, looked at us sheepishly, and rolled his eyes. Once we got home, Stan refused to follow doctor's orders and played tackle football with Shayne. I was in terror of Shayne's stitches tearing. As I screamed for Stan to stop, he screamed back at me as if reprimanding me, saying that Shayne was tough and he wasn't being hurt. When we returned to have the stitches removed, they had indeed torn, leaving Shayne with a larger, deeper scar.

The beginning of December brought snow, the start of the Christmas season, and my mother on our doorstep with her hand out for rent. Every month, she made sure to get her piece of the pie before the pie was gone. I worked hard to find gifts for the kids before Stan spent the money. We spent Christmas Eve at the farm, then left the next day for Milton to be with Stan's family. I felt Cap's absence all day and blinked away tears more than once.

When the calendar flipped into the New Year, Stan started school. His first semester went rather well. His grades were great, and he seemed much happier. In fact, we all seemed happier. Happiness, however, is like a bird at the feeder. It pecks and feasts, then flies off to parts unknown.

It was Saturday, and I needed a dose of the fresh spring air. A light green blanketed the Ocooch Mountains. A few days before, I had spotted my first robin. I called Mom, who said sure, bring the kids over, she'd take them horseback riding. It gave her an excuse to be outside with the horses, and it gave me a few minutes to myself.

As I drove up the driveway, I could see Starlight and Sam already saddled, standing near the granary. Shannon and Shayne jumped out of the car and raced toward the horses. I yelled for them to go to the house first and see what Grandma had in mind, then unbuckled and lifted Shawntel from her car seat, took a deep breath of lilacs and fertile earth, and headed to the house. Sharon was already giving Shannon and Shayne instructions for her horseback-riding plans.

My mother walked into the kitchen. "Sharon, take the kids outside. I'll be out in a few minutes."

"Okay, Mom," said Sharon, "but remember, they have to ride with me. They don't get to ride by themselves." Mom suppressed a smile. They all ran out the door. I held Shawntel on my hip as she fought to get down.

Mom went into the living room and I followed. She rearranged items on the oak table near the stairs, all the time muttering about gathering clothes for the church's mission trip down to Mississippi. At least that's what it sounded like. She stopped moving and clearly said, "Have you heard about Isabel Conrad, Charlotte's friend?"

For the past year, Isabel had been hanging around the farm. Other than the few times I had seen her with Charlotte, I knew little about her. She was an attractive, strawberry blond-haired teenager with hazel eyes, plump lips, and a loud, high-pitched voice that drew attention. She had moved to Steuben during middle school from somewhere down south like Mississippi or Georgia. She lived with her mother and a handful of siblings. Rumors had it that her father was in prison. Now a sophomore in high school, fifteen, she had earned a reputation of being a wild child—promiscuous, ready to drink and party, and who knew what else.

"The only thing I've heard is that Isabel's pregnant and Roger Williams is the father," I said.

"Well, he's going to marry her. I've already talked to Doreen, and she agrees," said Mom. Doreen was Isabel's mom. I wondered why my mother sounded so upset and why she would be interfering in Isabel's life.

"Doesn't Roger want to marry her?" I said.

Mom looked at me oddly. "Roger?"

"Roger Williams. Who else would Isabel be marrying?"

"Walt, of course!"

"What do you mean, Walt?" I said, now the confused one.

"He had sex with her, and he's going to marry her!"

"You mean our Walt?" I said.

"Yes."

Well, this was news to me, maybe even news to Crawford County. "Are you sure he's the father? Has there been a paternity test?"

"It doesn't matter," Mom said. "He said he had sex with her. The baby's due in September."

"But don't you want to make sure it's Walt's baby?"

Mom paced back and forth, distracted. I reminded her what the doctor had said about Walt. When he was six, Walt contracted the mumps. Three years later, after gorging on popcorn balls that Kathy made to celebrate the Packers being in the playoffs, he suffered severe abdominal pain. Kathy thought the popcorn balls permanently damaged him. Mom brought him to the doctor, who attributed the pain possibly being related to the mumps. The prognosis was that Walt would not be able to have children.

Mom humphed. "I guess it's a miracle then," she said.

"You know, Mom, he could go to jail for statutory rape. He's twenty-one and Isabel's only fifteen."

"Don't I know. I considered sending them to Missouri, where Rick and Phyllis got married, but Doreen and I don't want that." Rick and Phyllis were second cousins and couldn't be married in Wisconsin. They had gotten pregnant while dating. Mom punched a couch pillow into shape. "They'll have to wait until the baby is born in September, then get married after she turns sixteen in September."

And that was that. She went outside, and the kids went horseback riding.

Charlotte gave me the scoop on Isabel. Before too long, Isabel couldn't disguise the obvious changes in her slender body. School administrators called her into the office. After she admitted she was pregnant, they expelled her, even though she begged to finish the school year. Isabel's sixteen-year-old sister, Autumn, was also pregnant and due in November, which further complicated Doreen's life.

A healthy baby boy arrived in September; about a month later, Walt and Isabel were married. Charlotte was maid of honor. Walt had been trapped into a marriage, just as Mom's parents had been, and like Mom, Isabel's son was a love child. Mom had few smiles to offer during the wedding and reception.

Isabel's sister Autumn delivered a beautiful baby girl in November, but tragedy struck during the childbirth. Autumn died. It was a devastating blow to everyone, especially Isabel. Although I knew there were new tensions at the farmhouse, I didn't get involved because as usual, I had my own challenges at the house in town.

I worried about Shawntel. She began acting out close to her second birthday in April. One night at supper, she deliberately spilled her milk. I sent her to her room and let her return to the table only after the rest of us finished eating. She gobbled her entire dinner. The next night the same thing happened. She spilled her milk, got sent to her room, and ate alone. Almost every night she deliberately spilled her milk, knowing she wouldn't be able to eat with us. Her behavior puzzled me, but I continued to send her a threatening glance as she climbed down from her chair and went to her room until we were finished. For some reason, she seemed to want to eat by herself. Then, just as unexpectedly as she started, she stopped. I chalked it up to one of those things kids sometimes do for reasons their parents never understand.

About the same time, I sensed Stan's growing dislike of Shawntel. When she didn't eat dinner, he would scream at her and call her names. More than once, he yelled at her for something and grabbed her arm and wouldn't let go. His behavior infuriated me. When I tried to rescue her, he pinned me down on the ground. One time, while sitting on top of me, he said, "See how easy it would be to rape a woman?"

I loved my children more than anything in the world, and I hated, absolutely hated, seeing their father torment them, not to mention torment me. He refused to take responsibility for his family. I was the banker, the baker, the candlestick maker. If I didn't do it, it didn't get done. Mentally, I was wearing thin. My kids and I needed to get away from Stan. To do that, I'd need to be financially independent, which meant I needed a new job.

I applied at 3M. My mother was now working there, but I refused to use her connections. In fact, I didn't even tell her I submitted an application. Every week I'd call or stop in the office and let them know I was still interested. Nine months later, in March, they honored my persistence and hired me as a manufacturing lab tech in quality assurance. I stashed away money from every check. I calculated that within the year, I would be able to divorce Stan and live with the kids on my own.

What I neglected to factor into the equation was Stan's

behavior. I saved. He spent. I came home at night. He stayed away, sometimes weeks at a time. Instead of moving forward, I spun in circles, around and around, like I used to on the merry-go-round in the schoolyard. Only this wasn't a happy joyride. This was more like the time when I was seven. I stood on the outer wooden bench, straddling the metal bar, my small hands wrapped around it. A group of high school boys hanging around pushed me, faster and faster, blurring the world, increasing the centrifugal force, trying to tear me from my grasp of reality. I couldn't duck my head. Couldn't stop the spinning. Couldn't sit. Couldn't move. All I could do was hang on for dear life and hope I survived.

I had been working at 3M for two years when we moved back to Prairie du Chien. We rented an attractive two-story framed house in town with a grassy backyard and separate garage. Grapevines wound around a fence near the back of the garage. An older woman named Anna lived in the house next door. Our basement was a perfect play area for the kids. It had small egress windows near the ceiling, a painted cement floor, and two staircases, one leading up to a door that opened to the outside near the garage and the other leading into the inside back hall. I stored all the kids' toys down there, along with an old mattress they loved to tumble on, and Stan set up a ping-pong table. My drive to work was all of ten minutes. The only downside: the railroad tracks, only yards away. With forty trains passing by each day, we quickly grew deaf to their clacking. I probably would have been very happy had it not been for Stan's erratic, harassing behavior. Most days, I was exhausted and would fall asleep on the couch in front of the TV that Stan insisted I watch with him until ten o'clock bedtime.

On a Sunday in June, I took Shannon and Shayne to church. Shawntel, now age five, wanted to stay at home, and I didn't have the energy to argue with her. When we returned from the service, she was sitting on the living room floor in her *I Dream of Jeannie* pajamas, her "yellow Jeannie jammies," as she called them, holding one of her dolls. She looked so cute with her short blond hair. Stan hated that I had cut her hair and used it as a tormenting device, calling her a boy.

"Shawntel, why don't you get dressed? We'll be leaving for the picnic soon."

Shayne ran to the pantry and grabbed a box of Rice Krispies, while Shannon got milk and bananas. An empty cereal bowl sat on the kitchen table, evidence that Shawntel had eaten. The kids were excited about going to my work picnic at Wyalusing State Park. Stan wanted no part of it. He had softball games that day and already had been giving me a hard time about taking the kids with me to the picnic rather than to the ball field.

"Shawntel, please, go change your clothes."

Again, she ignored me.

Just then, Stan came into the room dressed in his uniform. Shawntel hugged her doll close to her chest. Stan went over to her and pulled at the doll. She clung tightly.

"You heard your mother; go get dressed," he said.

She stuck out her jaw and flung the doll. Good grief, I thought. It's starting already. I went upstairs to change my clothes, thinking their sparring would end quickly, as it usually did. The ensuing commotion, however, sent me scrambling back down. Stan had pushed Shawntel to the floor and was sitting over her, holding her hands above her head with one hand and poking at her ribs with another. She was trying to kick her legs and screaming at him to stop. With each jab, he mimicked her voice. "The little baby wants to play with her dolls. Waa. Waa."

He just never stopped with her. It seemed like every day he tortured her in one way or another. My yelling at him never seemed to halt his horrible antics, and I would end up consoling Shawntel after each episode. But today I was out of patience. I lost it.

"Stop it, you stupid idiot! For God's sakes, leave her alone."

Stan jerked around. The look in his eyes scared me, but it didn't stop me.

"Get off her now," I shrieked.

"Shut the hell up. The neighbors are going to hear you."

I couldn't have cared less. Stan slowly got off Shawntel. "She's such a baby," he said, glaring first at me, then at Shawntel.

"Go play ball and leave us alone," I said.

Stan grabbed his ball bag, stalked out the back door, and squealed out the driveway.

Once he stepped out the door, I sat in the rocking chair and held my arms out to Shawntel, who by now was standing with her arms crossed over her chest, determined not to cry. I coaxed her onto my lap, wrapped my arms around her, held her close, and stroked her hair. Tears streamed down her face. She wailed as if releasing every morsel of hurt from her heart.

"It's going to be okay, honey," I whispered. "I'm not going to let him do this anymore." She wept and wept, and I joined her.

I took the kids to the picnic, acted like I was having a great time, all the while plotting how I would give Stan the news that we were getting divorced.

When he came home late that night, I sat up and simply said, "You need to move out. I'm filing for divorce." This time, I wasn't giving in—not to the dictates of the Catholic Church or my mother's pursed lips. My children were my everything. I needed to protect them and keep myself sane, and the only way to do that was to be a single mother.

Stan moved out in July. I contacted an attorney and initi-
ated divorce proceedings. He tried to cajole his way back, but
I remained resolute. He showed up at my work parking lot and
begged me to let him come home. He came over to the house at
different times, saying he missed the kids and wanted to come
home. Sometimes he whined, sometimes he yelled. His hounding
drove me loony, but his absence gave me sanity.

After I kicked Stan out, Mike Doll introduced him to the
Bible Baptist Church. Stan joined and religiously attended
services. He now tossed in biblical quotes when he harassed the
kids and me. Shawntel and Shayne auditioned for a Pepsi commercial. Shawntel won over the producers when she winked one
eye after another. Stan berated me for using her to make money.
I put the money she earned in a savings account to be used for
school. I kept telling myself that by this time next year, we'd be
divorced and life would be normal.

It was a Saturday morning in August. I was putting away
the vacuum when I heard the front door open. Stan walked in
wearing a T-shirt, shorts, and tennies. The first thing I noticed
was how thin his legs looked. Then I noticed the machete in his
hand.

"Mary, I want to move back home," he said. His eyes had a
strange gleam. The tip of the machete touched the floor.

"What the heck are you doing, Stan?"

"This is my house, and I should live here!" said Stan, raising
his arm, the machete slicing the air.

A herd of footsteps ran across the upstairs floor, and Shayne
headed down the staircase, Shannon and Shawntel in tow. My
heart jumped.

"Stay right there," I said to Shayne, pointing to the stairs. The sharpness in my voice stopped him. He plunked down on a step. The girls did the same, huddling close to him.

Stan and I began to argue. I moved between him and the kids. The machete went up, it went down, a gauge of his anger. I tried to speak calmly, reasonably, a tactic that had never worked before but I prayed would work this time. Every muscle fiber in me tensed.

"Who do you want to live with, Shannon?" said Stan, pointing the machete at her.

"Mom," said Shannon right away.

"How about you, Shayne?"

Shayne looked thoughtful for a moment. "I have to think about it," he said.

It was such a great response, so genuine and sincere. I stifled fearful laughter.

Stan pointed the machete at Shawntel. "And you?"

"Mom," she said, defiant.

Stan looked at me. "See what you've done? You've poisoned them against me." The machete went up, inciting a new round of rants.

My senses were on high alert. "Shayne," I said, talking under Stan, "go over to Anna's and tell her to call the police." Shayne scooted past me toward the kitchen. I heard the door shut.

"Stan, we haven't had a relationship in years, and you know it," I said. He tilted his head and looked at me, the circles under his eyes seemingly darker than when he arrived.

"We can try again. Hell, I can be a good father, a good husband. You aren't giving me a chance."

We bickered back and forth. Finally, I heard the back door open. Behind me, Shayne said, "Anna said parents fight. It'll be okay."

This can't be happening, I thought. "Go back and tell her to please call the police." I remained between Stan and the girls. They were hunched over, pressed against each other. I kept talking to Stan, trying to get him to calm down without giving into his demands. The minutes ticked by. At last a squad car pulled up in front of the house, and two police officers approached the house.

"Whatcha doin', Stan?" said one of the officers. They knew him. They calmed Stan down, escorted him out of the house, stored the machete in his trunk, and told him to leave. I was appalled they let him go. They asked me if I wanted to press charges. I said no. I didn't feel safe pressing charges. Then again, I didn't feel safe not pressing charges. The man with the SERE training, who manipulated his daughters and almost everyone in his life, that man frightened me.

In September, the part-time babysitter I had hired when we moved to Prairie quit to attend school. My sister Charlotte took a new job nearby and agreed to move in with us. I started work at six in the morning, but she didn't start until nine, so she could get the kids off to school. I would then return home before school ended.

All was going smoothly until the day I went antique shopping with my girlfriend, Pix. I had the day off, so Pix and I drove to La Crosse to browse antique and consignment shops. Something kept bugging me to turn around and go home. I told Pix that I was sorry, but we needed to get back to Prairie du Chien. When I walked in the house, I found a terse note in unfamiliar handwriting that said, "Come to the farm right away." I called Mom.

"Stan's in jail," she said. "He pulled a knife on Charlotte. She talked her way out, and he left before doing anything. She and the kids are here."

What the hell?

Once at the farm, I heard the entire story. Stan had come to the house before Charlotte left for work. This time he had a butcher knife. He held it to Charlotte's throat as he pushed her toward the upstairs steps, saying crazy things about raping and killing her. Charlotte kept her cool and kept talking to Stan. Whatever she said made Stan rethink his plan. He left. Charlotte immediately called a friend who worked as a speech pathologist a few blocks away at the grade school. The friend came over, called the police, and brought Charlotte and the kids to the farm.

Mom ended up bailing Stan out of jail. I couldn't believe it when she told me. I could understand rescuing the underprivileged, the starving, the sick, the homeless. But rescuing a man who threatened to kill her daughter, a man who was a schmuck of a son-in-law, was beyond my understanding. Mom insisted Stan live with her for a while until she could help him relocate to an apartment in Prairie.

After Mom died, Charlotte's husband, Ron, convinced Charlotte to tell me the part she had never revealed. During Stan's short stay at the farm, Mom insisted that Charlotte meet Stan at the Baptist church in Prairie so Charlotte could offer *her* forgiveness in person. Mom, Stan, the minister, and Charlotte sat in the church office. Accepting someone's request for forgiveness was part of Stan's indoctrination into Christianity. Basically, Mom used Charlotte to help poor Stan become a good Christian—the man who threatened women with a machete and a butcher knife. My mother just couldn't see when her children needed her help more than anyone else needed it.

"Come on, Mary," said one of my coworkers as we walked to the parking lot. "Just come out for one drink. It's Friday night."

She nudged my arm. My social life had been almost nonexistent. Stan hadn't succeeded in running Charlotte off. She still lived with the kids and me and was dating Ron. Tonight, they were at a fish fry. I didn't trust Stan to stay with the kids, though he saw them regularly. A night out sounded like fun.

"If I find a babysitter, I'll be there," I said.

Fortunately, I found one. When she arrived, I told her I wouldn't be long. I took it easy at the bar, drank a few glasses of tap beer, played foosball, put on my happy face, and mingled. It felt good to be out again, but at the same time, a chill ran down my spine. Something felt amiss. I soon left and went home. The babysitter was surprised to see me back so soon. She had the kids upstairs in bed sleeping. She lived close and offered to walk home, but I felt better driving her. I locked the door behind me.

I returned within five minutes. As I got out of the car, I had the sensation that someone was watching me. I scanned the streets and railroad tracks. No one in sight. I tried brushing off the creepy feeling. I unlocked the back door and stepped inside. The closed basement door was a step in front me. A surge of adrenaline made my heart pound. Although the outside basement door was kept locked, I knew Stan had been there earlier in the day with the kids. Would he have unlocked that door? Terror gripped me. Surging adrenaline sent me sprinting down the steps, across the cement, and up the other stairs two at a time, scared that Stan would burst through the door at any second. The door was unlocked. I flipped the deadbolt, my heart pounding. Relief flooded through me. We were safe.

I was halfway down the staircase when Stan stepped in front of it. I almost stopped breathing. I'm going to die, I thought. He's going to kill the kids and me. Or just me and leave my body for the kids to find. I almost screamed, but who would hear me?

"What in the hell are you doing in here?" I said through

clenched teeth. "When did you unlock that door?" I needed to maintain calm.

He smirked. "You should pay more attention to your kids. I had Shayne unlock it this afternoon."

I considered running back up the stairs and out the door, but I knew he'd catch me.

"I don't want a divorce," he said, his shoulders slumping. "I just want to move back home." He sounded pathetic.

I took a chance. "A person who loves someone," I said, starting down the stairs, "doesn't do the things you do to me. You've had more chances then you deserve." I reached the last step and turned my body as if to go around him.

He grabbed my wrist. "If I can't have you, then nobody's going to have you!"

"Leave me alone! You're insane!" I tried to twist my arm loose, but I was no match against his strength.

He pushed me toward the old mattress and shoved me onto it. He flipped me on my back, climbed on top of me just as he had done to Shawntel so many times, and with a sick-ass grin practically ripped off my clothes.

"You're my wife, and there's no law against me having sex with you. If you call the police, they won't do a thing. It's my word against yours." Madness filled his eyes.

I gave up and lay there, thoughts of being killed and the kids finding me dead floating through my head. It was unimaginable.

When he finished, he stood up, zipped his pants, and said, "Guess I'll leave now." He walked up the steps to the outside door. When he got to the top, he turned. "You oughta make sure to lock this door so no one gets in and hurts you." Then he left.

Shaking, I ran up the stairs and locked the door. Back at the bottom, I collapsed, sobbing, my face buried in my hands so the kids wouldn't hear me. I never told a soul what he did.

Before month's end, I served Stan with divorce papers. I needed to be physically away from him so I applied for a research position with 3M in St. Paul and was hired. On Halloween, the kids and I moved to Minnesota. Stan had moved to Milton, found a job he hated, and visited us on weekends. I had no legal recourse to prevent him from doing so. He was playing Mr. Nice Guy. He was fun. He was attentive. He was responsible. The kids fell for it. They wanted him back. They were still young: ages ten, eight and six. Four against one.

On March 22, 1977, the day before the divorce was final, under pressure from Stan and the kids, I vacated it. Reluctantly, I agreed that Stan could move into my apartment. At the time, I told myself that I'd always loved my dad and wanted my children to have a father like him. Now, my kids were clamoring for their father. How could I deny them their father? I didn't want to live with the guilt of taking that experience away from them. Plus, I wanted to believe the seeds of goodness were somewhere inside Stan. Maybe his recent behavior was because those seeds had finally bloomed. He was paying child support, which he had never done. Maybe he was growing up and was ready to be a loving father. I fell for my own convoluted arguments, opened the door, and let him return. I didn't know what would happen if I didn't. I was afraid of him, didn't trust him. At the time, however, I wasn't able to admit this. I couldn't yet disengage from deep, complex patterns that governed my life.

PART FIVE

Dr. Orr shifted his gaze from me to Stan. "I really think surgery is the best option at this point," he said. Stan squirmed in his chair and turned to me, his eyebrows raised. After many years of excruciating symptoms, I had been diagnosed with endometriosis. I didn't particularly want the hysterectomy Dr. Orr was recommending, but we had exhausted available drug therapies, and I was weary of living with pain and massive blood clots. The doctor had spent the last twenty minutes explaining what the surgery entailed. Stan was getting a long-overdue sex education class.

"Okay," I said. "Let's schedule it."

As Stan and I hurried through the frigid air back to the car, I tried to recall my benefits at work. I was pretty sure I would get six weeks off at full pay.

"Do you think that guy gets off sticking that Donald Duck thing up women's twats?" said Stan. I looked at him in disbelief. "And what about sex?" he added. "How long do we have to wait to have sex?" The questions continued. I got in the car, blasted the heat, and tried to ignore him and his immaturity.

In four days, the calendar would flip to 1980. Stan and I had managed to remain married. He'd been working for over a year at Leasco, a trucking company, and spent more time driving cross-country than he spent in Lakeland, Minnesota where, three years ago, we had purchased a house. The kids liked the area and had many friends, though Shawntel, now in fifth grade, challenged her teachers. I had more than a few parent-teacher conferences about her defiant attitude and sharp tongue. Shayne, athletic and hyperactive, was the distractor and seventh grade class clown, and Shannon, a ninth-grader, remained the good student and child. Stan's violent behavior had stopped, maybe because he had settled in unfamiliar territory where he didn't know many people. The affairs with other women seemed to have stopped too, although he still had a knack for playing hurtful mind games with me. At least he was grateful for our house. Cap and Betty had never owned a home, and he was aware that we owned one because of my income and hard work. Gone was his whining that we would never be homeowners.

Surprisingly, Stan agreed to accompany me to surgery. The day after, however, he would need to hit the road. Mom insisted another adult be with me after surgery, so she arranged for my dad to stay with me for a week. Work confirmed that I would get six weeks off with pay.

The surgery proved to be no big deal. I was out of the hospital in a few days, had my energy back in a week, and thought wow, I could go back to work. Yeah, right. I knew when to stay put. My time with Dad proved to be the highlight of my recuperation. One day, after lunch, we were lingering at the table talking, and he began reminiscing about Grandpa Krachey. Dad told a story that he heard from his close friend August Borth. Apparently, Grandpa went to August's older brother and asked him if he would buy Grandma and their three kids. At first I thought Dad was kidding, but then when I saw the look in his eyes, as if he had said something he regretted, I knew he was telling the truth. The incident had occurred during the Depression.

"You must never tell your ma," Dad said. "She doesn't know. She still thinks the world of her dad. She was the oldest and felt responsible for him. And she's still angry that she didn't get willed more than the other kids."

Over the years, one of Mom's favorite lines to mutter was, "The one who works the hardest should get the most." Even though she resented her dad for dividing his estate equally among his children, she stuck by him. Just as I stuck by Stan. When people asked me why I stayed married to him, I never had a good answer. I wasn't sure if he was like a burr that I couldn't pull off of me or if I was the burr that no one, including myself, could pull off of him.

The results Dr. Orr and I had hoped for didn't happen. For another three years, I suffered symptoms. Severe monthly pains. Other daily discomforts. In addition, Stan's inconsistent behavior seemed to keep turmoil a constant source of contention, especially with Shawntel, who was thirteen and had taken to dressing provocatively. Stan frequently told her she looked slutty. He didn't like that boys looked at her and she looked at them. He was gone over-the-road most of the time, but insisted when he was home that I drop everything and pay attention only to him. But the kids also needed me, though my erratic emotions frustrated and probably perplexed them. I felt like a single parent caught between the devil, the deep blue sea, and my raging body. Dr. Orr couldn't do anything to solve the emotional angst and trials at home, but he thought he could mitigate the physical pains. This time he recommended removing endometriosis tissue that might be growing on vital organs and also to remove an ovary. He called the surgery an oophorectomy.

"I'll do my best to save one of your ovaries," he said to me during our consultation.

"Just take them both out," I said. "I really don't want to have another surgery."

Dr. Orr shook his head. "You don't know what you're saying, Mary. If we can save any part of an ovary, we need to do that. It's a very important part of your body, one that plays a vital role during menopause."

I was thirty-six years old. Menopause seemed far away.

I scheduled the surgery for a Monday. Stan talked to his boss and arranged to be in town. Stan's mom, Betty, was living with us and was a more-than-willing caregiver. The hysterectomy had been a piece of cake. I assumed this surgery would be too.

The day before surgery, Stan called. "Plans have changed," he said. "I'm stuck in Kentucky. My time limit for over-the-road driving is running out, so I don't think I'm going to make it back by tomorrow." For once, he sounded truly apologetic.

"Shannon can take me," I assured him. She was sixteen and had her driver's license. "And your mother can come too. I'll be fine, don't worry about it." Everything would be fine. Of course it would.

I heard the noises first, voices crisscrossing, mechanical beeps, and soft swishes. Gradually it dawned on me that I was in the recovery room. I inhaled deeply, breathed out, and repeated, as I had been instructed to do before surgery. My body felt leaden. Part of me knew I needed to wake up, but another part of me argued for the right to drift off into quiet and comforting oblivion. I dozed in and out of the internal discussion, vaguely aware of nurses talking to me about pain, drugs, and a hospital room.

When Shannon and Betty walked into my room, my eyes searched behind them. No Stan. The lingering hope that he somehow would have made it fell flat on its face in a puddle of disappointment.

"How ya feeling, Mary?" said Betty.

I held up my thumb. "Okay," I whispered. That's when I realized I wasn't in physical pain. A few more beats of my heart, however, and I felt something else, something welling in my head, something threatening to overwhelm me. A sea of anger washed over me, followed by a volcanic hot flash. I fought for control. Then the pain erupted. My stomach burned. It was pure agony. It felt as if every emotion and thought I had swallowed or buried deep inside me over the years was exploding outward. I couldn't concentrate on Betty or Shannon and had to shut my eyes. My thought processes became chopped and intermittent. I'd start a thought, search for the ending, and conclude with confusion and misery. Anger filled every pore, vein, nerve, muscle, and cell. Here I was, in a sterile hospital room with stupid thin blankets and creaking pillows. Everyone going about their daily routines. Doctors diagnosing disease, prescribing treatments. Nurses pricking patients with needles. Patients healing or dying. And all of them had someone behind them, holding them up with a supporting hand. But it wasn't like that for me. I was lost in a fog, with no sense of direction, and mad as hell. It was as if something had been ripped out of me, taken away from me, and it was never going to return.

Life settled on a landslide. As it turned out, Dr. Orr had not been able to save an ovary and had to remove both. I returned to work part time in an effort to give my body and mind more time to heal. My new persona scared my male bosses. I was compliant and nice one minute, ornery and mean the next. I had fifteen-minute hot flashes every fifteen minutes. All I could think about was sleep. I knew I needed sleep, *wanted* sleep, but mostly I felt as if I were hovering above the mattress never touching the sheets. Deep, comforting sleep never came. I began to crave alcohol, salty food, and red meat. By nine o'clock in the morning I was planning where I could have lunch to satiate myself. My sense of smell was heightened, as it had been when I was pregnant. Every time I visited the farm for a holiday or long weekend, I just about threw up at the ever-present smell of hay.

Stan stayed on the road as much as possible. The kids avoided me; they didn't come home on time, didn't do their chores, and sassed me. I had always been the pillar of strength; now they were watching me crumble. They called family for help, but I refused to talk to anybody. Suicide was a constant thought. I knew what was right in my mind, but I couldn't control my emotions. I didn't know me anymore. It was as if I had developed a split personality. One was the analytical woman I left in the operating room, and the other was the tormented maniac who haunted others. If I did not get some help, I might kill myself or someone else.

Out of pure desperation and a final last-ditch effort, I sought help from human resources and employee assistance. Louise from human resources took care of reigning in the discriminating and bullying male department manager, who had informed me that I had to work full time or not at all. I continued to work part time. Marie from employee assistance funneled me names of counselors, social workers, and organizations. To that point in my life, I had only consulted priests for help and a few social workers. I'd talk about sexual abuse, and they'd look at me blankly and end the conversation with, "You seem like a strong woman. You'll be okay." The priest I had put my highest hopes in, the one Stan even agreed to see, brought out a bottle of bourbon to our meeting and kept filling our glasses. We got drunk but didn't solve any problems.

It took six months to find Bob McCormick. When I first met Bob, he reminded me of Bozo the Clown, with wild bunches of hair on each side of his head. Better Bozo than Mr. Green Jeans. I grew to know him as a kind and gentle soul. I talked Stan into seeing him with me, and eventually the kids, though they put up a fight about going. It took losing my ovaries to finally get help.

It was our last family therapy session with Bob. After eighteen months of counseling, our conversations had become circular, with no one offering new insights into the problems we continued to face. "At this point, we've done about as much as we can. Some things have changed, but there's some resistance in the whole family to work harder. It seems that Mary wants to stay, but the rest of you just want to be done."

I glanced at Shannon. She slumped, looked at the floor, and nervously twisted her hands in her lap. I watched her give her dad a sideways glance. God! Why can't you see it, Bob? I silently screamed. Why had I spent all this time in therapy to end up still not knowing the truth?

As Bob droned on, recapping some of the communication skills we had recently discussed, I kept hearing the roar of other words: We're not done! There's more! Shawntel was fourteen and had just run away. She wore provocative clothes and was in relationships with boys, probably sexual relationships. Some of her boyfriends were black, which did not resonate well with Stan. Stan hated his job, again and was acting like Mr. Big Shot, again. He continued to challenge the rules and routines I set up with the kids and treated them as if they interfered in his life. "Write your question down, and I'll read it tomorrow," he always said. But tomorrow never came.

The biggest issue for me was my increasing suspicions that

Stan was molesting the girls. The media was starting to expose sexual abuse and domestic violence. *Psychology Today* printed an article about those and related topics almost every issue. The articles listed some of the red flags to watch for including sudden behavior changes, withdrawal, acting out, and drawing attention in a negative manner. I recalled how Shawntel, then ten, asked me as I was walking out of my bedroom, "Were you and Dad mating?" The unusual question disturbed me. But when I asked her why she wanted to know, she shrugged and walked away. During family therapy with Bob, an incident in the sleepy town of Jordan, Minnesota, population twenty-nine hundred, caused quite the commotion. A sexual-abuse scandal broke involving almost two-dozen adults, including village leaders, who were accused of sexually abusing their children, as well as others. The press covered the story for months. If Shannon were in the room when a news story came on TV, she'd leave. Shawntel remained glued to the set. Shortly after, Shawntel, of her own volition, called social services and reported the abuse of a friend. She had witnessed her girlfriend being beaten by her dad with a belt. The parents didn't want their daughter to be friends with Shawntel anymore.

Bob continued to ramble. I looked at Shannon, nineteen now, and doing well in community college. She always had done well in school and had many friends. Self-doubt swooshed in, towing its first cousin, guilt. Maybe I was as crazy as Stan proclaimed. Maybe Stan had never done anything wrong. Maybe the kids' acting out was rebellious teenage stuff exacerbated by a father who was still a teenager himself. No, no, no, my internal voice screamed. And yet, here we were. Almost one and a half years of intensive therapy, and the teams remained the same. Mary vs. Family. Stan's face showed smug satisfaction. Was he thinking that he got away with some inexcusable, maybe even heinous behavior?

"Mary?" Bob's voice interloped on my thoughts. "Mary, would you like to schedule one final appointment for you and Shannon?" He peered over his glasses at me.

Bob knew how much it bothered me that we never discussed Shannon's abduction when she was five. I felt there was more to Shannon's story because of my own sexual molestation at the same age. I feared her experience lay dormant, just as mine had, with no one to validate that it had happened and that it was not my fault. I looked over at Shannon, who rolled her eyes toward the ceiling.

"Shannon, would you be willing to come one last time?" I said.

She shrugged. "I suppose, if I have to. I know if I don't, you'll never stop nagging me."

"Okay, let's schedule for next week, November thirtieth," Bob said. "I suspect we won't need to meet after that."

The next Friday, I met Shannon in the 3M parking lot, and we drove the fifteen minutes to Bob's office. The session seemed particularly hard. Initially, Shannon resisted giving details, but then she relented. Her memory seemed clear. I found it disturbing, however, that she didn't feel the event affected her life in any way. Were we two different people responding to a similar event differently? Or was there something else overshadowing that incident?

"Has anyone else ever touched you inappropriately?" I asked. She was frustrating the daylights out of me.

"No," she said. "I don't remember anyone else ever having done anything to me." That same sheepish look that didn't match her answers.

Then, for the first time, I shared my experiences with her. She looked at me empathetically but didn't change her tune.

The hour ended. Shannon and I left Bob's office, none the wiser about what really happened. We walked to the car through snow flurries twisting and turning through the air, clouding vision. As I merged onto the freeway, I felt a sudden urge to drive like a maniac, to race between cars, past them, to race past the roadblocks that continually slowed me. My head ached. My heartbeat pounded in my ears. I turned on the windshield wipers. I know he did it! I know he did it! I pressed my foot harder against the accelerator but then remembered my daughter next to me. She didn't need me scaring her like Stan used to scare me. She needed my protection. She needed me to help her reveal the truth. Shannon flipped on the radio and sulked against the window. Then it hit me. I had one other person I could go to for help. My sister Sharon. She was now a grown woman and married. Maybe it was time to ask her about what really happened fifteen years ago. I dropped Shannon off at her car, found a parking spot, and went into work. The rest of the day passed in a fog, my mind mulling over how to approach Sharon.

She lived in Alaska, three hours behind Minnesota time. If I called her as soon as I got home, before the kids arrived home from school, I could speak to her privately. If she answered. Yet I hesitated. After all these years, I still felt the need to protect my younger sister. The topic was sure to bring up uncomfortable memories. Would she claim, as Shannon did, that the incident didn't affect her life? Surely, Sharon would not have forgotten what Stan had done to her, if he had molested her. I wanted the truth, but did I want to hear it from my sister? What would the truth look like? How would it impact my future? Would I be left high and dry again without help? For the rest of the afternoon I pondered answers to the endless questions whizzing through my mind.

I drove home as fast as possible over the now slippery roads, rehearsing what I would say to Sharon. The house was empty. The kids wouldn't arrive for another hour. I hung my coat in the closet, then settled in the chair next to the telephone that hung on the kitchen wall near the backyard window. I found Sharon's number in my address book. I stared outside at the bare trees. I felt as stripped and cold as they looked. Nervous, I punched the numbers. The phone rang several times before I heard a hello. It was Sharon.

"Hi, Sharon, this is Mary." I did my best to put a smile in my voice.

"Oh, hi!" she said cheerfully. "I didn't expect you. What's going on?"

"Is this a good time to talk?" I asked.

"Yeah, I'm just hanging out. Ed is still at the base."

I pressed the receiver against my ear and concentrated on keeping my voice calm. "I have something I want to ask you," I said. "Something that's bothered me for a long time."

"Sure, go ahead. I'll do my best to answer," she said.

"It's a really hard question, and I need you to be truthful and honest."

Silence...then a cautious, "Okay, tell me what you need to know."

"Do you remember the time when you were a little girl and you came to our house to stay? When you were about five or six?"

"Yes. I do," Sharon said, her voice soft, as if she already knew what the next question was.

"Did Stan molest you?"

"Mary, I don't want to hurt your feelings," said my sister, her concern coming through the line loud and clear.

That was not a response I had anticipated. I assured her not to worry about my feelings. "The truth is more important to me now than anything," I said.

Sharon said, "Yes, it did happen, but that was a long time ago. A really long time ago."

What had been red-hot coals of anger earlier in the day now cooled into relief and exhilaration. Relief that Sharon revealed what happened. Exhilaration at being validated. All those years, I had been right. How could he lie all this time to me? What other despicable acts was he lying about? Then there was my mother. Why on earth had she corroborated his story? She had protected a sexual predator even after I had shared my story of being molested. Who was this woman? Why hadn't she protected Sharon, her own daughter, especially after I, her other daughter, had impressed upon her the horror of what Bushey had done to me that day in the barn?

Before hanging up I told Sharon that I suspected Stan had abused Shannon and Shawntel too, then reassured her that what she shared would help me get to the bottom of things. We agreed to talk again soon. We hung up, and I called Bob. Surprisingly, I caught him in his office. He told me to again question the girls. The statute of limitations had run out on Sharon, and from a legal standpoint there was nothing that could be done.

I hung up the phone and looked at the clock. Hopefully Shannon would arrive home first, as she usually did. I dreaded bringing up a subject we had squirmed over earlier in the day. Maybe if I explained what Sharon said, she would melt and let it all pour out. I could only hope.

At last Shannon came into the house and bounced up the steps into the kitchen. "Hi, Mom, what's for supper?"

"I haven't had time to think about it yet," I said, leaning against the kitchen counter for support. "But I do want to talk to you."

Her smile swooped down into an exasperated frown. "What?" She must have known from my look it was serious.

"Well, I called Sharon this afternoon."

"Yeah, so?"

"I asked her if your dad had sexually molested her, and her answer was yes. So, I want to ask you again, do you remember anything about your dad doing that to you?"

Shannon's face turned ashen. The sparkle in her eyes faded. "No, he hasn't done anything like that."

Her answer threw me for a loop. I had been certain she would change her story from this morning. Her expression turned defiant, as if challenging me to say another word.

"I'll be at Diane's. Don't expect me for supper," she said, her back to me.

Damn it! I had followed Bob's instructions, and now I was back at the beginning of the maze, trying to figure out which way to turn. There had to be a way to get the truth out, but how? Maybe I needed to ask Shawntel the same question. All those years of Stan needling her and her rebellion against him always fed the feeling that something was going on between them. But I could never catch Stan at anything. Like a well-trained soldier, he outmaneuvered me. I'd have to rethink how to ask her; if she denied that Stan had done anything, I was finished. I could discern no other option for extracting the truth and without the truth, no action could be taken against Stan.

The bright sun had melted much of the snow, sending rivulets of water down the driveway as I headed out a few days later to

pick up Shawntel from work. She was waiting tables at a restaurant in Bayport, about ten minutes away. She hopped in the
car smelling of grease and showed me her wad of tip money. She
looked and sounded so happy, so innocent. I hated to puncture
the moment, but I was determined. We needed to talk. I teased
her about how much money she was making in such an off-the-
beaten-path restaurant. I told her the customers must really like
her outgoing personality. She smiled.

"Shawntel, I have a question for you," I said, "but first I need
you to promise to tell me the truth no matter what the question
is."

"I don't want to make a promise without knowing what the
question is," she said.

"Nope, you have to promise. This question is just for you
and only you." I counted on her curiosity to get the best of her. It
worked. She sat in the seat, giggling.

I willed the steering wheel to become a lightning rod for my
anxiety. "Shawntel, has anyone ever touched you in a way that
you felt was inappropriate?"

She leaned against the door and lowered her head. "I don't
want to answer that question," she said.

I reminded her that she had promised to answer my question
truthfully, whatever the question. I held my breath and waited.

She looked out the window, then down at her hands. "Yes,"
she said.

"Who was it, Shawntel?"

She twisted in her seat as if trying to think of a way to escape
from the moving car. "I don't want to tell you, Mom."

"Was it someone in our family?" I just knew what the answer
was going to be. I inhaled calm and tamped down the wrath I
felt rising.

She tugged at a ring on her finger. "Yes," she said.

"Do you understand how important it is for me to know the truth, Shawntel?"

"But Mom, I don't want to hurt your feelings."

I slowed down below the speed limit. "Was it one of your uncles, or a grandparent? Was it Shayne? Was it your father?" And finally, feeling with all the craziness in her life that even I was not above suspicion, I said, "Was it me, your mother?"

She tittered at the absurdity of my question." Of course it wasn't you; you always try to protect me…us."

"Well, with all the crazy things that have gone on in my life, I just wanted to make sure." I hoped that gave her the permission and freedom to tell the truth. The car went quiet.

"It's Dad," she said. She sounded sad.

I wanted to feel the relief, the exhilaration I had when Sharon finally admitted what had happened, but all I felt was a bolt of overwhelming sadness. I had failed her. "Shawntel, I promise you've done the right thing in telling."

"I don't want you and Dad to get a divorce."

My first thought was that divorce was too good for the bastard. I wanted to take a gun and kill him. Then confusion set in. Why didn't she share the same hatred? He had abused her for months, maybe years. Yet, she wanted him around. I'd have to grapple with that conundrum later.

"You need to know that I love you very much," I said. "More than you know. And what I want most right now is for you, and all of us, to be safe." I turned in the driveway and put the car in park. "Look at me and tell me that you understand."

Shawntel's eyes met mine. Tears. Fears. They were there. I reached over, seatbelt and all, and pulled her close. "We're going to be okay," I said. "Please promise me you won't say anything to your father until I have a chance to talk with Bob, and for God's sake, stay as far away from him as you can. Do not engage in any confrontations with him."

Shawntel went directly to her room, and I went to mine and closed the door. I needed to collect myself. I had suspected for so long that Stan was molesting her, and most likely Shannon too, and now my theory had become reality. Although I felt stronger knowing the truth, regrets bombarded my sanity. Rage rolled over my heart like a bulldozer crushing it. My poor daughters. The thought of what they had endured sickened me. Over the years I had wished for Stan to have a heart attack and die, for another woman to take him away, for him to just leave. Now the part of me on the verge of insanity wished that I could kill him. Throughout the months of family therapy, Bob had reminded us of his responsibilities to report all abuses disclosed during therapy. But he had never said what would happen when such abuses were reported. I picked up the phone. It was time to find out.

My hopes that Stan would be arrested in the next days were dashed by the reality of legal procedures. "It's a process, Mary," said Bob. "It takes time." First, Bob needed to contact the Washington County authorities and report what Shawntel said. Before filing charges, social services needed to interview Shawntel to confirm her accusations. I needed to go to the courthouse to pick up papers to file an Order for Protection petition. Bob suggested that he have a private face-to-face with Stan to get him to admit to the abuse and take full responsibility for it. He wanted the blame off Shawntel's shoulders and placed squarely on Stan's. After that meeting, the sheriff's office could do its thing and arrest Stan. To complicate matters, I was supposed to fly to Philadelphia, then Wilmington, Delaware, for work and would be gone most of the week.

On the one hand, I needed to go on the trip. I didn't want to raise suspicions at work that anything was amiss. Plus, looking ahead, I needed to be able to financially support the family. This trip was part of my ongoing training, learning new and very intricate equipment and operations theory. At least on the plane I would have some space to cool down, regain a rational edge to my thinking. On the other hand, I dreaded leaving.

Bob asked the sheriff's office to wait until I returned home to request that Stan come in for questioning. I, in turn, asked Bob to delay his meeting with Stan until I returned. In my mind, I kept seeing an image of Stan's machete. I was tempted to remove all the knives from the house. Even a lamp, scissors, a full beer can could become dangerous in the hands of a madman. Stan was about to be laid out for what he did to his family. At what point would he become a raging lunatic?

Every day, whether I was home or gone, I talked to Shawntel. She was nervous but had found ways of avoiding her dad for quite some time, though I didn't know that then. She and I hadn't told Shayne or Shannon anything about what was happening. Stan wasn't the wiser either. I continued to leave early in the mornings before he got up, and he usually came home late and stayed up watching TV after I went to bed. I attempted to have normal conversations when necessary. At night, I hugged the side of the bed. Just the sight of him repulsed me.

I had returned from my trip and was at work attempting to focus. Tomorrow, the sheriff's office would be calling Stan. The confrontation would begin. The phone rang and I answered it, my mind elsewhere.

"Mom, why is the Washington County sheriff looking for Dad?"

"What?" I said, stunned. Shayne didn't usually speak in a whisper.

"Yeah, the sheriff called and asked for Dad."

Oh, for Pete's sake. How could this be happening now, a day early? "What did you tell him?"

"I told him he was at work."

I tried to keep my voice even. "Did you give them an address or a telephone number?"

"I just told them the name of the company."

"Okay, good."

"Mom, what's going on?"

My mind splintered in different directions. What were the authorities thinking? What if they had already reached Stan and he was driving hell-bent for home, hell-bent on hurting someone? Me. The kids. "Shayne, do not call your father! Do you understand me? If he comes home, do not mention that phone call. I'm leaving work right now."

When I got home, I told Shayne and Shannon that they needed to stay at home with me, that Shawntel had said her dad sexually abused her. Neither of them said much. They looked more scared than surprised. Shayne had spoken with Stan and knew he was mad. Thankfully, Shawntel was at work. I told both kids that I'd tell them what was happening later. Right now, I needed to make dinner, and they needed to line up a friend's house to stay at overnight, get their clothes packed, and all their school gear ready to go. I went about my chores as normally as possible, while playing out what the future held for my kids. What would they do? Where would they go? How would they survive, and whom would they tell? How could they tell? It was such an embarrassment, such a taboo subject. Fear gripped me.

I was taking the tuna casserole out of the oven when I heard the garage door go up. I braced myself. A minute later, Stan raced up the steps into the kitchen.

"What the fuck did you do?"

I looked up in mock confusion. "What are you talking about?"

"The police want to see me. What did you tell them?"

"I didn't tell them anything."

Shannon and Shayne came out of their rooms and sat at the table.

Stan began to pace. "I'm not going. I don't know what's going on."

Stan did most of the talking at dinner, conjecturing what the cops wanted, rationalizing whether to go or not. He finally talked himself into going to see what they wanted. "Otherwise, they'll just come here." I breathed out relief.

The kids and I did the dishes while Stan prepared to leave. As soon as he drove off, we packed the car. I dropped off Shannon at her friend's, dropped off Shayne at his friend's, then picked up Shawntel at the restaurant. In all the chaos, I hadn't gotten around to finding a place to stay. Shawntel and I drove around for a while, weighing the options. I found a pay phone and called my good friend Linda.

"Can I come and stay with you without telling you why?"

"Of course," she said. It wasn't until months later that I explained the reason for our intrusion.

Shawntel was afraid Stan would come back home, find us gone, and kill himself. Secretly, I wished he would. Before she went to bed, she called the house. Stan answered. She hung up without saying anything. I found her behavior odd, but was too distracted by everything going on to question her about it right then.

Late that night, a snowstorm hit the Twin Cities and made for some very slow driving the next morning. I had called Bob in a panic about the turn of events, but we didn't speak until morning. Bob was upset with the sheriff's office. He had told them that they didn't have to jump the gun, that Stan wasn't a candidate for going on the lam, and that Shawntel wasn't going to change her mind. But those folks had their own viewpoint. Bob was worried, however, because he knew Stan was a bully and might act out. He suggested that Shawntel and I come to his office.

Our cars pulled into the parking lot at the same time. The three of us had been talking in Bob's office for about forty-five minutes when Stan burst through the door. We all jumped. Bob was a tall man, fairly large framed, but wore a back brace. He quickly moved between Stan and me. Stan tried to reach around him to grab me. My heart was pounding so hard. For a moment, I thought Stan might punch Bob. Then Stan turned on Shawntel. "You lied! You're making all this up."

"Dad, you did it! You know you did it! Leave Mom alone."

Stan settled down a bit.

Bob said, "Mary, you and Shawntel leave."

Later that day, Bob called. He had gotten Stan to admit that he abused Shawntel. The night before, the police had gotten Stan to admit the same thing. His guilt was on the table for everyone in the family to see.

I was bound and determined to divorce Stan. The attorney I consulted, however, flashed the yellow caution sign. Stan hadn't been convicted yet, though he had been charged with one count of intrafamilial sexual abuse in the first degree and another count of second degree intrafamilial sexual abuse. Technically, he was still innocent and would be until a judge declared him guilty and eventually sentenced him. With all this pending, the attorney advised me to go easy and not push for an immediate divorce. It would only complicate things. As if things weren't complicated enough. He did say that he at least could get financial support for the children. I didn't argue. I was too weary. It felt as if my internal framework were on the verge of collapsing. I needed advice, but even more, I needed support.

The thought of help sucker-punched me in the stomach. I could still hear my mother's sharp comments and disapproving sighs when she learned of family, friends, neighbors, even strangers who asked for help. They were failures. All of them. I finally had the gumption to overcome my fear and take action to uncover the truth about Stan's behavior and succeeded. Yet, as I worked to help my kids get through this trauma, all I felt was guilt for having failed them. Stan and I were still married. I dug for strength, turned down the volume of my mother's voice, then picked up the phone and called Marie. She was the one who had directed me to Bob. Maybe she could recommend someone new.

She gave me a list of suggestions. From there, it was trial by dial. I talked to a male counselor who seemed to insinuate that I was the one to blame for Stan's incest. Huh. I called Catholic Charities. The sister with whom I spoke asked if I were interested in a family treatment program. I had never heard of such a thing. She recommended Wilder Child Guidance Clinic; they offered such a program. No, we don't, said the Wilder receptionist. So I moved on to a program called Face to Face and took the girls with me to one of their meetings. That counselor suggested Wilder. "But they don't have a program," I said. The counselor knew otherwise. I called Wilder again and this time connected with the right person. I went in and filled out an application. By this time, I had learned to say the words "incest," "sexual abuse," and "treatment" without flinching.

Stan now rented his own place and was prohibited from having contact with Shawntel. The statute of limitations had run out on Shannon. I continued to work full time at 3M and was the sole supporter of the family. The reality of what Stan had done to the girls in our house haunted me. I had to get out of there. My attorney suggested I sell the house myself to avoid having to pay a broker's commission. I got busy painting For Sale signs to post in front of the house and near the freeway. The kids weren't happy that we had to move. It had been the longest I had lived in one place besides the farm. Seven years, to be exact. On an unseasonably warm day in February when melting snow piles cowered near the trunks of the poplar trees, I pounded the sign in the front yard At the end of the month, our family was accepted into the Wilder program, and in May, I sold the house.

Every Thursday, we attended family counseling. The kids went to their groups. Stan went to his. I went to mine. Once a month, parents met as a group. Each week, all families ate supper together and afterward convened for a wrap-up session.

Diane Dovenberg was one of the founders and leaders of the program. She was a soft-spoken, methodical thinker. During sessions, she balanced a notebook on her lap and leaned forward, elbow almost resting on her knee, her forefinger and thumb on her chin, and ducked her head as she listened. When she resurfaced, she would paraphrase, then offer thoughts, suggestions, and ideas. If she were confrontational, she did it in the most kind, gentle way. She had never been married or had children. Everyone in the family responded well to her. I adored her.

As we progressed through counseling, I learned much about the complex subject of sexual abuse. It's not about sex but about power and control. Furthermore, incest tends to be generational. Parents need to learn to watch for red flags and never be ashamed to ask bold questions of their children. Even bold questions may not elicit answers. In order for any social service organization to step in, however, at least some of the truth has to be on the table. I was shocked and appalled to learn just how devious and deceptive child molesters are at convincing children not to tell. The abusers instill fear in those they are abusing. They hold power over their victims. Just like heroine and cocaine own substance abusers, sexual abusers own their victims. They know how to make them feel responsible and shameful for the situation at hand. These invisible, tangled bonds of fear, guilt, and shame can keep people in place for years, even lifetimes, and keep patterns replicating through generations.

While I knew tough times were still ahead, I naively believed all the counseling we were doing was going to save our family. After so many years of secrets and torments, we were on the path to becoming normal and whole. We would be the poster family of incest recovery and togetherness.

I needed to tell my parents what had transpired. I left it up to Stan to tell Betty and the rest of his family. I drove to the farm on a slushy, damp Saturday in early spring. It was a déjà vu experience. Mom, Dad, and I sat in the red room at the farm in the same exact chairs we had perched on fifteen years earlier when I suspected Stan had molested Sharon. I said that Stan had sexually abused the girls, we were in counseling, and he would be going to jail or prison. We wouldn't know which until sentencing occurred, probably in the summer.

My mother put her head down and spoke in an uncharacteristic small, weak voice. About the only thing she said was, "I just can't believe he would do something like that." She couldn't stop shaking her head. Dad looked me in the eye. "I'm so sorry, Mary. So very, very sorry."

At Diane's suggestion, I asked my mother to drive up to Minnesota to join us in a counseling session.

"If it will help you, I'll come," she said.

Diane was skilled at getting people to talk, but even she found my mother a tough nut to crack. But she got her to open up a little. I'm not sure what led up to the story that Mom shared and I had never heard.

My mother was six years old. Grandpa was struggling at the time with the farm. Money was tight, and he could never get ahead on anything, financial or otherwise, besides the number of children in the family. One day he walked into the kitchen. My grandma was in there with Mom. Grandpa had a dazed look in his eyes and pistol in his hand. He ranted about his life and how everyone would be better off without him. He held the gun to his head and yelled, pointed it at the floor and cried. Grandma and Mom were frightened. Mom held onto Grandma and didn't know what to do. Then Mom took the initiative. She talked to Grandpa, calming him down, telling him he needed to live. She didn't stop until he dropped the gun and walked out of the house, defeated.

"You saw all of that?" Diane said.

"Yes," said Mom.

"You talked your dad out of killing himself."

Mom tilted her head to one side. I saw a sadness I'd never seen before. She let out a soft sigh. "I guess I did," said Mom.

So this is where she first gained power, I thought. At the tender age of six, she learned that she could control the outcome of events. She was the one in charge. For years, she saw her dad as the underdog, an underdog who needed her support. All these years, she had seen Stan as the underdog too. And Walt. And the teenage hitchhiker from Texas she had picked up the week before. And countless others she tried to help. The problem was that she never recognized that some underdogs won't ever learn new tricks, no matter how hard you try to teach them, nor are underdogs the only ones in need of help. Sometimes the people closest to you—the ones who may wear masks of strength and are too afraid to speak up—are the ones who are really drowning.

As Stan's sentencing date approached, the kids grew increasingly nervous. They were worried he might be incarcerated at Stillwater State Prison rather than the local jail. The counseling had eased my anger toward him. I still felt he should be punished, but not with a twenty-year prison sentence, the max he was looking at, in a penitentiary rumored to be violent, especially toward those who committed sexual crimes against children.

Diane encouraged the kids and me to attend Stan's sentencing in court. Shayne refused to go. He was very angry with Stan and at that point didn't want anything to do with him. The girls and I drove to the courthouse in the middle of August. As soon as I stepped out of the car, I felt sweaty from the humidity and also nerves. The girls looked even more nervous.

We found a seat in the air-conditioned courtroom. A few minutes later, Stan and his public defender walked in and took seats at one of the front tables facing the judge. Stan was dressed in street clothes. He fidgeted, tapping his fingers on the table, leaning forward, backward. I still saw him once a week at counseling. If we needed to talk or argue about some practical matter, I would stop in at Price Mart, where he worked full time.

The sentencing got underway. The judge flipped through a file and asked questions of Stan and his attorney. Then he closed the file. I knew it contained recommendations from Diane Dovenberg and Bob McCormick for a lenient sentence.

"Mr. Havens, in light of the fact that you are pursuing counseling at Wilder and are working full time, I am going to sentence you to six months in jail and a work-release program."

The girls' shoulders relaxed. The judge ordered Stan to report to Washington County Jail to begin serving his sentence. He would have a probation officer; ironically, the same probation officer that Shayne had for his high school truancy. He could work as many hours as he wanted. He would continue to attend the Wilder program. I was relieved at his sentence, relieved that this part of the process had ended. Maybe I could sleep through a night again.

Stan was released in February 1987. Before the year ended, we bought a house, moved in, and became a couple again, at least on the surface. I didn't really want to be married, but Stan had made an effort. He said all the right words to convince me that he would work on our marriage, be a better husband, and be a good father. I didn't completely believe him. Trust is hard to restore once it has eroded. His behavior was in many ways different and better, but I had long ago lost trust. It's one thing to have your partner betray you by having an affair with an adult, but an entirely different thing when you're married to someone who has an affair with your children. I couldn't believe him, yet I couldn't leave him. Right next to his words were planted my mother's admonition: you stick by the man you married. All of them seemed affixed to me like Krazy Glue.

Although we had gone through legal and social service systems in stellar fashion, which is not the norm for most families, I felt something still needed addressing. I just couldn't put my finger on it. Incest history repeats within the family system, sometimes for generations. As I learned in Wilder, it's a proven and well-known fact. Somehow, I would have to figure out how to break the cycle and leave a legacy of safety and happiness for the next generations.

In January 1992, I wrote Oprah Winfrey a letter. Oprah, herself a victim of child sexual abuse, was dedicating many of her shows to creating awareness about sexual abuse and provided invaluable resources to men, women, and children dealing with the lasting effects of sexual abuse and incest. I watched every *Oprah* show on incest and sexual abuse. I suggested to Oprah that she consider working on shows that included entire-family treatment, because it seemed she was missing the point that it is a family problem. I made my plea, sent the letter, and forgot about it until April, when I shared with a close friend that I had written to Oprah. That afternoon, I returned home from work to a message from Mary Kay Clinton of *The Oprah Winfrey Show* asking me to return her call.

I did, and she answered. After a few questions, Mary Kay said, "We'd like to have your husband on the show. Do you think he'd be willing to do that?"

I hadn't told anyone in the family that I'd written the letter. "I can ask him, but I really don't think he'll do it." I knew he was going to blow a cork.

"Would you and your daughters be willing to come on the show?" Mary Kay asked.

I told Mary Kay I'd ask the girls and get right back to her. I immediately called Shannon and Shawntel. Their first instinct was to say no, but before I had a chance to reply to Mary Kay, Shawntel called me back and barraged me with questions that I couldn't answer. She now was a mother of a two-year-old and had to consider his care. Once Stan got home, he exploded as expected and refused to go on the show. Shannon and Shawntel feverishly talked, finally deciding to go. It was exciting and scary.

Mary Kay made arrangements for Shannon, Shawntel, and me to fly out less than forty-eight hours later on Sunday, spend the night in Chicago, and attend the show on Monday. If Stan changed his mind, they would accommodate him. A limousine picked us up at the hotel. In the green room, we learned we weren't going to be on stage but in the audience. Shannon opted out of being interviewed; Shawntel and I chose to be disguised in wigs.

The show, "Why Mothers Don't Tell," was intense, with many hard, personal questions lobbed at the guest panel of people who had suffered incest. The feisty audience applauded and booed. We had been told that if Oprah had time, she'd venture into the audience, approach us, and ask us some questions. I was sweating bullets as I kept looking at my watch, wondering if we'd be interviewed. Finally, Oprah headed toward us. I felt faint with fear because I didn't think this audience would appreciate that I was still living with a man I knew had molested my daughters. As it was, Shawntel did most of the talking.

"I totally feel comfortable with my son being left with my dad," Shawntel said. The audience's boos terrified me. Shawntel pressed bravely on. "My dad has gone through five years of counseling. Now he understands the things in his life that have gone on and why he did this, and I believe you have to give people who do that the benefit of the doubt."

I held my breath wondering how Oprah would respond. She nodded and emphasized that the benefit of the doubt is relative to each situation and that the important thing is that the rampant, hidden abuse needs to be stopped and the women in the families need to recognize the role they play. I silently added: and understand how to extract themselves from the fear that binds them to these uncontrollable, demented, lunatic men.

That was the end of our appearance. We were ushered briskly through the lobby and outside to a waiting limo. Someone would let us know the date the show was set to air.

Either we did a good job or the show had a good filing system, because five months later Mary Kay called back. Oprah was doing another show about incest called "Scared Silent." Would Stan, the girls, and I agree to be guests? I told Mary Kay to call Stan directly at work and ask him. I asked the girls, and the three of us decided yes. I wasn't thrilled about being on the show, but once again responsibility and guilt drove my decision. I had been unable to stop Stan's abuse; if our story could help others and even positively contribute to our family's healing, then I would do it. That night, the first thing Stan said when he walked through the door was, "I'm going to be on the *Oprah* show."

This time we were on stage. We shared it with another man and his daughter, whose dislike of each other was palpable. None of us wore wigs. I think we all were a little nervous, especially since we had not been briefed on Oprah's questions. When I eventually watched the show, I was quite proud of the job we did. I particularly was pleased with some of the information that found its way to public ears.

Oprah opened the show by saying, "My next guests want you to know that incest can happen to any family no matter how normal the family seems from the outside."

Oprah first asked Shawntel if she remembered when the abuse began.

"About three," Shawntel said.

"About three," Oprah repeated.

"I wasn't in school yet."

Oprah tilted her head. "And Shannon, how old were you?"

Shannon said about three.

Oprah then asked Shawntel if she knew what was happening to Shannon; Shawntel replied no. Oprah turned to the audience. "As you will see, it's revealed on tomorrow night's special on CBS and PBS that many times daughters in a family, especially, will allow themselves to continually be abused, thinking that they're protecting the other people in the family. And it's never that way." She returned her attention to Shannon. "Why did you deny what was happening when your mother asked you, Shannon?"

"Didn't want to admit it."

"Didn't want to admit it," Oprah said.

"No," said Shannon, looking down at her hands. "No, still protecting…"

Oprah waited. "Protecting your father?" she prompted.

"Yes," said Shannon, nodding her head.

Oprah then asked me when I first suspected abuse. I shared the story about Sharon being abused at age five. Oprah asked Stan how he got away with it.

Stan said, "With Sharon, I convinced Mary's mother that it

didn't happen. I told her that Sharon made me mad, and that I threw her up against the wall and she made up the story. Mary's mother believed that."

"So sexual abusers become very adept at lying, don't you?" said Oprah.

Stan looked rather smug. "Yes, oh yes. You haven't much choice. You have to keep everything under wraps, otherwise you're in deep trouble."

"Why did you do it, Stan?"

Stan shifted in his chair, then looked toward Oprah, let out a sigh, then leaned back in his chair, and looked away. He nervously laughed. Stick it to him, I thought.

Oprah changed tactics. "The first time. Do you remember the first time?"

Stan looked directly at Oprah. "No."

Oprah pointed her finger at Stan. "This is what I want everybody to know because this is what's so interesting about this whole case of sexual abuse is that by the time you catch somebody doing it, I don't know of any case where that is the first time the person has ever done it."

I couldn't have agreed more. I chimed in. "I tried on numerous occasions. I'd come back to the house thinking that I'd catch him doing something and I'd be so embarrassed because everybody would be kind of looking at me like, oh, what are you doing back? Then I'd feel guilty and ashamed like, you know, I was thinking something was going on and then it turned out I was wrong."

"But if you suspected—" said Oprah.

"I did ask the girls!" I said, feeling the well-worn need to share the truth. "I would ask them, but they'd always say no."

Oprah turned to Shawntel and asked her how old she was

when she told me what happened. Shawntel said about thirteen or fourteen. Oprah confirmed that the abuse by Stan continued for ten years.

"Well, it stopped about when I was twelve," Shawntel said.

Oprah looked at her quizzically.

"It just got less and less and less, and I knew how to avoid it."

"I'd asked Stan earlier, why he did it. Why, Stan?" said Oprah.

Stan's shit-ass-eating grin made me want to puke. He said, "We went through therapy and stuff, and we came up with several different reasons. One of them was because of the way I was brought up. One of them was a situation I had in Viet Nam. The other one was of my feeling of inadequacy to my wife. I think we came up with a hundred reasons, but never did we find an excuse. You can come up with all these reasons as to why you did it, and they never add up to an excuse no matter what you think." He laughed and the audience clapped. "When I came back from Viet Nam, I didn't care about life. Life didn't matter. Everything was just a big bore. There was nothing going on, so I created different problems."

"Was it for sex?" Oprah asked. "You know, rapists don't rape for sex."

"No, it wasn't."

"So, what was it for?"

Stan said, "Sometimes in my mind it was to get even with my wife. Because for some reason, I was below her. So, one way to harm her was to harm our children. I didn't want children, and the first thing I said to my wife, one of the first things was, I didn't want children. I was afraid to have that responsibility. But, of course I wanted to have sex with my wife. I'm not sure I knew that's how children came. I really thought they came by the stork."

Never in all the years of counseling first with Bob, then with Diane Dovenberg at Wilder did I hear Stan say this. Get back at me? Harm me? I sat there in front of millions of people bearing a façade of calm, but inside rage twisted and flowed through me. And on top of it, the stork had flown back again. Embarrassment joined rage.

Oprah looked at Stan. "Let me ask you this: when you were having or sexually abusing your daughters, did you feel more powerful? Did you feel in control?"

"Yes! I felt like I owned the situation," said Stan.

"And you couldn't be told no."

"Ummmm . . . no, not right away, no." He quickly looked at Shawntel. "Ah, Shawntel, was...Shannon told me no. When Shannon said no, it stopped with Shannon. It didn't with Shawntel right away."

Shawntel jumped in. " I didn't really say no. I just made up a lot of excuses. Like my foot hurt," she said, laughing, "and whatever I could think of."

Stan said, "With, with us, there was never, ah, penetration. There was the attempt. But, I never—"

"But it doesn't make any difference," Oprah said.

"No, it doesn't," said Stan. "It doesn't matter. I mean, just if you touch them in any way that they don't want to be touched, that's the beginning of it. That's where it starts." He coughed, uncomfortably I thought, then said, "But I can come up with all these reasons, and it's not going to have no excuse for anybody."

Oprah said, "I know on the special tomorrow night there is a case, and we're gonna meet this family. The wife walked in and found her husband with her ten-year-old, and they were able to put the family back together. I'm always amazed at when the family can come back together, and I want to know how that happened with this family." She cut to a commercial.

When she returned, she asked the girls if they wanted to be

back together as a family. Shawntel said not at first, but after being in Wilder, she changed her mind. "There is no one in this world that I can be angry at but my dad. There is no one that I could have gone to counseling for or got help from except from him. He had to be there to hear it. No one else mattered. I could scream at all of you, and that would not get rid of that pain. He had to know."

"You know, what I think is so still not understood," said Oprah, "is a lot of people associate abuse with just the sexual act. I know for me the sexual act was the smallest aspect of the abuse. It's what it does to your mind, and the anger and the sense of shame, and how if you're not allowed to be angry with the person who did it, you spend the rest of your life getting angry at people who didn't do it."

Shawntel nodded. "Yeah, and I don't think you grow past that age. I don't think you grow past that…I think that you stay in that little child, and I know for myself, I know Diane helped me with this a lot…That I, I needed my dad to heal that little child, and I needed that little child in me to know that it wasn't my fault, to know—"

Oprah interrupted. "Because did you also think it was your fault?"

"Well, I felt like it was my fault, felt like I provoked it. I don't know why, but we protect them."

Sitting straighter in his chair, Stan said, "But they need the father to be able to say, 'I did this to you.'"

"So when were you able to do that?" Oprah asked Stan.

Stan exhaled and laughed. "When she made me do it…no, when I was able to. When we stayed together in the program and worked through it."

Oprah said, "So, I think it is important for all of you, because I believe this is so rampant. I think this happens to more people than it doesn't happen to. Everybody is really so scared silent that nobody talks about it." The audience broke into applause. "We are going to take a break. This family has been through years of therapy to put their lives back together. So those of you who are going to find out or who find out today, you suspect it's going on…don't…think…that…you…can keep the family together all by yourself without help. Forgiveness is one of the last steps. You need to get mad and do something about it first."

Word was out on the Wauzeka streets that we had been on Oprah. At least that's what Isabel said when she called me to find out what Oprah was really like and to discuss details. No one in Wauzeka ever brought up the subject to my face, which didn't surprise me. It's not exactly as though you banter about incest. I didn't mind talking to Isabel about the experience, or anyone for that matter. After all the counseling I had been through and all I learned about incest and sexual abuse, I shared Oprah's feelings: the more people knew about the topics, the more likely it was that the cycles of abuse could be stopped.

I had assumed our *Oprah* careers had ended. In 1995, however, we were called back for a reprise. The show was "Men of the Cloth" and focused on sexual abuse by priests. I never figured out why we were asked to appear. Maybe at that time the producers couldn't convince enough priests to participate. Shawntel was eight months pregnant with twins, and the producers didn't want the liability of flying her to Chicago, so Stan, Shannon, and I were America's poster family for incest recovery.

We were on the air for six minutes, part of which included clips of our previous appearance. Oprah asked similar questions, and we repeated our stories. She concluded the show by saying, "We want to know why Mary stayed. We don't have time to find out today. I promise you another show about it in the future." All I could think was, thank goodness I didn't have to answer that question, because what in the world would I have said? Logically, it made no sense that I was still with Stan after all these years. All I had to do at any point was just leave! Every viewer of every *Oprah* show knew that. What I didn't recognize, and wouldn't recognize for many years, and what is so hard for others to understand were the complex powers at play that bound me to my dysfunctional husband, to long-established patterns of abuse and guilt, and to fear. Especially fear. It rendered me immobile and silent. When you have no voice, you can't even answer a simple question.

PART SIX

During the last two weeks of June 1998, a series of storms blasted into southwestern and central Wisconsin from Minnesota. Straight-line winds gusting at sixty, seventy, ninety miles per hour, were even clocked at one hundred and twenty miles per hour in a few places. The winds uprooted trees, knocked over power lines, and created prolonged outages. Branches littered county roads and highways. Campgrounds and RVs were destroyed. One squall lifted a roof off an elementary school, another the roof off a bowling alley. Outside of La Crosse, gusts collapsed a large circus tent on five hundred folks, injuring thirteen. Vicious winds bullied silos and chicken coops to the ground, while torrential rains swelled rivers, streams, and creeks, flooding lowlands and fields of crops. Intermittent hail inflicted further damage on land and buildings. By month's end, ten counties in western Wisconsin had been declared federal disaster areas, with damage estimates exceeding five million dollars.

On Thursday, June 25, my mother phoned in the afternoon. A storm had just moved through Wauzeka. She, my dad, Walt, Isabel, the kids, and some farmhands had fled to the farmhouse basement, where they listened to the wild winds and golf-ball-sized hail assault the property. The house lost roof shingles and suffered siding damage. The new crop of corn was stripped and the alfalfa flattened. One of Walt's cows was killed. And the old barn had blown down, though the silo remained standing.

My God, I thought. The barn had blown down. I only half-heard the rest of what my mother was saying about how poor Walt would be burdened with the time and cost of cleanup and repair. As it turned out, insurance covered most of the destruction and Walt even received one thousand dollars for the cow. As my mother prattled on, all I could think about was the barn, that old gray building that had held me hostage all these years. Ironically, the weekend before, I had visited and snapped a photo of the structure. A therapist had suggested I do so. When the shutter clicked, I thought, someday this barn will be gone. Now it was. The barn was gone. Who would have thought a violent storm could destroy the source of the guilt and shame I felt each time I saw the faded hulk of a building? No therapist that I knew. But I could feel it happening, a letting go. During the cleanup party some weeks later, I happily hauled pieces of gray lumber to the dumpster, and with every toss exorcised some of the darkness deep inside me. It lifted like a funnel cloud returning to the sky.

The next spring, March roared in with more winds of change. I was at work when Isabel called. Usually she waited until evening, so her voice caught me by surprise.

"Neither of your parents are feeling well," she said. Gone was her usual cheeriness. "And neither has showered. They smell terrible. I don't think they've vacuumed for a month, and dog hair is everywhere in their apartment." She sounded completely put out. "My thyroid's been acting up, and I'm not running on full energy here. My hair is dry as straw, my nails are breaking. I called Barbara earlier today to see if she might come down and help, and I was wondering if you could too. Besides, your mom is such a *private* person. It would be better if you two handled this."

I told her I could come that weekend. She thanked me and

said she had to skedaddle. I sat for a moment, digesting the thirty-second conversation. Isabel had been traipsing in and out of my parents' apartment for years. Why now did she consider my mother to be a *private* person? Weird. A timer rang in the lab, and I set the thought aside.

If Mom had had more respect for doctors, she might have agreed to the colonoscopy her doctor recommended in 1994. As it was, she waited two years, even though colon cancer had killed her mother and her mother's sister. She ignored the genetic testing Aunt Loretta had, which showed the marker for familial adenomatous polyposis, a marker linked to colon cancer. Years later, that marker also would be linked to cystic fibrosis. Mom's colonoscopy revealed a right-sided colon lesion. Though benign, it was suspicious for early carcinoma, especially considering the FAP marker and our family's history of colonic polyps. Instead of having the lesion surgically removed, Mom decided to self-treat. She had taken herself off of thyroid medication using herbal remedies and a diet filled with fruits, veggies, and little meat. This time, she bought a juicer, did colonic coffee cleanses, and who knows what else.

"There's a lot of fiber in my diet," she said when I called to check in on her. "All that roughage is removing the polyps."

I wasn't so sure. "If you get colon cancer and die, I'm going to be so goddamned mad at you!" I said. She was stubborn and opinionated and could be a real thorn in my side, but she was my mother. She just laughed and continued juicing vegetables from her garden.

On Friday, I picked up Barbara on my way through Hastings, and our cleaning service headed south to Wauzeka. Winds pushed against the car and swayed semitrailers on the freeway. The Mississippi flowed dark and deceptive. Barbara and I caught up on family happenings. Four hours later, we turned the car into the farmhouse driveway. The new white barn looked fresh, even in the dimming light.

We parked alongside the garage, retrieved our luggage from the trunk, and entered Mom and Dad's apartment. The smell hit me first. A foul smell of mold, garbage, and body odors. Mom was lying on the couch, her skin gray. She managed a weak smile. Dad sat in his recliner; his eyes sparkled when he saw us. Dirty dishes were piled in the sink and on the counter. The butter dish was uncovered, boxes of cereal were open, and Mom's desk had a stack of what at first glance looked like unopened mail, magazines, and newspapers. I popped into their bedroom. It stank of urine. I glanced at Barbara. She looked as if she were forcing calm.

"Where's Isabel?" I asked.

"Somewhere," said Mom.

Barbara opened the door that separated Mom and Dad's apartment from the rest of the farmhouse and went into the living room. I followed. We could see Isabel standing in front of the kitchen sink, a cigarette hanging from her mouth. She jumped, startled to see us.

"I didn't hear you come in," she said brightly, removing the cigarette and blowing smoke out the window above the sink. Then, in a low, conspiratorial voice, she said, "Walt thinks I've quit." She put the cigarette to her lips and turned toward the window. From there she could see the front of the new barn. "Now y'all won't go tellin' him about my one little bad habit, will ya?" she said, affecting her little girl southern voice. "Like I said, my honey thinks I quit." She sucked in her cheeks, turning the end of the cigarette bright red, then exhaled swirls of smoke out the window. "I tell you, this thyroid business has me all out of sorts. I can put on weight just by looking at food." She waved the smoke out the window with her hand. She said she had trouble sleeping, but she couldn't get out of bed in the mornings to help with chores—or anything, for that matter. She caught sight of Walt walking out of the milk house. She doused the cigarette, threw the butt in the garbage, and dashed to the bathroom. Barbara and I heard her brushing her teeth.

Walt stomped through the mudroom. He had barely taken a step into the kitchen when Isabel rushed up to him, wrapped her arms under his, and passionately kissed him. Walt looked at us, face flushed and embarrassed. "Hey," he said to Barbara and me. He tried to push Isabel away, but she clung to him. Was this demonstration for our sake? Did she really think he wouldn't notice she had been smoking? I lived with a smoker. I knew exactly how a smoker smelled and tasted, even after chewing gum. I squelched an urge to laugh.

Stan's words came to mind. On our way home from Christmas at the farm, Stan had said, "Isabel is so full of shit her eyes are turning brown, the way she gets all lovey-dovey with Walt. She only cares about one person. Herself." At the time, I thought to myself, "Just like you." But that was Stan, a man of many lies and performances, who had no clue he was sharing the stage with his sister-in-law.

We could count on Isabel for two things: good coffee in the morning and perfectly popped corn for nighttime movies. Indeed, the next morning I awoke to the smell of coffee. Isabel, in her bathrobe, stood at the sink, yawning and trying to wake up. I grabbed a cup and then headed back into Mom and Dad's apartment. Barbara was already there. She had cleared and opened their small drop-leaf table so we could all sit together and spread a clean tablecloth over it. I opened the refrigerator to search for eggs. It smelled moldy. Bits of dried lettuce, jelly, peanut butter, and meat stuck to the shelves, the sides, and the bottom. I opened the cheese drawer and discovered the source of the mold. I quickly shut it. I'd have to deal with this later. In between frying eggs and making toast, I washed the salt and pepper shakers, jelly and honey jars, and the butter dish and returned them to the wooden lazy Susan that Kathy had given them years ago from England. Dad sat on a kitchen chair, drinking his coffee. He looked happy to have us there.

Barbara and I made plans for the day. We'd tackle the apartment, then I'd take Mom to her MRI appointment in Boscobel while Barbara did a grocery run.

Dad piped up. "I'd like to go visit Aunt Liz," he said. His sister Liz lived in Wauzeka. She recently had turned one hundred. I said we could drop him off on the way.

After breakfast, Barbara and I dug in, knowing we wouldn't be able to accomplish as much as we wanted. I opened the fridge. The hunk of bluish cheddar cheese promptly went into the garbage.

"Your dad will still eat that," said Mom. She was sitting on the couch, one eye on the morning news, the other eye on Barbara and me.

I said, "No wonder Dad never gets sick. He's immune to everything." Dad chuckled. I knew he wasn't wearing his hearing aids and was surprised he heard me.

The Minion Sisters' Cleaning Service forged full steam ahead. The vacuum whirred. Fresh, clear water filled plastic buckets; gray water was dumped from them. I changed sheets, toted urine-smelling clothes from the laundry hamper to Isabel's washing machine. Now, why couldn't Isabel get a load of laundry done in her new fancy washing machine mom bought her? At one point, Mom got up from the couch. "I'm going to feed the horses," she said, putting on her jacket. She didn't think she needed anyone to go with her.

While she was gone, Dad grabbed his cane and walked over to the window to look at the birds in the feeder, then to the window facing the horse barn. I suspected he was watching her walk across the yard. "Wish I could get out there some with Walt," he said. "Those cows will be dropping calves soon enough." He leaned on the counter. "Looky there. A robin." He stumped back to his recliner and huffed into it. "Your ma has that back pain still," he said. "Wonder what's going on? She doesn't sleep well and keeps me awake sometimes with her moans."

I slid a refrigerator shelf back into place. "The doctors will get to the bottom of it," I said. At least I hoped they would.

Mom returned, looking pale. She asked me to find her another sweater. Then she laid down on the couch and fell asleep.

Mom's MRI was uneventful. On the way back, she sat in the passenger seat, hunched in her heavy winter coat, hugging herself, a scarf tied under her chin. I turned on the windshield wipers to fend off the sleet. Maybe someday I would live in a place that had sunny, warm springs instead of misty, cold ones.

"I don't know how Walt is making it," she said. "Isabel spends and spends and spends. She has to have the latest hairdos, manicured nails, even massages." Mom snorted. "And there's Walt. Working everyday to support the family. I don't know how in the world he's going to make it."

I was irritated with Isabel for being a spendthrift, but I knew Mom wasn't exactly easy to be around either. She could get ornery with whomever was around and never addressed problems directly with Walt and Isabel. When I encouraged her to do so, she jumped to a new subject, as she'd always done.

I pulled up to Aunt Liz's house, and we went inside for a short visit. Dad must have confided his worries about Mom to Aunt Liz. I could see the concern in her eyes when she asked Mom how she was doing.

"Oh, gettin' along, gettin' along," said Mom.

By the time we returned to the farm, it was edging close to supper. Barbara hadn't returned yet with the groceries, so Mom went to take a nap.

"When I heard you were coming down, I made sure to get into town," said Dad. He shuffled over to the end table next to the couch, opened the top drawer, pulled out a few decks of cards, pad of paper, pencils, then a pint of brandy. "If Isabel sees this, she'll take it faster than a hawk snatching a field mouse." I heard an edge of irritation in his chuckle. "Thought we might have a shot."

"Or two," I said with a teasing smile.

We were sitting at the kitchen table sipping our brandy and chatting when Barbara walked in, a bag of groceries in each arm. She went back out to the car to get the rest. I stood up to help but decided to make a pit stop in the bathroom. Dad said he wanted his slippers, so he headed to the spare bedroom where he had left them. When I returned, Isabel was at the table digging through one of the grocery bags, her back to me. She turned around as if ready to march off, but jerked to a halt, seeming surprised to see me. A bottle of extra-strength Tylenol was in her hand.

"Found the Tylenol!" she said. "Grandpa is gettin' so forgetful these days. I've taken to monitoring all of his meds, even these little things. I'll put them in his pillbox and make sure this gets put in my cupboard with his prescriptions." She quickly left. She must not have seen Dad standing in the bedroom doorway or the bottle of brandy on the kitchen table.

Dad walked over to his recliner and settled in. "I don't know why she says those are for me. I never take them, but she always adds them to my grocery list. Wants me to pay for them, I guess."

"Just make sure she doesn't find out about this," I said, picking up the brandy bottle and stowing it in its hiding place.

Two weeks later Isabel called with jarring, though not surprising, news. Mom's March colonoscopy showed a positive B-II lesion in her right colon. Surgery was scheduled for April 20. She was considered low risk with a good chance of recovery. Isabel didn't even have to ask anyone to come down. All five sisters immediately got busy setting up a round-robin schedule of care. I volunteered to be there the day of surgery.

Stan opted not to accompany me, which was fine by me. I drove down to Wauzeka the day before surgery. Mom had been hospitalized two days earlier with excruciating back pain diagnosed as musculoskeletal related. Her doctor prescribed a muscle relaxant and ibuprofen, neither of which she took. I worried about her and Dad, of course. Isabel might not be the fastidious household manager, but she had a medical background, and she basically shared a living space with my parents. I pulled into the farm, the crescent of a waxing moon heralding my arrival. Dad, clad in pajamas and robe, greeted me at the door.

"Couldn't sleep, so I thought I'd wait up for you," he said, giving me a warm hug.

I hauled my bag and some groceries inside. Dad disappeared into the spare bedroom. I heard his file drawer slide open. When he reappeared, he was holding the pint of brandy. "Thought you might like a little nip before bed."

Did I ever. It had been a long day at work, and after four hours of driving with only my thoughts for company, I was too wired to sleep. I filled two glasses with ice and sat for a father-daughter catch-up chat. As I headed to bed, I heard noise on the other side of the fireplace. Mice, I thought. Maybe Mom and Dad needed a cat.

The next morning, Dad had the coffee hot when I walked into the kitchen. He shaved, washed, and dressed while I fixed break-fast. While we ate, I noticed he nervously circled his thumb over his middle finger, a habit I inherited. I half-expected Isabel and Walt to pop in, but all remained quiet on their side of the house. Dad didn't know where they were.

When we arrived at the Boscobel hospital, Mom was lying in bed with her eyes closed, looking tranquil and thin. An IV tube snaked from her hand to the drip bottle. Dad, cane in hand, shuffled to the bed and gently set his hand on top of hers. Tears filled his eyes. Mom's eyes opened, and a weak smile appeared on her face.

"Hello," she said. He leaned down and kissed her on the lips. He looked relieved.

Nurses and doctors popped in and out of the room for what seemed like an eternity. Finally, a nurse and attendant loaded Mom onto a gurney. She winced and groaned. Dad kissed her again, I kissed her cheek, and the attendant rolled her out of the room. An antiseptic emptiness filled the space. "Turn on the TV," said Dad.

Good idea, I thought. We needed a distraction. We were about five minutes into watching a game show when the station inter-rupted with a news alert. There had been a shooting at Columbine High School in Littleton, Colorado, and the place was in chaos.

Talk about a distraction. "What's with the world?" I said. Dad just shook his head. We remained transfixed.

Sometime later, the surgeon dressed in scrubs, his mask hanging down, knocked at the door. He explained that he had removed the right-side colon, and although the left-side colon showed an area of red irritation, he decided to leave it alone. He had left the gallbladder in, even though it had stones. Mom would not need a colostomy bag. He was uncertain where her back pain was coming from, but he didn't believe it was from her colon. He said if the pain went away, he would take credit for it. If it continued, she would need further testing.

After he left, I called Kathy. I told her Mom was doing fine and to relay the news to everyone and have them wait until tomorrow to call Mom in the hospital. "I'm uncomfortable with the surgeon leaving the irritated section," I said. "But he's the expert."

Mom was wheeled back into the room shortly after, not yet awake. Dad scooted his chair close to the side of the bed. He kissed her cheek. We went back to watching Columbine unfold. I glanced at Dad. His face was soft, and he caressed Mom's arm. I'd never seen this side of him, the tender, loving husband worried about his wife. It surprised me. Even the stress of losing four children had not created a chasm between them.

During a commercial break, he looked at me and said, "I don't want to live without your ma. I don't think it's possible."

"I know, Dad," I said, wanting to gather him in my arms. I thought of the times Stan had visited me in the hospital and the many times he hadn't. I could understand the literal meaning of Dad's words, but that's where the understanding stopped. I lacked the real-life experience to relate to them. The TV cameras zoomed in on a reporter relaying the latest details about the Columbine tragedy. A teacher had died. The students held a photo of his wife and children in front of him as he tragically slipped away, deprived of the chance to say good-bye.

In June, Mom put out the call for a Fourth of July family reunion, saying Dad wanted everyone to be together at the farm. It was too short of notice, not to mention that everyone had just been there taking their turn caring for Mom. I planned to be in Alaska visiting Sharon. Kathy couldn't make it, nor could a bunch of the grandkids. Charlotte and her husband, Ron, ended up driving to the farm from South Dakota for the weekend. It was late afternoon and the two of them, Dad, and Isabel sat on the deck. Mom had recuperated enough to run errands. Dad asked Charlotte to make him some coffee to drink while watching the five o'clock news, and the two of them went inside. After she settled Dad, Charlotte returned outside to visit with Isabel. They had remained very close friends and didn't get to see each other much. Tired of the girls' chatter, Ron went inside. That's when he noticed Dad sitting in the recliner, his head oddly tilted back and to the side, his tongue hanging out. When he looked closer, Dad was gasping for breath, the whites of his eyes showing. Ron raced out to get Isabel, who immediately suspected a stroke, called the hospital, and was instructed to bring him to Emergency.

Isabel had been correct. Dad had had a stroke. By the time Charlotte called Sharon and me in Alaska, Dad was lying conscious and comfortable in the Boscobel hospital, and Isabel already had taken Mom home. I returned to the Monopoly game I had been playing with Sharon and her kids, but the niggling thought that this was a life-changing event distracted me. I forgot to collect rent on St. James. Later, after everyone was in bed, I called Kathy in Washington, DC, and woke her up. I told her what I knew: Dad was stable, and everyone had gone home.

"You mean no one stayed with him?" She sounded fit to be tied.

"No, he's there alone."

"Someone should be there with him," she said. "He shouldn't be alone."

Her insistence made me nervous. We hung up, promising to keep in touch with each other. I was just drifting off to sleep when I heard the distant ring of a phone. Then, Sharon's voice. Then footsteps. Then a knock at my door, and Sharon saying, "Mary, Dad's had a massive stroke."

It took less than twenty-four hours for our bicoastal family to converge in the middle of the country at Gundersen Boscobel Area Hospital. The staff set us up in a family area that became command central. Visitors traversed between Dad's room and the continuously crowded family room, where bodies draped over chairs and lounges and sprawled out on the floor, trying to find a comfortable place to rest.

On July Fourth, despite the heat and humidity, someone opened a window when the town parade began. I walked to and from Dad's room to the family area, talking with whoever was there, getting something to drink, remembering it was the Fourth, gazing out the window at the high-school marching band, the drumbeat vibrating the air. Dad's wish for a family reunion had come true. The thought that he couldn't enjoy it made me sad. The day stretched like the day before, one hour inching toward the next, to the next, to the next. Dad's condition didn't change. No one wanted to leave, so we all stayed and ventured in small groups to the Unique Cafe, a few blocks from the hospital, the hospital I knew too well, where lives came and went. I was afraid to think that another life might be going.

246 MARY A. HAVENS

The next day, dad's sister, Aunt Liz, asked to visit. Word had gotten to her, and she wanted to see her baby brother. I secretly hoped that she would inspire him to awaken. When she came through the doorway hunched over in her wheelchair clutching a hanky in her soft hands, she looked delicate. Dad lay flat on his back, eyes closed and hands to his side, his chest rising and falling. When she caressed his arm, his muscles twitched, sending hope to everyone who had squeezed in the room that he would awaken.

"Ab, you need to wake up," she said in her soft-spoken voice. Dad's eyelids fluttered. "Illene needs you to help her get well. Besides, you can't go before me. I'm older, and you still have much to live for." She talked to him about good times they had growing up, about family, about farming. Although Aunt Liz remained vigilant, her brother never opened his eyes. Exhausted, she asked to go home.

The doctor requested a meeting with Mom and another family member. Mom wanted Bobby present as her power of attorney, executor, and her oldest son. She asked if I would join them. Though uncomfortable with life-and-death decisions, I agreed. The meeting the next morning was brief. The doctor explained that as long as Dad's pacemaker kept his heart beating, his organs would continue to function, which challenged the body's natural shutting-down process. He suggested removing the oxygen tube, and if need be, administering morphine.

Mom gasped. Her voice almost inaudible, she asked, "It won't be euthanasia, will it?" Over the years, Mom had made it clear that she was against any human purposefully taking the life of another, especially by abortion or euthanasia.

I gathered my strength. "It's what Dad wants. If he can't have a good quality of life, he wants us to let him go. We're just honoring his wishes." Bobby nodded in agreement.

Everyone gathered, and the doctor removed the oxygen tube. Nothing happened except for a communal sigh of relief.

The next morning, the doctor informed us that Dad's system showed progressive decline, He suggested we say our good-byes. He would return in the afternoon to administer morphine. As the sun mellowed in the western sky, the entire family crowded into the hospital room. The doctor instructed the nurse to push the drug into the line connected to my father's arm. Stop! I wanted to scream. I don't want to do this anymore! The sorrow on Mom's face further shattered my heart. The thought that I must be strong for her came crashing down on me. Dad's breathing slowed. Later, Allan and Barbara told me, each in a private moment, that they saw Dad open his eyes for the briefest of moments and smile.

Elbert Mullikin passed away on July 7, 1999, at 5:40 p.m. A month earlier, he and my mother had celebrated their fifty-sixth wedding anniversary. Before we left the hospital, a nurse pulled Barbara aside and told her that shortly before Dad died, the doctor had been called into labor and delivery. The nurse assisted. When the baby was born, she heard the doctor whisper, "You can go now, Bert. Your replacement is here."

The shovel scraped against the earth. Family and a few close friends began to congregate around the hole the grandkids were taking turns digging near the farmhouse deck. Earlier, Bobby's daughter and her husband had delivered a flowering crab apple tree to be planted in Dad's honor. Walt and several grandsons lifted the small tree by its root ball, carefully placed it in the hole, and snipped off the surrounding burlap. Mom watched Walt's every move, her shadow falling across the little tree. The shovel was passed round-robin and the dirt replaced. I was surprised to see Walt participating. He hadn't been around much at the wake a few days ago and had remained in the background of activity at the church funeral, stuffed as it was with the many people who dearly loved Elbert Mullikin. Somewhere behind me a cardinal burst into song.

Sharon grabbed Mom's hand and began to pray. Heads bowed.

"…and may this tree bear fruit through the years and bring happiness to new generations, just as Dad brought happiness to us. Amen."

"Make those apples grow, Bert," said someone in the back. People smiled. I wiped away tears, amazed I had any left.

The group slowly dispersed. No one seemed to be in a rush to go anywhere. It was as if we all wanted to be where Dad loved to sit on the deck, where he could look out over the entire farm. To the north, the pasture near the granary and beyond that, the hay and cornfields, split by the road leading to the cabin that Allan and Bobby had helped build for Mom. To the southwest, across the county trunk road, the pig barn and the fields and woods that stretched into the horizon. So many memories he and Mom created on all that land.

I walked up to the deck, grabbed a Coke from the cooler, and went into the kitchen to help Barbara and Kathy prepare hotdogs and burgers for the barbecue. Sometime later, I looked around for Mom. I suspected she had escaped for a rest. Sure enough, I found her sitting in Dad's recliner in their apartment.

She held up socks, still bound to each other by a tag. "What do you think I should do with these? Your dad never wore them."

Had I heard her right? A pile of Dad's clothes lay next to the chair, and next to them was a toolbox, the one he kept in the apartment in case he needed a screwdriver or hammer. "Please, Mom, let's wait to give Dad's things away. I'll come help you, and we can take our time. Sort through them. Decide who should get what."

I sat down on the couch and reigned in my irritation. Mom's eyes were glassy, probably a combination of exhaustion, grief, and physical pain, or perhaps painkillers. I couldn't remember if Isabel had given them to her or not. Warm, moist air pushed through the screened door. Someone laughed. My body felt heavy. The cushion springs seemed to compress under the weight of the past few days.

Mom smoothed the socks on her lap. "I told Bobby he could have Uncle Bob's picture. Dad wanted him to have it because he was named after Uncle Bob. Bobby told me to leave it on the wall. And I insisted Allan take the guns and some of Dad's tools. He said he'd come get them, but that we should leave the toolbox here." She never looked at me.

I leaned my head back against the couch, confused. How could she even think these things through? Were these the actions of a deeply bereaved widow? She had never been materialistic, and yet sometimes her actions were all about material things.

I took the socks from her. "Mom, I'll come back some weekend, and we can do this then. But let's not do it now. Let's do this as a family."

She lifted her face. I couldn't place her expression. Worry, embarrassment, guilt? It was too fleeting; she returned to looking pale and sad.

"Do you think we took your dad's life with that morphine injection?"

For a moment, I missed Dad so much it hurt my bones. "No," I said. "It was what Dad wanted." I tried to assure Mom that the healthcare directive had stated very clearly that Dad didn't want to live unless he could function with a sound body and mind. That seemed to appease her.

I thought about Dad's bottle of brandy stashed in the filing cabinet and was tempted to dig it out. Instead, I walked over to the window to see if the bird feeder was full. The cardinal sitting on the ledge pecked at a seed, tilted his crowned head toward me, then flew away. My stomach growled. I gathered Mom, and we followed the scent of barbecuing burgers and hotdogs, the thought of food a welcome distraction from the chaos I felt creeping closer.

Fortunately, before I left for Alaska, I had scheduled a chiropractic appointment, thinking I might need an adjustment after the stress of flying.

"How's your mom doing?" Dr. Kranz said after I related the reason for the knots in my shoulders, neck, and back.

"She's hanging in there," I said. "The will reading is on Wednesday."

Dr. Kranz looked surprise. "Are you driving back for it?"

"No, I wasn't invited. I think just two of my brothers are going."

"I'm surprised you weren't invited," he said, pushing hard on a very sore trigger point.

"Should I have been?"

"If you're included in the will, you would have been asked to attend the reading."

I explained that my parents had signed their wills back in 1981. I was pretty sure my brother Walt knew how everything was to be handled and divvied up between all of us. Dr. Kranz said that if there were any issues or confusion, he could give me the name of a good attorney friend who handled his family's estates.

Wednesday evening, Carol and Bobby called. They both had attended the will reading because Bobby, who had never handled anything related to wills and estates, was uncomfortable going alone. Carol was the town clerk of Wauzeka and had a good business sense. "Something doesn't seem right," Carol said to me. "It sounds like everything is going to Walt." Indeed, that did sound odd. I asked who was there.

"Your mom, Walt, Bobby, and me," she said.

"Does Mom have a copy of the will?" I asked.

Carol said, "It's at your mom's house."

"The next time I'm there, I'll take a look at it." I said.

"And we found out Mom is going to Alaska," added Bobby.

"What?" I said. "Alaska? That's crazy."

Bobby went on to explain that Mom, one of her cousins, and a good friend were driving to Anchorage in the friend's RV. They planned to stay with Sharon and Ed for a week.

Good Lord. She was actually going to go. For quite some time, Mom had tried to coerce Dad into going on an extended trip to Alaska with their friend, but Dad had started saying things like, "You go, Illene. You're the frontier woman. I'm staying put right here. My bones don't have enough oomph to get me that far."

I hung up and instant messaged my sisters about Mom's trip. I was far more concerned about her plans than I was the details of the will reading. Turned out my sisters were, too. By the time I wearily crawled into bed that night, I knew it would be futile to suggest to Mom that she cancel or even delay the trip. Once she made up her mind, she was not going to change it, regardless if she just lost her husband of fifty-six years, regardless if she was on pain meds. I pulled the blankets over me and punched a snoring Stan. I realized I had forgotten to mention the will to my sisters. Oh well. My siblings and I implicitly trusted my parents and Walt. I turned out the light and drifted into a dark sleep.

A few weeks later, I called my mother. She had just fed the horses. "I need to pack for Alaska," she said. "Do you think my blue jacket will be warm enough?"

"Yes, but take a few sweaters, too," I said. We chatted about her trip. Before we hung up, I said, "Mom, I was wondering why some of us weren't invited to the will reading. I mentioned it to Dr. Kranz, my chiropractor, and he said that if you're not invited, you're not included in the will. I'm confused. Were some of us left out of it?"

Silence followed.

"You there, Mom? I just want to make sure everything is how you want it and you're taken care of. Do you have a copy of the will?"

My mother answered softly, her voice trembling. "Yes."

All at once, I hurt for her. She had been through so much lately. Months of pain and then the death of her best friend, my father. But beneath my sadness, something squirmed. I had a sneaking suspicion she knew exactly what the will said.

"When I visit after you get back from Alaska, we can talk about it."

There was another pause. "Yes, I suppose we can do that," she said. "I just know that I want Allan to have the cabin and some land below in Plum Creek so he can build rental cabins. He is going to have a hard time making ends meet with Carmen's MS. She might very well end up in a nursing home, and he could lose everything."

"Is Walt still making installments to buy the farm from you?"

"Oh sure," she said. "He's done some of that."

After I hung up, I sat at the dining room table rehashing a past conversation. I swear that a while back I had asked Mom if Walt were renting from her and Dad. Oh sure, she had said. But what else had she said? Maybe the rent payments had turned into purchase payments? Before the definitive thought could surface, my reverie was interrupted. Stan walked in dressed to umpire the local women's league softball game.

"Let's go," he said impatiently.

I set aside everything else in my life and once again attended to him.

If I hadn't felt so tired, I would have been livid. I'd been at the farm for less than an hour. Mom had returned from Alaska a few days before and was napping when I arrived. I could hear the tractor grinding in the distance. Isabel was nowhere to be seen. I went into cleaning mode. When I brought the garbage outside, I discovered Dad's dirty old barn-smelling bib overalls on top of cantaloupe rinds. Who'd had the audacity to toss them out? I grabbed them, located an empty grocery bag under the kitchen sink, stuffed them in it, and put the bag in the trunk of my car.

When I returned, Mom was awake. I didn't bother mentioning the bibs. It would be a draining, frustrating way to begin our visit. We caught up on her trip, on Shannon, Shawntel, and Shayne, and poor Stan, as Mom still called him. The sun slanted through the window. The blue sky had gotten the best of the earlier cloud cover.

"Mom, let's sit outside. I'll get your sweater and you get the will so we can go through it together."

Mom twisted the tissue she was holding, then nodded in a resigned sort of way.

We settled into chairs on the deck. Yellow elm leaves were scattered across the grass, and the first scent of autumn filled the air. Geese flew overhead, and I thought of Bonnie, as I always did in the fall. Mom handed me the will.

"It doesn't take a rocket scientist to figure this one out," I said, flipping through the pages. "Right here, it says I give to my son, Walter Mullikin, all real property that I own or have any interest in at the time of my death."

Mom pulled her sweater tighter. "That's really not the way I want it to be." Her voice was hesitant, confused.

How did this happen, I wondered. In July 1993, we'd had a family meeting. Just my parents, my seven siblings, and me. No spouses, no kids. We had sat around the kitchen table and decided how the farm would be divided. Everyone agreed that Walt could buy it for eighty percent of its value and pay everyone over ten years.

"I'm not going to have the government taking this farm away," Mom had said at the meeting. Although it was one of her broken-record comments, we all had heard stories of widows who had lost their farm after their husband died, and eventually had to contend with nursing homes or hospitals hounding them for back payments.

I had zero interest in the farm. I recalled saying, "When it comes time, I'll just give my share to Walt." Mom had mentioned Peter Taylor, an insurance agent who could help get a trust in place to protect their assets. Later that month, she sent me a birthday card with an added note asking if I had read the trust pamphlet and to pass it on to Kathy after I did; she planned to invite Peter over that September to further discuss the issue.

I looked at my mother now slumped in my dad's favorite lawn chair. She was looking any place but at me. My dad's bibs in the garbage annoyed me. Oddly, the will did not. The will just left me with an unsettled feeling in my stomach. Mom was plunk-dab in the middle of a confusing situation that she didn't seem to want to be in and was certain to piss off some of her children.

By October, I had obtained the name of Dr. Kranz's lawyer friend.

"Come on, Mom," I said, on the verge of childish pleading. "I'll come pick you up and take you back to the Twin Cities. The leaves are turning, and the drive up here will be gorgeous. We'll meet with the lawyer, then have Shannon's and Shawntel's families over for dinner at my house."

My mother rebuffed my invitation yet again. I assumed she didn't want to admit what the will really said. In November, I found out otherwise. Isabel called to say that she had taken Mom to the doctor for more tests. The results had just come back and showed that my mother had stage III colon cancer. A bomb exploded in my stomach.

"She really hasn't been feeling well since she returned from Alaska," Isabel said. "She tells Walt and me that all the time."

On Thanksgiving Day, another bomb exploded. Kathy called Mom from Virginia to check in and wish her a happy holiday across the miles. She discovered that Mom was not invited anywhere, not even to Walt and Isabel's. Isabel had arranged for her family to be at the farm, and they had not included Mom. Kathy was irate. So was I. What did Walt and Isabel think Mom was going to do? Sit in her apartment while the smells of turkey and stuffing and the sounds of people laughing and enjoying themselves drifted across the fireplace? Isabel's mom, Doreen, was still Mom's good friend and would be at the dinner. What the hell was this about? Kathy called Allan, who'd also assumed Mom would be included in farm festivities. He immediately offered to pick her up and bring her to their house. Later, Kathy called Walt and asked him why Mom wasn't invited to join them. He said they assumed she knew all she had to do was walk through the door and join them. No apologies.

In early December, Isabel sent out an e-mail to the sisters informing us that she and Walt thought it best that she take a leave from work in order to be a caregiver for Mom. After much research, Mom had decided to pursue treatments at the Cancer Center of America in Zion, Illinois. The protocol combined chemo and radiation with holistic approaches like nutrition therapy, massage, and acupuncture. At first, I didn't think much of her going so far from home, but as we discussed it more and I read the literature she brought with her at Christmas, I became comfortable with her plan. My sisters and I felt she needed to make her own decision; our role was to support that decision.

"I want to make the best choice," said Mom, "because I don't think it's fair for you kids to lose two parents in one year." I did appreciate that. I didn't think I could handle another major loss so soon. I suggested that before going to Zion in early January, she visit with the lawyer I had found in Minnesota. This time she agreed.

It was so odd to see only a few inches of snow on the ground. Normally in late December, the Twin Cities would be covered in white, and plows would be grumbling up and down streets, creating snow banks and dropping sand to make the roads less slippery. Charlotte and I each held one of Mom's arms as we headed toward a small brick building. We had an appointment with Frank Rheinberger, the attorney referred by my chiropractor.

Mom had driven herself from Wauzeka to my house in Minnesota. I would've gone down to get her, but my work schedule didn't allow me to get away, and once again Walt and Isabel had not offered to assist. Could they not see beyond themselves? Since her return from Alaska, Mom sounded sad and lonely.

The three of us entered a small foyer with wooden chairs along the walls. We could hear Mr. Rheinberger talking in his office on his phone. He didn't have a receptionist or other staff. Within a few minutes, he came out and greeted us. He had a serious but pleasant face and looked to be in his forties. We followed him into a conference room lined with bookshelves and law books. A large curtained window looked out onto the parking lot.

"I understand you would like me to look at your mother's will," he said to me, my cue to hand him the folder I was carrying. "I'm sorry for your loss," he added, opening the folder.

It didn't take him long to scan the will. "This is pretty simple and straightforward," he said. "You've given your farm to your son Walter and nothing to your other children. Is that correct, Illene? May I call you Illene?" He peered over his glasses at my mother.

"Yes, of course," she said, leaning forward. "But that's not what I want."

"What do you want, Illene?"

She sank back into the chair, and her chin and lower lip began to quiver. She nervously twisted her fingers and hands in her lap. Then, as if determined to defend her position, she sat up straight, put her elbows on the table, and said, "I want Allan to have the cabin." She began to explain how poor Allan was going to have a hard time making ends meet. She then catapulted into poor Walt and how he, too, would have it difficult, especially with a wife who only spent money and never lifted a finger to help.

Mr. Rheinberger sat and listened until Mom finished her

case. He asked her about the farm and questioned why the will had been written this way, giving everything to only one of eight children. He went on to explain how the law affords farmers certain advantages to prevent them from losing their property.

Then he said, "Don't you love your other children?"

Mom's eyes lit. "Of course I love my other children!"

"Oh, excuse me, maybe I jumped to conclusions. Do you have other assets to give your other seven children?

Mom seemed to know he had her on this one. She sank back into the chair. "No, no I don't."

"What do you have for your other sons and daughters?" he asked. "Perhaps other bank accounts to leave them equaling what you've given Walter?"

She looked down at her lap. "I have about five thousand dollars in the bank, which will go toward my funeral, and a ten-thousand-dollar life insurance policy."

"Do you have a POD on those accounts?"

"What's a POD?" she asked.

"Payable on Death," he replied.

"No, I don't."

"I suggest that you go to your bank, get the POD set up, and put your other seven children on it. But make sure Walter isn't added. That's the least you can do for your other children. And, I would insist that Walter pay for your funeral expenses."

Mom went into protest mode. "That's what the life insurance is for, and besides, he can't afford to do that. He works so hard and barely can make ends meet. My husband and I have been paying the taxes, insurance, and other farm expenses because he doesn't have the money. Isabel spends like there is no tomorrow."

Mr. Rheinberger wasn't interested in her excuses. "Now, what about that cabin you are talking about? Where is it? On the farm?"

"Yes, the cabin is on the farm, and access is across the fields."

"Is there any other access to the cabin? And what about the property for your son Allan to build cabins on?"

"There is no other access to the cabin, but the land below is in Plum Creek, and that would be a place to build cabins."

"You do understand, Illene, that your son Walter owns it all and does not have to give anything to Allan, right?"

"I want Allan to have the cabin," said Mom.

Mr. Rheinberger interrupted. "Illene, you can say you want *me* to have the cabin and I would appreciate that you want to give it to me, but it doesn't mean a thing. You can tell your son Walter that you *want* Allan to have the cabin and hope that he will honor your wishes, but he does not have to do so. He owns it all! I suggest that you go and have a talk with Walter and tell him what your wishes are. He might make promises, but no one can hold him to them."

Mom never looked the lawyer in the eye. "Walt wants the Allis-Chalmers tractor, and I would like it to stay on the farm. I always wanted Bert to polish it up and drive it in the parades, but he wouldn't ever do it." She looked at Charlotte and me. "And Walt should get that big picture of Dad hanging over the fireplace because he paid for the picture."

Mr. Rheinberger sighed and closed the file folder. He seemed ready to wrap things up. "Illene, you have a few things to take care of when you get back home. I'm sure Mary will help you with an inventory list."

Mom nodded. "Yes, she's already started one for me."

We left the office. I anticipated anger and disappointment among my siblings. Walt getting everything, imagine! Sure, I was confused by the favoritism, but to be honest, I didn't want anything to do with the farm. I had wonderful memories of it, but I also harbored dark, shadowed ones. Mostly, I was just too damn tired to care.

The next day Mom flew out of Minneapolis to Virginia to visit Kathy. Upon returning, she'd drive with Isabel to Zion for her first treatment. In the meantime, an event that I had wished and prayed for was about to happen. Shawntel's five-year-old twins, Vanessa and Valerie were going to have a sleepover with Grandma Mary.

The girls became aware that their brother Vincent and Shannon's boys, Jacob and Jonah, occasionally stayed overnight with Stan and me, they pestered Shawntel to do the same. Shawntel did some fancy dancing with excuses. *Oh, it would be too much for Grandma. She's too busy.* Never could she state the real reason. Shawntel and I had long ago agreed that the girls would only stay overnight if Stan were not there. Even I didn't trust him despite all we had been through. After all, Shawntel had told me once during treatment that he had been so daring as to molest her while I slept on the couch, and they were on the floor.

"If I let the girls come over," said Shawntel, "you have to promise that Dad sleeps downstairs on the couch, and the girls sleep in your locked bedroom either on the bed or in sleeping bags on the floor."

I promised to make that happen. First, I told Stan about the plan and suggested he leave, but as usual, no way José. He gave me the worn excuse of not having friends. Both Shawntel and Shannon had commented many times that their dad never seemed to go anywhere without me, and it wasn't because he loved me head over heels. At least Stan agreed to stay downstairs, where he slept most nights until the wee hours of the morning, when he would come upstairs and flop next to me in bed.

Shawntel brought the girls over late Saturday afternoon. I'm not sure who was more excited, the twins or me. I fixed hotdogs, macaroni and cheese, and for a treat, we walked to Dairy Queen for ice-cream cones. Vanessa wanted to put blankets over the table and build a fort, so the three of us worked on it. By eight o'clock, they were yawning. They climbed in my bed, security blankets in tow, and chose a few books for me to read. Valerie lay pretty still, while Vanessa just couldn't get comfortable. I assured her that the bedroom and bathroom doors were locked so no one could come into the room. But she twisted and turned, and finally moved to the floor next to the bed. I turned out the lights. Still, sleep wouldn't come. I did my best to comfort her. Valerie sat in bed looking sad because she wanted to stay, but knew if Vanessa went home, so would she. I called Shawntel.

The twins' only overnight never happened. In my heart, I felt that their mother's fears had transferred to them, along with my uncertainty and lack of trust in Stan, regardless of the locked doors. I resented Stan for taking that experience away from us all. Just one more layer of hurt, frustration, and anger. The poster incest family was not the success I'd dreamed it would be.

Isabel called me the day before she and Mom were supposed to leave for Zion. It was Sunday, and I was folding laundry, waiting for the Green Bay Packer game to start.

"Mary, I have to tell you something," she said. "I'm not going to be able to take your mom to Zion tomorrow."

"What's going on?" I held up one unmatched sock.

"I have to go to Madison. I'm going into rehab."

I dropped the sock. That was about the last thing I expected to hear. Then she spilled the truth. She had developed an addiction to prescription drugs. She hadn't actually taken a leave of absence from work in early December; she'd been fired. Someone at the clinic discovered that she'd been taking drugs from inventory and reported her. Management agreed not to press charges if she quit and promised never to work in any type of clinical or healthcare setting.

Isabel started to cry. "I know I can get through this. But please, don't tell Illene. Not just yet." If she had a tail, it would be dragging between her legs.

"What do you propose we do?" I said, feeling a bit sorry for her, but at the same time irritated with her for lying.

"Would you be able to take her to Zion? I know you have to work and it's inconvenient, but I can't ask Barbara, and everyone else is too far away."

Barbara was not Isabel's favorite person. My theory was that Isabel was jealous Barbara was a certified nursing assistant and knowledgeable about healthcare, not to mention very adept and talented at it, too. Isabel could have asked Bobby or Allan, of course, since they lived in Wauzeka, but she kept those families at arm's length. Later, I would learn that she spread rumors about them, which probably explained why during family get-togethers, their families usually sat off to the side.

"I think you should be the one to go with Grandma," said Isabel.

"What do I tell Mom?" I said. My mother proudly mentioned more than once that Isabel would be taking her to Zion.

Isabel laid out the scenario. Isabel needed to pick up her youngest son from jail in Appleton and bring him to the jail in Prairie du Chien, where he'd serve out his sentence for stealing drugs from nursing-home patients. He had just been convicted, and I was to say that Isabel had learned last minute that she had to do this. It sounded far-fetched to me, but Isabel insisted it was the best story to present.

I told Stan I'd be gone for at least a few days.

"I told you Isabel is a lying bitch. She's as phony as a three-dollar bill." He gave me the now-do-you-believe-me look. For once, I had to agree with him.

I packed my suitcase, feeling sorry for Mom, Isabel, and myself. Yet again, I was in a place where I didn't want to be. Still stuck with Stan. Still stuck with chaos. And now stuck with a lie that I was being arm-twisted to tell. At least the Packers beat the Bears thirty-five to nineteen.

It was a little less than four hours from Wauzeka to Zion. Mom must have said at least five times that she wished Isabel could be with us, that she was sure she would appreciate the facilities, and why was Isabel the one who had to transport her son between jails? Wouldn't someone in law enforcement do that? That's why we pay taxes, for heaven's sake. I tuned her out as much as possible.

"This is why I can't travel with her," Dad said to me one time. We were sitting in my kitchen and could hear Mom preaching to the kids about watching too much TV. Stan had started an argument with her. I also knew Dad was uncomfortable traveling long distances because he easily tired and had become incontinent. Mom never seemed able to accept either. I felt such a hole in my life when I thought about him. I wondered if I had fully grieved his passing. It seemed as if I had gone from one drama to another. Complications with the will. Kids. Grandkids. Work harassments. Mom's cancer. Keeping up with all my siblings, their spouses, kids and grandkids. No family is without its drama. Hopefully Zion would turn out to be hassle-free. Mom had contracted to stay there for one week out of each of the next twelve months.

"I wish Isabel could see this. She'd really like it," said Mom.

I glanced around the fourth floor solarium. The place looked more like a posh hotel than a cancer center.

"Mom, it's probably better that you know where Isabel really is and why she couldn't bring you here today." My mother looked directly at me in surprise. I continued. "She's in Madison, not Appleton, checking into a rehab program. She's addicted to prescription drugs."

Mom pushed the idea away with her hand. "Isabel? Addicted?"

"She called me last night and told me. She asked me not to tell you. But I don't want to lie to you."

By the time I finally got Mom to at least tentatively believe the truth, suppertime had arrived. We got up from our comfy chairs and walked to the elevator.

"Well, I know she would approve of this place. I just know it," said Mom.

Why she wanted Isabel's approval, I wasn't sure. Now that Dad was gone, Isabel was the one person who Mom saw daily and who was versed in medical care. Maybe she trusted her more than anybody else.

A few days later, a subdued Isabel called me from rehab. "Mary, my sister brought me here just in time. They had to hurry and give me methadone. A few more minutes later and I would have died," she said in a breathy voice.

"What happened?" When I picked up my mother to go to Zion, Isabel hadn't appeared sick, distraught, or anything but lucid enough to elicit sympathy for her son's situation while covering her own ass.

Isabel mumbled something about trying to detox herself and the effort backfiring.

"I'm glad you're doing okay," I said into the phone, not wanting more details to doubt. I confessed about telling Mom why Isabel hadn't driven to Zion. Isabel practically screamed the roof off rehab, she was furious at me that I told Mom the truth. Our conversation came to a screeching halt. I must not be the ally she's looking for, I thought to myself.

Isabel's rehab program was quicker than grease lightening. Seven days! That was the extent of her stay. A few days after her release, I received an emailed update from one of Isabel's family members. Isabel would live with her sister in Madison and attend individual and group therapy sessions. The rest of the family would attend Al-Anon meetings and do family counseling. Kathy sent an e-mail to the sisters saying she was uncomfortable with Isabel administering Mom's medication because of her addiction. Kathy had a son dealing with addiction and knew all too well what games addicts play. I had no arguments with that reasoning. The only things I didn't have were the mental and physical energies to make the argument. Someone else would have to handle this one.

It had been almost fifty years since I had seen Johnny Payne. Throughout that challenging span, he occasionally popped into my mind. The images and memories I stored of him would tumble down into my heart, fueling hope that someday we would see each other in person. My mind thought it silly, futile, even absurd to think that we might meet again, while my heart warned that if we did, I might not be able to stay true to my marriage.

Johnny had visited Wauzeka while Stan and I first lived in California. Mouse told me he knocked on her door one day. He had learned that I had moved to San Diego and was wondering if Mouse had my phone number, because he was stationed in San Diego and would love to have a cup of coffee with me. She told him on no account would she give him my number. When she related the story to me, she emphasized how adamant she had been. Johnny left Wauzeka without any way to contact me. I left San Diego none the wiser that he had been close to me, maybe within miles, maybe blocks. When I heard how Mouse had protected me, helped keep my marriage intact, I didn't say much, just swallowed my disappointment.

At times, I thought about calling Roy and Jean Kemerling and asking how I might contact Johnny. But something always prevented me from dialing their number. Fear that a conversation might tarnish the glow of memories. Embarrassment that Johnny might not remember me. Shame that a married woman would allow passion to tempt her. I tried searching for Johnny on the Internet, but to no avail. Perhaps Johnny's real name had escaped me or I no longer had the correct spelling. I'll always wonder if Johnny felt something similar. Did he think about going to the farm and asking my parents how to reach me? Did he type my name in a search engine?

In September 2001, before the Twin Towers imploded and shook the world, I learned of Johnny's whereabouts. I was visiting the farm over Labor Day weekend. Stan had to work, so Shannon, her kids, and I drove down from the Twin Cities. While they went horseback riding, Mom and I drove her Plymouth Fury to her cabin. As we bumped over the ground, my mother said that she had just seen Roy Kemerling. Apparently, Johnny had been in Wauzeka in the spring. His marriage had dissolved, and he was heartbroken. He was drinking quite a bit. After three weeks, he left and returned to New York. Roy recently received notice from a relative of Johnny's that Johnny had died shortly thereafter. Mom didn't say much else. I gripped the steering wheel to prevent my hands from trembling.

For the rest of the weekend, I put up a good front. Laughed. Smiled. Told funny stories. Behind my facade, the one I had learned to construct in an instant, sat a lump of sadness and disappointment. For so long I had played the movie reel in my mind. Johnny and I meeting somewhere, maybe a bar or ball game, ordering a beer or wine, talking, him eventually sharing that he had kept me tucked in a corner of his heart. That's where the shorter-than-short movie ended.

My Internet searches from that point were limited to finding where he was buried. I gave up trying. What difference did it make? The dream of us reconnecting couldn't become reality. Johnny had been the one person who had tried to protect me and respected me, and who truly loved me. I would always love him. Deep down, I don't believe we ever forget our first true loves. It wouldn't surprise me one bit if the day my mother told me about Johnny's passing, she thought of Rube Infield—where he was, what he had been, how he had affected her life. Maybe like me, she resigned herself to waiting for the day when a corner of her soul could join with a corner of his and validate their brief, glorious time shared on earth.

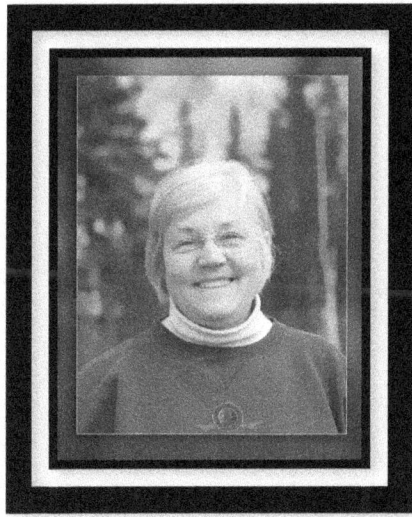

PART SEVEN

Since placing her first SOS call for cleaning five years earlier, Isabel had been relying on others to clean Mom's apartment, including the Minion Sisters' Cleaning Service. "It's so bad this time," she said to me over the phone. "The smell is leaching from Grandma's apartment into our home. Walt insisted I call." She reiterated her line about Grandma being such "a *private*" person that she didn't want to invade her space. This from the woman who didn't think twice about borrowing towels, toilet paper, and Tylenol from my parents. "Besides, you girls do such a good job," she said.

I told Isabel we would be there this coming weekend to celebrate Barbara and Mom's birthdays. We'll clean, I promised.

"Four hours. That's what we need," I said to Barbara, cranking up the car's heater. "Between the two of us, that makes eight hours of cleaning." The apartment was eight hundred square feet. One hour per one hundred square feet should do it.

During the drive, Barbara and I talked about Mom and how she seemed to be losing energy of late. It had been two years since her treatments at Zion. We agreed to visit as often as possible. We moved on to what was happening with our kids, grandkids, and jobs. I had started a new job that I loved at Kodak. On weekends, I tried to see my grandchildren. Shannon had three kids, and Shawntel had four; it was the highlight of my week to spend time with them. Shayne was still single. I purposely avoided discussing Stan. This was my time to not think about him. Although he had stopped his affairs, I wanted to be rid of him, but I could never seem to make that happen. At least he had a decent job that seemed to suit him. He was managing a warehouse in shipping and receiving. When he started, the warehouse was a mess and hindered business. Pretty soon, his coworkers relied on him. He mostly worked alone, which he preferred. When he had to work with others, he complained relentlessly about them. It was much later that I learned his boss had required him to take anger-management classes.

Stan told his coworkers that I looked like a sumo wrestler. He laughed and teased me about it. One day, I had to stop by to see Stan at work. One of his coworkers came out on the shipping dock where Stan and I were talking and asked me several times if I really were Stan's wife.

"What were you expecting," I said, "a sumo wrestler?" The guy looked embarrassed.

Since being on Oprah's show, Stan had had three heart attacks and had quit smoking, only to start again. Although I frequently considered leaving him, I couldn't bring myself to do so. He intimidated and scared me. He never punched me out, but there were times when he grabbed me and held me until it hurt, a certain crazed look in his eyes. I almost never resisted or fought back when he did that. Somehow I knew that if I did, he would physically harm me. At times I would pray for him to have another heart attack and die. Or for another woman to woo him over. Or for him to just disappear. That only made me feel guilty and sinful. If I tried to walk away, he'd follow me and force me to listen to him. My thoughts drifted elsewhere, just as they did when Mom ranted. I had long since learned how to respond to his manic behavior. It would be years before I could step back and really look at how deeply the talons of fear had sunk into me. I didn't have SERE training like Stan did. I couldn't figure out how to escape.

I turned the car into the farmhouse driveway. The moon cast shadows on the crystalline snow. As always, I felt Dad's presence. Thankfully, someone had shoveled the steps up to the door. We stomped our boots on the mat and stepped inside.

The first thing I saw was Mom asleep on the couch. Then, I almost gagged. The stink that greeted us wouldn't have been acceptable in the barn. Dishes were piled in the sink, on the kitchen table, on the coffee table. Dirt littered around the door. Barbara beelined to the bathroom. "Oh, gross!" she said.

What the heck? Isabel and Walt were in charge of Mom. The will had decreed that. If the health department knew what was happening here, they would've condemned the place. Had we arrived during working hours, I might have called them, I was so mad. Barbara gently shook Mom awake. She smiled, happy to see us. I cleared a space at the kitchen table, retrieved the bottle of brandy that Dad and I had never finished, and prepared for a long weekend.

The next week, Isabel sent an e-mail.

Walt and I have talked and we decided that I'm going to take a leave from work for a while. It seems uncertain as to how well Grandma will do with the radiation and neither of us is comfortable having friends responsible or for that matter seeing her sick like she has been. If everything improves as we are sure praying it does, we are sure that she would enjoy different company then. We really hope our decision gives us all some peace of mind knowing that Grandma will not be alone and that

we won't have to wonder if she is getting enough care.
Love Isabel

Without us conferring, Kathy, Barbara, and I sent individual e-mails to Isabel. Each of us thanked Isabel for her concern, then assured her it wasn't necessary for her to take time off. We also had been talking to Mom and would set up round-robin visitations. We each expressed our desire to be involved in this last leg of Mom's life. We wanted to spend as much time with her as possible, and we knew her feelings were mutual. Though none of us mentioned it in our e-mails, we knew my mother was dying. Isabel knew it, too. So did my mother.

A few days later, Stan shook me awake. I had gone to bed early and for once, had fallen asleep without tossing and turning. His presence startled me. My first thought was that I had crossed the bed's centerline and invaded his territory; he didn't like being touched while sleeping.

Stan said, "Isabel's on the phone. She needs to talk to you." His gruff voice sounded pissed off, probably because he had to interrupt his TV watching and climb the stairs to wake me.

I hadn't even heard the phone ring next to me on the nightstand. Still in a daze, I fumbled to find the lamp, then the phone. "Hello," I said, closing my eyes against the light.

"Walt and I are with your mom in her apartment." Isabel's sharp voice quaked my brain awake. "She wants to talk to you."

The next sound I heard was muffled crying. Then Mom managed to get out, "I don't want any fighting." I sat up in bed. Fighting? "You don't have to worry about me," she said. "Isabel is right here and should be the one in charge of my care. She said she'll e-mail everyone about what's happening."

I could envision Mom sitting in Dad's recliner, flanked by

Walt and Isabel, tears running down her sallow cheeks. Anger swelled through me. How utterly conniving! Every ounce of me knew that Isabel had planted those words and somehow forced Mom to say them.

"Mom, don't worry about this," I said, trying to remain calm. "We'll work everything out. We all want to spend time with you at the farm. That's the most important thing."

Mom continued to speak, but I couldn't hear what she was saying, only sense the tremble of her chin and feel her intense sadness. Here she was, being bullied by the son and daughter-in-law to whom she had given everything. Everything!

Isabel's voice came through the line. She whispered for me to hang on while she stepped onto the porch. I heard a door shut, then the strike of a match, followed by a long inhale and exhale as if she needed the buzz to stoke her courage for another attack.

"Are you worried about me caring for your mom because of my prescription drug addiction?"

It had been three years since Isabel was in rehab; I hadn't given much thought to her past. "Isabel, the only thing I know right now is that I would like to be with my mother. For as much time as possible while she's still on this earth. That's what I would like."

There was a long pause. "I have to go now," said Isabel, and hung up.

I tapped the base of the light. The room plunged into darkness. I found myself in a state of wonder. Had Walt and Isabel really just bullied Mom? I pulled the covers up to my chin. I didn't know if Isabel still had an addiction or not, but she was coming across as one self-centered caregiver who had not a clue what we meant to Mom.

It had taken us a while to get Mom ready for the Memorial Day parade, but it was worth every minute. She was riding in her brother Larry's convertible, sitting in the front seat. The wind had kicked up, and we had bundled her in her heavy coat and warm shoes and socks. Then they proceeded down Main Street, past Stuckey's grocery store, the house where Uncle Bill killed himself, the local tavern and restaurant, the post office. As they drove past family and friends scattered throughout the crowd, she waved, her expression one of contentment. The scarf tied under her chin streamed behind her, and for a moment I saw the girl in her, the one who had lived here all her life. This was her territory. If ever there was a matriarch of Wauzeka, she was it.

The parade ended at the Catholic church cemetery. My sisters and I found Mom and walked her over to Dad's grave. The headstone showed his name, birth date and date of death, and her name with birth date. A chill ran through me. What would be her date of death? June, July, December? David, Bonnie, and Stevie's graves, next to Dad and Mom's headstones, told their own story; a few feet away was my baby brother Johnny's headstone. We placed bridal wreath and lilacs on each one, just as I did in grade school when I carried the flowers in the parade and felt sick to my stomach. The crowd quieted as a trumpeter played "Taps." The last mournful notes echoed off the church. The flag snapped in the breeze. Then the first reverberating bang of a twenty-one-gun salute honoring those who had fallen.

A few days after Memorial Day, An email arrived from the Walt and Isabel camp decreeing that Mom would be receiving fewer visitors and only at scheduled hours.

"But I like visitors," Mom said when I asked her about it.

Allan was so peeved that he went over to the farm and confronted Walt.

"Get the hell off my property," said Walt. "And don't you
ever step foot back here again."

I wondered if Mom heard them arguing below her window.
Allan left angry and crushed. Walt was the big brother he had
always looked up to.

Much to my surprise, Mom asked to have a private conversation with me and another one with Bobby. I knew Barbara
was hoping for one, but Mom never requested one with her. My
intuition said to have mine away from the farm. I didn't know
what Mom wanted to discuss, though I anticipated her asking
me to return to the Catholic Church. Regardless, I didn't want
anyone eavesdropping on us, so I asked Allan and Carmen if
Mom and I could talk at their house the next time I came into
town.

Carmen had moved two chairs near one of the windows
in her sunroom. The smell of freshly cut grass drifted through
screens. I helped Mom get situated. The veins in her thin hands
seemed more noticeable. For a moment, I could see her kneading
bread, hanging freshly laundered sheets on the clothesline,
pushing fabric through the sewing machine, trimming my
bangs with scissors.

I grasped her hand. "Mom, it's important for me to look
you in the eyes and tell you that I love you and how much I
care for you."

Mom looked at me, then at her lap. "You don't have to do
that," she said, her voice barely audible.

"Yes, I do. It's important you know that. This has been a
really hard time for me. It's been hard for everybody. We all

love you and want to spend time with you. We're all fighting. It's crazy and not like I want it to be."

Mom kept her eyes down. "I don't want it to be like this either."

"I don't know about drug addicts," I said, "but I know that someone who has an addiction and puts herself in places where she's at risk deeply concerns me."

"You're talking about Isabel," Mom said weakly.

"Yes, I'm talking about Isabel. I know you want Isabel to take care of you and there was never any—"

"It's the convenience," said Mom, her voice rising. "She's my best caretaker and knowledgeable, and I don't like her not being able to work."

I really didn't want to upset my mother. She was the one who had suggested we talk. I gently explained that I had consulted an expert who said that a healthy recovering addict would never risk putting herself in the position Isabel had put herself in, because it's too dangerous, too easy to slip back into old habits.

My mother sighed. "I can't imagine, just can't imagine, being without Isabel."

"The thing I have trouble with, Mom, is that Isabel seems to control everything. You and I have not had what I would consider a glorious relationship over the years, which I'm sorry about."

"Me too," whispered Mom, her mouth swooping downward.

"I feel that Isabel is in between us right now, for whatever reason." I could hear my voice start to quiver. "It breaks my heart, because I want to be able to be a part of this journey with you."

Mom twisted her hands. "And I just want time because we didn't have some things, you and I. There are so many things that I did wrong."

It was the first time in my life, and perhaps in hers, that my mother admitted to doing something wrong. With that admission, something happened. We talked. Mom and I really talked. About how she knew Bonnie was going to die and how incredibly difficult it was watching her slip away; how she never thought I was culpable in any way for Bonnie's death; how Johnny had died without anyone around; how she wished she had been less hard on Bobby when he was young.

She paused, pensive. "After all that news broke about priests molesting young boys, I started wondering about Bobby. Do you think anything happened between him and Father Cassidy?" Her eyes held a pain I had seen too often in my lifetime.

"I don't know, Mom," I said. "Did you ask him?"

"I asked him the other night. He told me that Father tried, but never did anything to him." She looked down at her feet and sighed. "I want to believe him. Do you think he's telling the truth?"

How could I give her peace? "If that's what he said, I think you have to believe him."

"At the time with all you kids, I thought his life would be better. We didn't have a lot of money, and Father seemed like a good man. Bobby never complained. Not once."

She looked out the window. The buzz of cicadas filled our silence. "I'm so sorry about so many things," she said, her voice tearful. "I should have known how hard it was for you in California, and I didn't help you enough."

"Mom, I was away in California. You helped me a lot. I only wished—"

"Not as much as I could have. Or should have."

"The only wish I had was that you would have been there with me, and that wasn't possible."

Mom started to interrupt, but her words melted into tears.

"Stan and I didn't have the money to fly you out," I said.

"Plus, you had kids at home, babies of your own. It's just a wish that you could've been there with me, and guess what? When my daughters had their babies, they didn't even want me to be there! And I was really mad, 'cause I wanted to be there with them."

Mom laughed and nodded. "That's kinda like how I was. I never wanted anybody there but your dad. I didn't want my ma; I didn't want anybody. I just wanted him. And he was there every single time except that one time with Johnny. He just couldn't be. There was nobody to do the chores."

"But he was there in spirit," I said.

Mom sat taller in her chair. "I'm not ashamed of anything, except what I did when you told me what Stan did to Shannon and Sharon. I'm sure I didn't act properly at all. I just didn't believe—couldn't believe it happened when you told me. It didn't register at all. I mean it did, but it didn't. It didn't go deep enough to make me realize how horrible, how—" She stopped and looked at her trembling hands.

Then Mom shared a story that I had never heard. She said that when she was fourteen or fifteen years old, she had gone to a movie about football with a friend and the friend's uncle. During the movie, the uncle molested my mother. I knew the movie. Years before, I had stayed up late and watched *Knute Rockne, All American* starring Ronald Reagan. It was released in 1940. Mom would have been fifteen years old. In that moment, I understood why my mother hated football. I wondered what else she hated because of that incident.

"You know what, Mom? You survived and I survived."

"I know, but—"

"How were you going to help me when I couldn't even find professional people to help me? I went to many professionals, and they didn't know what to do. The fact that you didn't have any answers for me is not your fault. We've been very fortunate in finding people like Diane Dovenberg."

Mom said, "I'll never forget the time Stan and I went up to the park above 3M, and he talked to me and said how sorry he was for what he had done to Charlotte. And I thought if I put him in jail, what good is it gonna do? If I thought it would have done good, I would have put him in jail. At the time, I didn't think the publicity would help anybody."

Her comment took me aback. I considered asking her why she thought it was up to her to put Stan in jail and not the law, but I didn't. She still saw herself in control of events.

She continued. "The way it turned out, do you think it was the best way it could have turned out?"

"Yeah, I do."

"I think you love Stan."

"No, I don't love Stan. I don't love him anymore."

"I think you do."

"He and I have a lot of differences."

"Oh, I'm sure you do."

I knew my mother. She had not believed me in the past, and she was not going to believe me now. Or maybe she didn't want to believe me because if I left Stan, who would I have? In her world, I would have no one. Maybe that was a sadness she didn't want.

"Mom, I have three absolutely wonderful children and six— no wait, seven grandkids. I'm very lucky. And we're all lucky to have you. I know that each of them would like something from you that they can remember you by." Where this thought came from, I wasn't sure, but I stayed with it. "Maybe it's time you go through your things and organize them. You know I'm an organized person and need to have my ducks in a row."

"And I'm the most unorganized person there is." Mom let herself smile.

"Your grandkids would love to hear what things are near and dear to your heart and why. Like that thing you made out of horsehair, or the fainting couch. I used to think those things were so silly, but now I see you had a flare for decorating and collecting. I wish you had been encouraged to do more of that."

Mom had a dreamy look. "I love elegant stuff."

"But you don't want to take care of it," I said, hoping my tone was teasing.

"That's exactly right," said Mom, getting into the moment, "and not only that, but then the other half of me doesn't want that stuff. I want the cowboy stuff. The pioneer stuff. The horses, the cabin, the gardens." She laughed and leaned forward. "You know, it's like you're a divided person. Have you ever felt that way? Divided?"

As my mother's health deteriorated, Stan's insults increased. It was bizarre. A partner in life is supposed to support you during trying times, but Stan never had been able to do that. Contending with his snarky comments, righteous indignation, and his ever-present needs was draining me of vital, sanity-saving energy. Sometimes during the drive to Wauzeka, I'd imagine taking a curve along the Great River Road and not turning the wheel. The car would careen off the road and over the bluff. In less than a minute, I could snuff out pain, anger, guilt, and shame. I was aware that no one knew how I truly felt. I was a pro at masking my feelings. During my most desperate moments, I learned to focus on my grandchildren. The need to love and protect Shannon, Shayne, and Shawntel had kept me going all those years before Stan's incest was discovered. Now, my love for my grandchildren kept my hands turning the car wheel in the right direction, kept them away from Stan's machete and the knife drawer, kept me going anew into each day. Without my grandchildren, I seriously doubt I would be alive today.

It was mid-June, and I was exhausted. Kathy had screamed at Isabel, refusing to leave Isabel's kitchen, until she returned Mom's important documents. Isabel coughed up the file with the healthcare directive in it. Our family seemed to be splitting apart. The thought left me despondent. I stood in the middle of the living room staring out the big windows framed by sheer curtains. A soft breeze filtered through the screens and brushed my bare skin. Tears began to brim. I feared that if I let them flow, I wouldn't be able to close the floodgates.

Stan was in the dining room on a ladder up near the ceiling, spraying water on the floral wallpaper in an attempt to remove it. He let the water soak in, then peeled the outer layer before scraping the adhesive. It was a laborious job. Why, I wondered, did he have to do this now, in the middle of my mother dying? I could hear him grunting.

His voice scorched through my misery. "Can't you fucking get in here and help me? You know this is hard work and I have a heart condition!"

A deep guttural sound began to build in me. At first, I hardly recognized it was coming from me. I couldn't hold it back. "My mother is dying, and all you can think about is what more you can take from me!" I screamed. "Wallpaper? Who the fuck cares about wallpaper?"

I could no longer control my emotions. I screamed and

sobbed. My throat began to hurt. Stan descended the ladder and gently wrapped his arms around me. For a moment, I relished the feeling of human touch.

"I'm sorry," he whispered.

His words jolted me. Words said too late. All I saw in that moment were patterns from years of abuse. For years he had pushed me into oblivion, kept my voice buried. Life had been all about him.

I shoved him hard. "Don't touch me! Don't you ever touch me again!" Hot, burning tears streamed down my cheeks. I wondered if our neighbor next door could hear me. I didn't care. The only thing I cared about right then was surviving and getting through the rest of my mother's life, however long that might be.

My mother was determined not to die in July. We had a boatload of family birthdays in July, including Bobby's and mine, and she didn't want anyone to be reminded every year of her passing. As if we wouldn't remember. Plus, she didn't want us to have to return her social security check for that month. The day before my birthday, the dreaded call came. Mom was declining quickly. It was time for the family to convene at the farm. I left for Wauzeka the next day, Monday. Stan stayed home, having visited the farm earlier in the month to say his good-bye.

Ironically, Mom's hospice nurse was out of town for a week. During my last visit to Wauzeka, I had met her when she checked in on Mom. In private, I questioned her about the hospice process and how Mom was doing. A caring and empathetic person, she took the time to relay much information. She ended our conversation by saying that she had told Illene to send a message from the other side. Mom had smiled and promised to do so. Isabel, now in charge per Mom's healthcare directive, hired a registered nurse to assist during the hospice nurse's absence. I prayed Mom's passing would be smooth and tried to ignore the feeling that it could very well be otherwise. When I arrived, I was happy to see Mom in a hospital bed rather than in Dad's recliner. The bed had been delivered the previous week and was set up in the middle of the apartment. Kathy and Charlotte were already there.

"Hi, honey," Mom said to me. She looked frail, but her blue eyes were alert. I still wasn't accustomed to her calling me "honey," something she had recently started doing.

"We need to stay ahead of that breakthrough pain," Isabel reminded us throughout the day. In addition to increasing the dose of the pain patch, the doctor, per Isabel's request, had increased the frequency of morphine from every four to every two hours. Mom didn't like taking the medicine. She'd purse her lips when she saw Isabel or the nurse approaching. More than once during the past months, she had told me that she didn't want what happened to Dad to happen to her. I knew she still felt that she had contributed to his death by agreeing to the morphine.

On Tuesday, I noticed that Mom's breathing seemed labored. Maybe it was the light in the apartment, but she looked paler than the day before. She even looked as though she had lost weight. Isabel alerted everyone that Grandma's time was near. She phoned Father Wolf, the parish priest, who soon appeared with Sister Donna to administer last rites. Walt came in from the barn, those milling around outside came in, and we surrounded Mom's hospital bed. The priest prayed. We prayed. Mom folded her arms on her chest and continued to breathe and breathe and breathe. After an hour, Mom perked up. Isabel and the nurse came to her bedside in the afternoon and kicked everyone out. When I returned, Mom was sleeping soundly.

Sharon arrived from Alaska on Wednesday. She set candles

and family photos around the apartment and looped music on the CD player. The apartment assumed a cathedral-like air. People used hushed voices when they entered. If Mom was alert, the whispers gave way to chuckling and laughing, occasionally crying. So many people passed through—extended family and friends toting casseroles or pans of brownies or scrunching Kleenex in their hands, depending on their personal mission. Always, there was the pulse of music playing and Isabel's voice rising above the fray, directing traffic.

Kathy's son, Sam, arrived from the East Coast. Mom seemed so happy to see him. They hugged and talked about the weather, Sam's job, and his new wife. Two hours later, Isabel announced that she was calling Father Wolf and Sister Donna because Mom wasn't doing well. Kathy and I looked at each other. They had administered the last rites only yesterday. Once was enough in the Catholic church.

When Mom saw the father and sister walk in, she said, "What are they doing here? I haven't sinned since I last saw them." She looked totally confused. The priest and nun stood at the end of the bed and began praying together. Isabel gathered everyone around the bed. Apparently yesterday had been a dress rehearsal. Would this be the real performance? I glanced around at the somber faces. If only someone would turn that music off. Sister Donna started to say the Our Father, and we joined her. She wanted to say it slowly, so we could understand the meaning of each word, but the pauses between words were so long that we all gave up reciting what we knew by heart. Then halfway through the prayer she skipped a line, and people started looking around at each other. Mom lay there, eyes closed, her hands crossed on her chest. The tissue box was being passed, and sniffles could be heard between the looping songs.

After a bit, Mom looked up and said, "I can't do this. I don't know how to do this."

This is it, I thought. I'm going to collapse on the floor. We're all here waiting for her to die, and she thinks she's going to die, but she's as alive as can be.

I was standing next to Sister Donna. She leaned over and whispered, "Yesterday, I told Georgeine McCloskey at the post office that Illene had passed. I guess I gave her the wrong information." I didn't know whether to laugh or cry. This can't be happening, I thought. This is insanity. The father and sister began chanting something that sounded like, "Let Jesus take you." We waited. And waited.

Finally, Mom opened her eyes and said, "I don't think Jesus wants me."

That night, after hamburgers had been grilled and Isabel's kitchen cleaned, I sat by Mom's bed. Candlelight flickered on the walls, and a new selection of music drifted softly through the room. Mom was commenting on one of her friends who had stopped by earlier in the day. As I listened, I noticed Isabel and the nurse walk through their living room toward the apartment. Mom saw them coming, saw the syringe in the nurse's hand. The duo stepped up into the apartment. When they reached the end of the bed, Mom clamped her mouth shut.

"Illene, you need to take this," the nurse said, moving toward Mom.

Mom turned her head away.

"Grandma, Grandma, we need you to take this to stay ahead of the breakthrough pain," said Isabel.

Mom's eyes grew panicked. She tilted her head back. The

nurse touched the syringe to Mom's lips and Mom arched her back. It was like watching a frightened horse rear its head back. Mom did not want the morphine. She had not mentioned pain. I wanted to stand up and scream at both of them, but I forced myself to stay seated. What good would it do? If I moved, I would lose it, probably lunge at Isabel, and cause unneeded commotion. Mom was enduring enough physical and emotional pain at the moment as it was. Mom had chosen Isabel to be in charge. The healthcare directive made that clear. Part of my heart was shattering for my mother, for what she had created and what Isabel seemed to be orchestrating.

"Come on, Grandma. Just a little bit," said Isabel. Mom sank into the mattress and opened her mouth a little. The nurse pushed the syringe between her lips.

"There now," said Isabel. "You'll sleep so much better."

Mom's death was not playing out like Dad's. Back then, we were a family united. Now, we were a family divided. Kathy told me in private that Sam had asked her what was going on in the family. He felt the tension, but didn't have the details about Walt and Isabel being willed the entire farm and certainly didn't know about Isabel's need to control Mom's care during the past months. Walt fueled the tension when he told Kathy that she had to choose sides. She told him in no uncertain terms that he was crazy and she wouldn't choose a side. The gulf grew wider. Charlotte, having been such good friends with Isabel for so long, was still trying to believe that all was good, as did Sharon, who did not see what had been happening because she lived so far away. How petty and ridiculous this all is, I thought. Mom is dying amid family strife.

I was the last person to speak to Mom. No one asked me

what she and I discussed, nor did I share parts of our conversation. Mom had requested that I follow my heart. Right then, I didn't have the energy to do so. Besides, my exhausted, fraught-with-emotion heart might not have led me in a positive direction. I tucked Mom's request in the back of my mind for future deliberation.

Ron arrived the following afternoon. I was sitting at a picnic table and watched him and Charlotte enter Mom's apartment. Charlotte later told me that after Ron spoke to Mom, he and Charlotte quietly sat at her bedside. Unexpectedly, her breathing grew loud. That's when Charlotte came out on the deck and yelled for Isabel. I knew what was happening. The hospice nurse had told us that at the end of life, a person can have a death rattle—noisy, irregular breathing caused by fluids building at the base of the throat. As I entered the bedroom, I noticed that the noisy hay elevator had stopped. I figured the boys working it had turned it off and were on their way inside.

Isabel was taking Mom's vitals by the time I squeezed alongside family members in the small bedroom. "She's gone," said Isabel.

Just then, loud voices from outside filtered through the window. I looked out and saw the three grandkids, who had been working the hay elevator standing next to it scratching their heads. It turned out the machine stopped of its own accord. No one could ever figure out why. Someone yelled through the apartment door, "There's a rainbow! Come look at the rainbow!" Everyone rushed outside.

Sure enough, a full rainbow arched across the perfectly cloudless blue sky. Right then, a flock of swallows swooped over the barn, dipped toward us, and turned toward the county trunk road. I watched until they disappeared over the fields.

EPILOGUE